They Used To Call Us Game Wardens

William H. Callies

Technical manuscript formatting and cover preparations by
Shawn Nevalainen
Proofreading/Editing by Ivy Hanson
Special thanks to Michelle and Ken Strukel
Manufactured in the United States of America by
Callies/Hanson Publishing

First Edition, March 2006
Second Edition, May 2006

Cover photo was taken by Patricia Callies.
Permission to print the cartoon on the back cover was given by
the artist, Roy Blomker. This painting was done in oils and
gifted to Bill by Roy.

ISBN: 978-1-4243-0075-4

To order books, send $17.00 for each book ordered to cover
costs, tax and mailing. Send a check or money order to
Callies/Hanson Publishing, 3308 1st Avenue, Hibbing, MN
55746 or call 218-258-7831. Reseller discounts are available.

Bill would most likely have dedicated this book to his wife, Patricia. Bill said marrying Patricia was the smartest thing he had ever done. They were married for fifty-one years and she often encouraged him to write another story. She was his best friend and a marvelous mother to their children. He said he was able to be the warden he was because Patricia was his helpmate and she was willing to be his assistant without pay at each station. She was mentioned in many of the stories but that does not really give the reader the complete picture. Patricia was a urbane city girl but she adjusted quickly to being a warden's wife. Besides being chief cook and bottle washer, she manned phones, monitored state radios, tagged pelts from trappers, chased shiners and even put on his hat and learned to wave at people like Bill did so that locals did not know he was staked out someplace else. He had many reasons to say marrying her was the smartest thing he ever did.

Our Dad, William (Bill) Callies, was always a great storyteller. Growing up, he would tell us bedtime stories about his life as a young man in Iowa. He always had exciting experiences to relate. His whole life was really extraordinary. We remember a Dad who went to work in a white shirt and a tie. He had been a journeyman floor installer in the carpenters' union but he rose quickly to be in charge of all of the floor installers for different companies and even to start his own floor-covering store, Modern Floors, in St. Louis Park, Minnesota. At age forty-three, he came home to our Edina home to tell us he had been offered a job as a Minnesota Game Warden. He said he would not make any money at it but he thought he might live ten years longer. The full story he wrote about becoming a warden and the training he experienced in 1960 is in the appendix of this book.

It was a culture shock for the family—we used to live in Edina and Dad was a businessman and then we lived in Waskish, Minnesota with thirty-two year round residents on Upper Red Lake and we were the family of the game warden and many of the people did not really want a warden.

Being a game warden, for Dad, was the BEST job in the world. The State of Minnesota gave him equipment and he got to play cops and robbers all day and all night. He absolutely LOVED his job and he worked hard at it.

When he was in Waskish, he was the only law enforcement officer for miles around so he handled lots of calls not really related to game and fish laws. He was stationed in Waskish for fifteen years, then he and Mom moved to Ironton to the Crosby/Ironton station. He spent a short time stationed in Orr, Minnesota and eventually bid on and got Baudette, Minnesota with Lake of the Woods in his territory—just forty miles north of Waskish. He retired from the Minnesota Department of Conservation after twenty years as a warden when they were living in Baudette. Dad could always mesmerize people with his stories. After he retired, with Mom we tried to get him to write stories and he finally did. He told us he would write but we could not publish them until after he died. He died September 21, 2003 and this is volume I of two volumes of his stories.

Most of the stories are written about his years stationed at Waskish. We think it was the area he loved the best but it also was where he spent the most years. Reading these, you might think he was prejudiced with his references to Indians, Blacks, Swedes, etc. He really treated everyone the same—if you broke the law, you should be held responsible. He would get very frustrated with Indian problems at Waskish because his area had the western border on the Red Lake reservation. When he was most upset with the members of the tribe, we would remind him he was one-eighth Native American. Knowing that might have actually caused some of his frustrations—he thought they should respect the law more and be better all around citizens.

Dad treated everyone the same. He wrote the stories as he saw them. Some people are going to be happy seeing their names in the print, others may not. The stories relate the history of his work as he lived it.

We hope everyone will enjoy reading this and realize what the job of Minnesota Game Warden involved during the twenty years from 1960 to 1980.

Ivy Hanson and Fred Callies

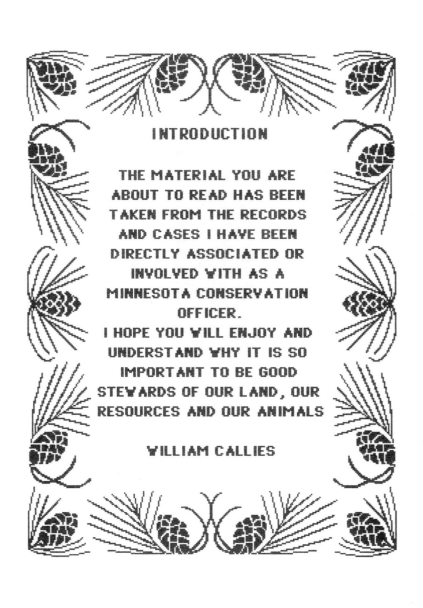

INTRODUCTION

THE MATERIAL YOU ARE
ABOUT TO READ HAS BEEN
TAKEN FROM THE RECORDS
AND CASES I HAVE BEEN
DIRECTLY ASSOCIATED OR
INVOLVED WITH AS A
MINNESOTA CONSERVATION
OFFICER.
I HOPE YOU WILL ENJOY AND
UNDERSTAND WHY IT IS SO
IMPORTANT TO BE GOOD
STEWARDS OF OUR LAND, OUR
RESOURCES AND OUR ANIMALS

WILLIAM CALLIES

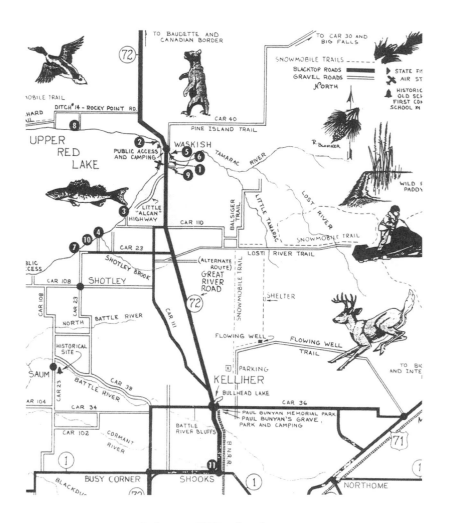

Map of Waskish area

TABLE OF CONTENTS:

Appendix

Chapter 1/ *WARDEN NEIGHBORS*

IN THE FALL OF 1960, while on probation, I had an opportunity to check out a warden station that was on the vacant list. It was at Waskish, Minnesota on the east shore of Upper Red Lake. I was assigned to work with Harland Pickett at Baudette, Minnesota, who, if I were fortunate to be assigned to the Waskish Station, would be my neighbor to the north. Eventually, while on probation I was able to meet Leo Manthei, of Blackduck, who would be my neighbor to the south.

Eventually, on January 16, 1961, I was assigned to the Waskish Station. No one else put in for it, partially on the advice of the last game and fish enforcement man to occupy the station. In fact, the station had been vacant for over two years. Its former occupant was Al Markovich, at that time stationed as the game warden at Warroad.

This station had a state house, a big old log house to live in, however, the Section of Game had scavenged it. The furnace, water heater, and sump pump had been spirited off to some other state building. Consequently, there was a lot of work I had to do before I could bring my family to this new, old home.

As I have told you earlier, I had met my neighboring wardens to the north and the south. My western boundary was the Red Lake Indian Reservation. I had yet to meet my neighboring warden to the east and come to a mutual agreement on our district lines.

Finally one day in February, a letter came out from our area supervisor, Dick Tarte, that we were to meet in Bemidji for an area meeting. It was here and then I was introduced to James Ces Richards, the game warden from Big Falls. My first impression was that he looked like the English caricature of John Bull. He was obviously the oldest man in the area—I would guess in his late 50's. At the time he seemed to want to know as much about me as I wanted to know about him. I noticed a round object in his shirt pocket that I assumed to be a Copenhagen snuff can. I was to become aware through future association that prior to his making a major statement, he would send a brown stream of tobacco juice onto the ground. He told me he was among the last of the old political appointees and was able to survive the changes of political parties. The method of selecting game wardens after 1945 was through the civil service system.

Eventually into the meeting Supervisor Tarte asked Ces, he being the senior man, where our mutual line should be. Ces responded with "Bill can come right up to my wood pile", which meant that whether I went by the logging road across Pine Island or by the black top through Kelliher, Mizpah, and Margie, I would have to drive over fifty miles to my eastern district line. Ces did relent before the end of the meeting and we settled on a north-south logging road on Pine Island about halfway between Big Falls and Waskish known as the Fiero Truck Trail.

Ces let me know that although there were hundreds of game and fish laws to enforce, the only ones he considered worth enforcing were those pertinent to trapping fur bearing animals and spot lighting deer.

Over the years, Ces always made it a point to get approval from our supervisor to come to Waskish for the opening of the walleye fishing season to assist me checking fishermen. However, because to spend any time checking fishermen was at the bottom of his list, we would spend that first weekend looking up old friends. We would catch a mess of walleyes and persuade my wife to fry them up for a good meal of fresh pike. Then he would want to catch one limit of walleye to take home to "Ruby", his wife. This was high on his priority list.

Having spent the first two years of the opening season in this manner and never recording any violations, and then the following weeks I would write up a number of violations, I became concerned that our supervisor, Tarte, would chew me out for not making good use of my assistant neighboring warden. So, on the third year of the opening fishing season I told Ces of my concern and that this year we were going out on the lake and check fishermen. This did not meet with his approval. However, he decided to humor me and go along with my decision.

Left to Right: Bill Callies, Ces Richards, Gil Keeler

So at daylight, we got into the state Alumacraft boat powered by an 18 horse power Johnson motor and proceeded out the Tamarac River and out to the closest boat on Red Lake. There were three men in the boat. When I pulled along side the boat, I observed the man in the back seat by the motor was using three fish lines (only one is allowed in Minnesota). All of the men had current angling licenses in their possession. So I wrote a summons and seizure slip for the man in the back. I spent a few minutes explaining to the violator where and how to take care of the summons.

I then started the outboard motor and headed for the next boatload of fishermen. I had gone about a hundred yards when Ces turned around from his front seat and signaled for me to shut the motor off. When the motor shut down and the boat came to a stop, Ces spoke up and said, "That takes care of the paper work. Now let's go fishing."

On another instance, Supervisor Tarte called me to go over to Namakan Lake to do some additional work in the state cabin. I was to meet Ray Appleby at the cabin. He was to bring the material up from Orr by way of Crane Lake, Sandpoint Lake and into Namakan. I was to bring the state 16-foot boat on a trailer to the access on the Ash River, then through Kabetogama into Namakan.

Somehow or other, Ces heard about this work project and made a request to Supervisor Tarte to deadhead along. Tarte ok'd this, so I picked up Ces in Big Falls, his sleeping bag, packsack and grub. We got to the Ash River access and off-loaded the boat, my tools, sleeping bags, packsacks and grub. I had two six gallon gas cans for the outboard motor, one can was full the other had about two gallons in it. We proceeded down the Ash River through Sullivan Bay, the Narrows, Lake Kabetogama and into Namakan Lake. Somewhere down near Cameron Bay, the can with the two gallons of gas went dry. When the boat came to a stop, I disconnected the empty can and was in the process of hooking up the full can. I happened to look up at Ces and was surprised to see tears running down his face. I was real concerned and I asked, "What the hell's wrong?" Ces let a stream of tobacco juice loose and he came back with, "God makes this country so beautiful and he only lets us stay for such a short while."

I could tell you hundreds of stories and instances about this man. He was very proud to be a game warden and there were some wardens he was proud to work with. I remember one instance that he couldn't wait to tell me about. He worked with and thought a lot about his neighboring warden to the north, Gil

Keeler of Littlefork. It seems this one fall and winter we had little or no snow cover through the deer season. This situation would find the deer coming out onto alfalfa fields, openings, and roadsides to graze at night. This situation left some of us working nights to curb deer shining. The particular instance Ces narrated to me occurred one night south of Big Falls on Number Six. He had Gil Keeler with him. Gil was driving, Ces was the passenger. They drove down Number Six until they located a deer out on an opening. Gil drove to a place near there where they could pull off the road and hide their car. Some time went by (actually, he said it was around one a.m.), when they heard one shot from a hi-power rifle in the direction of where they had seen the deer. Gil started the car and pulled out on to the black top without the use of his lights. They drove slowly and quietly eventually coming to a car stopped on the road ahead of them with their lights out. Then out in the opening, they could see two men with a small flashlight messing around with something on the ground. Ces then told me he took his five-cell flashlight and flipped the light onto the two men. Ces said he recognized the older man. He lived in Margie. He then called out the man's name and instructed the two men to come to him in the patrol car. That man knew it was no use to run because the wardens had his car and Ces would pick him up at his home in Margie the next day. The other man was not so cooperative. He took off into the bush on a dead run. This brought Gil out from behind the wheel and with his five cell flashlight in hand, he took into the woods in hot pursuit.

The older man Ces called up to the car told Ces, "You might as well call your partner back because he never will in God's world catch my hunting partner." He went on to tell he was a young, husky farmer, a logger and a good woodsman. At this point Ces told me, "I whipped out my pocket book and threw a ten dollar bill on the car seat and I told that fellow, "Your five dollar bill will get that ten dollar bill if he doesn't." Then according to Ces they waited about two hours and they could see the glow of a light coming through the bush. Eventually, they could make out the two men. Gill had his jacket and shirt over his arm. He was down to his underwear and it looked like Gill was surrounded by fog. He had the man's arm and was pulling him. Needless to say Ces picked up a fiver.

On another occasion to further understand this man, Ces asked me to come over to Big Falls to give him a hand at something. At this date I do not remember exactly what we were to do. Ces suggested I bring my wife along so that our wives could get better acquainted.

Left to Right: Leo Manthei, Les Borning, Bill Callies

We arrived at the Richard's home early that Saturday morning and were invited in for coffee from Ruby's bottomless coffee pot. We were sitting at the Richard's kitchen table when an elderly man, (obviously an old logger or a "Jippo" as they were known as in those days) came pounding on Richard's back door. The man was very excited. It seems there was some property on the east side of Big Falls that was owned by a local individual. This property had an old house, a barn, and several small buildings on it. The house was rented out to another Jippo that had a wife and several small children. The owner of this property propositioned the old Jippo into tearing the barn down and for his services he could have the lumber he salvaged. By so doing, the owner could get a reduction on his property tax. The Jippo went over to this property to check the barn to see if he could handle the chore and the quality of the salvage. He was up in the haymow when two shots rang out from a high power rifle. The bullets came through the wall and out through the roof sending a shower of splintered wood all over the hay mow. The Jippo had enough of that and he jumped down from the hay mow door on the back side of the barn and headed for Ces's house on a dead run. Ces being the only law enforcement in Big Falls at this time and place to spill out the story of what happened.

Ces jumped up, grabbed his hat and jacket, and instructed me to come along. The Jippo elected to sit this one out.

Ces and I arrived at this old house that hadn't seen any paint for many years. A lot of the windows were broken and old blankets were hung over the openings from the inside. Ces pounded on the front door. We stood on the front porch listening to a lot of scrambling from inside the house. Eventually the door was opened by a cruddy looking person in his late thirties. He growled, "What do you guys want?"

Ces explained that we had a complaint from a logger that someone fired two shots at him while he was checking out the barn and then asked the man if he knew who might have been doing the shooting.

The man spoke up and said, "You're dam right I know who was doing the shooting at that son of a bitch. It was me. I pay rent on this place and no one has any right to come in on this place unless I say so."

Ces said, "You wouldn't mind if we looked around?"

The guy said, "Like hell you will. Get off my porch." And with that he pushed past us, went out into the yard west of the house to a good sized German Shepherd dog that was chained up there. Ces and I went back to Ces' car from where we observed this man removing the chain from the dog. He seemed to have a good hold on the dog's collar and started to walk back to the house with the dog.

Ces opened the car door, reached under the driver's side seat and pulled out his service revolver, a .38 special Smith and Wesson with a six inch barrel. Ces slapped the gun into my hand with the instruction, "If he turns that dog loose, kill him." Things were getting pretty tense. The man went into the house with the dog.

Then Ces turned to me and said, "You stay out here on the road where you can watch the out-buildings. I'm going to go look for Miller, who is the justice of the peace, and get a search warrant for this place." Ces took off in the car. I had the revolver stuck in my back pocket and I was standing out on that dirt road feeling very conspicuous.

Suddenly the inside door opened and then the screen door was knocked open so hard I thought the hinges would come off. This guy lands on his feet on the porch and he has got a 303 British Army rifle in his hands. The action was open and I could see the glint of the brass shells as he was shoving them into the magazine. He slammed the bolt shut, which I knew chambered the first shell. In a flash, the stock was on his shoulder and I'm standing looking at that little black hole pointed right at my belly. There was no place to run for cover and to reach for that pea shooter in my back pocket would surely set this man off. Then the man hollered, "I can split a wand at a hundred yards."

I was only thirty yards away and a lot wider than a wand. All I could do was holler, "Hold it mister. Whatever your problem is now, is nothing to what the problems you will have if you pull that trigger."

He stood there like a statue for what seemed like an hour. Then real slowly, he started to lower the gun. Then he said, "Yeah, I guess you're right." I then suggested he go back in the house unload the gun and put it away. I was really relieved when he went back in the house. In fact, as I remember, I started to get the shakes. Then it started to rain, not hard, but it seemed to make me shiver harder. Then the front door opened again, slower this time, and there was this man again. I remember I quit shaking then. Of all things, this man invited me to come into the house out of the rain. I declined his offer, told him I would wait out on the road 'til my partner came back.

Eventually Ces showed up with the warrant. I told him about my incident with the tenant. Ces then got on his car radio, called the dispatcher at Virginia and instructed him to get hold of the sheriff at International Falls and have him come with a deputy to pick this man up and hold him.

With that, we went to the house. Ces pounded on the door again. The man came to the door and Ces announced, "I've got the paper. You want me to read it to you?"

The man said, "No, you've got the paper so go ahead and look around."

The first little building southwest of the house had the carcass of a small deer. It was dressed out, skinned, and cut into four quarters. The four quarters were fresh and had been hung on nails on the wall. Outside in the grass I could see a bloody trail that I followed to a big hole in the ground that might have been an old well pit. In the bottom of this pit, we could see several deer heads, hides, and legs.

We loaded the dressed out carcass into the car trunk and then we went into the house. We met the man, his wife, and three young children. Everyone looked pretty cruddy and poorly dressed. There was an old round oak table in the middle of the kitchen and in the middle of the table was a big bowl of boiled meat. They told us it too was venison. Other than the venison, there was no other food in the house. There was an old barrel stove to keep the whole house warm. Actually, it didn't even keep the kitchen warm. Ces sat down at the table made out the summons and seizure receipt for the deer meat.

We waited for about an hour until the sheriff and his deputy arrived. They took the man, the rifle, and the ammunition out to the sheriff's car, then on up to International Falls where the man was locked up. The first day of court he was taken before the district judge and charged with threatening to shoot me.

Ces and I went over to his house where we spent some time trying to calm a couple of concerned wives. Ces then told Ruby to put together a lot of canned goods and potatoes from their vegetable cellar. We then made out the confiscation papers for the meat. Ces took out his pocket book, took out a dollar that he stuck in an envelope along with the confiscation papers. He addressed the envelope to our supervisor. He then put a stamp on the envelope and we gathered up all the canned goods, spuds, and bread and headed for the post office where Ces left the letter in the mailbox. The next stop was back to the house where the woman and her three children were. We hauled in all the grub plus the four quarters of deer meat. We then cut up some firewood that would hold them until Ruby would get the welfare down to take over.

The man got a sentence of 90 days for threatening me and a hundred dollar fine for possessing a deer in closed season. Later the sheriff advised me the family came from Montana and that the man had been released from a mental institution.

Chapter 2/ FISHERMEN FROM CEDAR FALLS

On one opening of the walleye season while stationed at Waskish, two other wardens and our area supervisor came over to assist me checking fishermen on Upper Red Lake. Usually Upper Red Lake is one of the hot spots in the state for walleyed pike and I am reasonably sure on the opening weekend we have 5,000 fishermen. It doesn't take any skill to catch a daily limit of six walleyes in an hour or less. Most of these fish run about a pound a piece and it is a common practice to go out on the lake, catch a limit of fish, return to their campsite, clean their fish, eat them and then go back out and catch another limit. I have reason to believe there are some would be sports that repeat this process up to a half dozen times on an opening weekend. It is hard to police this problem where there are so many boats and people coming and going and evidence is hidden in their bellies. However on occasion, we do get a break and the following stories will testify to that.

On this particular opening, I had the assistance of these three wardens. They stayed over until Monday, so they could enjoy a businessman's holiday. We caught a mess of fish off the dock in back of the house. I filleted them out and my wife fried up the fish along with other goodies. After this good feed, I suggested we go down to the Kansas City Resort and run a fish check on their guests. Now the Kansas City Resort is located about two and a half miles southwest of Waskish. The last two miles is down a winding one-track road through the woods, with occasional turnouts in the event you meet oncoming vehicles.

The owner of the Kansas City Resort dubs this trail or road "The Little Alcan Highway". On this particular day, we met an old school bus converted into a kind of motor home, coming out from the Kansas City Resort on the Little Alcan Highway. We all came to a stop and I left my patrol vehicle to check this vehicle and its occupants out. There were two men and two women on board. I could see through the window they had fishing gear on the outside and there were several cane poles tied onto the vehicle. I asked them if they had any luck fishing and they let me know fishing was good. They said they had caught their limit, brought them into camp, cleaned them, and had a big fish feed. I then asked to see their angling licenses and the men each produced a non-resident combination husband and wife license. I noted that they all had the same last name and

THEY USED TO CALL US GAME WARDENS

that they were all from Cedar Falls, Iowa. It turned out the two men were brothers and they said they were in the scrap-iron business in Cedar Falls.

I then told them I wanted to get on the bus and check to see if they had any fish and how many. They were reluctant to let me do this but as my partner wardens had, out of curiosity, moseyed up behind me, they decided to let a couple of us come aboard. We were in for quite an eye opening. These people had enough supplies, gasoline and home canned goods to stay in Minnesota for a month and never have to purchase anything. They had two large wooden boxes full of worms and night crawlers for fish bait. I had heard some of the resorters comment about fishermen from our neighboring state and they would say these people come up here with a clean pair of overalls and a twenty-dollar bill and they don't change either of them.

We continued our check through their belongings and we eventually came upon a large round washtub full of fish fillets. There was some ice on top of the fillets (two fillets constitute one fish) and when we finished counting, we had one hundred forty-six walleye pike. If we had come onto them before their big fish feed, I'm sure we would have eight or ten more fish. Allowing that they could legally have twenty-four walleyes they ended up with one hundred twenty-two walleyes over their legal limit.

We wrote the two brothers up for over the legal limit of walleyed pike. We did not charge the women. I booked the two men into justice of the peace court in Kelliher, Minnesota. They were to appear before Justice Clara Quale. We all drove first to my residence to pick up my helpers' patrol cars so they could return to their assigned districts. I took the two men with me to Kelliher, about fifteen miles south of Waskish. Their wives followed in their converted school bus.

When we arrived at Mrs. Quale's office, the two brothers and myself went in. Mrs. Quale owned and operated the

Kelliher Independent newspaper, which put out a small weekly newspaper with the aid of one female assistant. Usually, when I came in the front door, Mrs. Quale would come through the door from the printing room with her heavy apron on, wiping ink off her hands with an old rag. Her usual opening statement when she saw me with some people in tow was, "Well, what do we have here?"

I offered her my copies of the summons plus the copy of the seizure receipt for the fish. The judge then sat down at her desk, inserted a form in her old typewriter, and typed out the complaints for each man. She would then announce Justice Court for Beltrami County was now in session. She would then have me read her typed out complaints with the statute section and subdivision of the law that these people were in violation of. She would then have me swear to it and sign my name. Then court would begin. The two men, knowing they had been caught with the goods, pleaded guilty.

She noted on the seizure receipt how many fish they had and commented on they must have really been biting. So she handed down her sentence—thirty dollars or thirty days for each man.

At this both men started to laugh so the judge asked, "What's so funny?"

They then told us they only had twenty-eight dollars between them.

The judge said, "That's no problem." She sat down at her typewriter, made out commitment papers, then she instructed me to take them to the county jail in Bemidji and turn them over to the sheriff, John Cahill.

I loaded the two men into the patrol car and with the two women following us in their converted school bus we drove the forty-five miles to Bemidji. We stopped out in front of the sheriff's office and I escorted the two brothers to the desk where a deputy sheriff started to book them. All of a sudden, these men began to realize this was all for real and right now we had a Donny Brook on our hands. We finally got them back into the cells and locked up where they would do their thirty days. I then went out to my patrol car and headed home to Waskish. Now days when I read in the paper the fines imposed on game and fish violations, if those two men were to come before our courts with that kind of a violation, they would probably get a fine of a thousand dollars and ninety days in jail.

To get back to our story, about ten o'clock that evening I got a long distance call from the county sheriff's office to the effect that these two fishermen did not like the counties' accommodations. They requested and got permission to float a loan over the telephone from their banker in Cedar Falls. The money was to come up via Western Union the following day. The deputy sheriff wanted to know if the men could be released. I told him that was up to the judge; however, I would call her and get back to him. Upon hearing of their request the judge said, "When the money is laying on my kitchen table, that is when we can unlock their cell door." The money arrived the following day around noon and they were released.

Two hours later they were at my headquarters wanting their angling licenses back. As I had only placed one charge against each man, I had no legal right to void their licenses.

When I turned their licenses over to them, I let these men know I was born and raised in Fort Dodge, Iowa and I could remember, as a boy, how some of the so called sports would go to Minnesota and see who could return with the most game and/or fish. I told these men, "You are just like a plague moving northwards across the state, cleaning out one lake after another." One day, they would go to Canada and start on those lakes.

Chapter 3/ SENIOR CITIZENS

It was about 6:30 p.m. of the first Saturday of the deer season in November of 1962. I was scheduled to work that night in a work party in Harland Pickett's area to start around 8:00 p.m. There were a half dozen wardens involved, plus John Parker would be flying in the Super Cub with our Supervisor, Dick Tarte, as observer.

I took a short cruise around the resorts in Waskish to see how the hunters had made out on the opening day and to look for untagged deer.

Just as I approached the lodge at the Sunset Resort, I noted a four-door sedan sitting in front of the lodge with its motor running. There was an elderly man at the wheel and two elderly women in the back seat.

They were motioning and calling to a man approaching with a gun case that appeared to have a gun in it. There was a lot of enthusiasm in the calls from the vehicle that caused the gun carrying person to break into a trot. There was a lot of chattering as he climbed into the front seat and set the gun case between himself and the driver. I thought I better nip this little program right in the bud.

I pulled the patrol car right across in front of their vehicle, got out with my five-cell flashlight in my hand and approached the vehicle from the driver's side. The driver rolled his window down. I shone my light inside and there between the driver and the passenger was a big spot light with about six feet of cord and it was plugged into the cigarette lighter.

I then asked, "What have you folks got in mind?" It was extremely quiet in the car now. Then I told them "It looks like we all have the same thing in mind."

"I'm going out and drive around the country until I locate a nice deer or two feeding in some alfalfa field. Only I'm not going to shoot at those deer. I'm going to hide my car real good so that a group of shiners like you folks can't see me. Then when you shine your light on that deer I will come out of hiding and if that gun has any shells in it I will pounce on you."

"I will seize your gun, the spot light, and your car. Then I will haul you down to Kelliher and put you in an iron cage with one straw mattress and a five-gallon can to relieve yourselves. I will go back out and look for more people that have the same thing in mind and bring them to the iron cage and stuff them in with you."

"Then in the morning, I will come to Kelliher and haul you down to Bemidji and lock you up until Monday morning."

At this point I stopped the narration because I could see one ladies' dress getting awfully wet—weak kidneys no doubt. That was the end of whatever they had in mind.

Chapter 4/ PREVIEW TO WARDENS' TACTICS BEFORE PRESENT LAWS

More specifically the title could be, "How we used to work to try to control night hunting for wild animals." It was a dangerous but thrilling method that even was condoned by district judges. It entailed driving at night without lights. Most of the wardens rigged up various kinds of sneak lights, which, in most cases, was the old black light used on army motor vehicles during World War II. To begin with you would by hook or by crook acquire one of these army black lights. I was fortunate in that one time when I was in Minneapolis, I went to Wilensky's Auto Parts and they had about a dozen of new army surplus black lights. He wanted $2.00 a piece. I had $10.00 so I bought five of them. They had a 6-volt light in them which had to be converted to a 12-volt light. I finally located a 12-volt tractor light that fit and I made the switch.

Next, was to get a good mount and a hook-up so you could turn it on or off. Also we had the light rigged so it could be easily dismounted during the day so that word wouldn't get out to the night hunters that we had a new secret weapon. We also had a switch to disconnect our back up and brake light and we would remove the dome light so that no light would give us away if we opened the door.

Now, we are set to observe these night hunters and get sufficient evidence to satisfy the county attorneys, the judges, and in some cases the jury, that we had a good case.

Usually starting around September 1st, I would go to some remote part of my district around sundown, park the car back on some old logging road out of sight of traffic on the side road (usually near a field that deer liked to come out on to graze), and there I would set up to wait for a spot lighter to come along. Also, I would check to see if my neighboring warden was out working and if he was close enough to maintain radio contact in the event either of us needed assistance.

Usually this was a very boring existence because you would sit all night every night for days on end and never see another car. The only thing to break the boredom would be eating my lunch that my wife packed for me every day. Occasionally my son-in-law or a close trusted friend would sit the night out with me.

But when that moment comes when a vehicle casting a spotlight or head lights from side to side or out across a field, you can't imagine the excitement and anticipation that comes inside of you. It's a greater thrill than the most fantastic hunting or fishing experience I ever had, and this is just the beginning of the experience.

Now the problem is to observe this vehicle and try to get the car stopped before the gun is shot. Of course, if you see someone shoot or there is a deer in the vehicle in closed season then you have the party dead-to-right.

Chapter 5/ *THE THREE SWEDES FROM GONVICK*

This little episode took place on the opening of the walleye pike season. J.C. Richards, the warden from Big Falls, Minnesota, had been sent over to work with me to check fishermen on Upper Red Lake. Ces had come over the day before the season and we spent the evening before seeing to it that no one started before midnight. Around one in the morning, we hit the sack to get a few hours sleep.

Around 5 a.m., I woke up from the roar of outboard motors on the Tamarac River in back of the house. My wife got up and made us a good, big, hot breakfast as we didn't know when we would find time for our next meal.

After breakfast, I told Ces we would take the patrol car and drive back to the stone chimney, which was located near where the Lost River empties into the Tamarac River, about ten miles east of Waskish. I knew there were still a lot of walleyes up-river left over from the spawning run. Where there are fish, you will find fishermen. To get there, you have to drive south of Waskish five miles on Highway 72, east four miles on a county road, then south two miles on a forestry road, east to the county line, where you get on the Balsiger Trail, north past the old abandoned town site of Norden, east across a small bridge over the Little Tamarac River, and eventually you have to turn north. After about four miles, you come to a bridge crossing the lost river.

I didn't mention it before, but this trail dead-ends about a quarter of a mile further on where the old stone chimney stands along side of the Tamarac River. As we approached the bridge, we could see a half dozen cars parked along side the trail. There were about ten people fishing off the bridge and at least ten more fishing from the bank.

As we got close to the bridge, three of the fishermen on the bridge jumped up and started to run north. In less than a minute, we crossed the bridge and caught up with them and I hollered at them to halt, which they did.

We got out of the car and started to quiz them about being so anxious to leave and meanwhile, we kept our eyes on the rest of the fishermen. These three men were nervous and we felt reasonably sure they had something to be nervous about. We walked them back to the bridge and started checking fish stringers and counting fish. All the fish stringers were claimed by the various fishermen. Also, there were three stringers with six fish on each one that were claimed by our three new friends. Then, I asked to see fishing licenses and every one came up with a license. There was no violation here unless they had fish in their car. They identified their car, unlocked the doors, and again we found no fish. Then I had them open the trunk. There were no fish in the trunk, but there was a two-burner gas plate, a twenty-pound bottle of propane gas, and a large iron kettle, about a four-quart size. In the bottom was about a quart of half coagulated grease. You could still feel some heat on the kettle. I stuck my nose down in the kettle and I could smell fish. I turned to these three men and asked them how many fish they had eaten and none of them opened their mouths. They were obviously nervous. In fact, two of them got the shakes and it wasn't that cold.

Finally, I told them the evidence was gone and we couldn't do anything to them unless we caught them later on in the day catching more walleyes. But just out of curiosity, when did they start fishing and how many fish had they eaten. After about fifteen minutes of assuring them I wouldn't do anything to them, they said they started fishing at midnight. They had caught three limits each, filleted them out, and each had eaten eighteen fish. They were just going to eat the eighteen more on their stringers when we drove up. I was amazed and inquired how they could eat so much. One of them, obviously a Scandinavian, said, "They are small and it's just like eating potato chips."

Chapter 6/ SPOTTING SCOPES

One summer day in 1962, I finally accumulated enough money doing side jobs laying floors to purchase a spotting scope. I always felt if I could observe individuals from a great distance, I could do a better job of enforcing the manner in which fish or game could be taken. Usually, when I made personal contact with the individual, I would note extra equipment laying about that had been used but at this moment of contact it would be laying about, not operating, and no way would the individual admit to using it.

So this day, found my wife and I in Herter's sporting good store in southern Minnesota purchasing one spotting scope with five eyepieces of various powers from 15x to 60x for forty-eight hard-earned dollars.

Eventually, we got home to our station in Waskish with my new toy and as soon as I could get my wife, luggage, and other purchases unloaded, I got into my patrol car with my new scope and drove over to the lake (Upper Red Lake) to see if there were any fishermen. The lake was so rough there were no fishermen out there. However, off to the north of me at the mouth of the Tamarac River, I could see a boat. I knew I could better observe the boat from the bridge across the Tamarac River, so I drove to this new observation site. I also had purchased a spotting scope mount that could be attached to the window of my patrol car. I could, under some circumstances, sit comfortably in my patrol car and observe individuals to see if they were violating any of the laws of the Conservation Department.

From the bridge, I could see there were two boats with two people in each boat. When I looked through the scope, I could see there was a man and boy in each boat and also that both men were angling with more than one line, which is a violation in Minnesota. I knew if I went home to get my boat and went out to apprehend these people, they would have plenty of time to get the extra lines out. Also, I would be too far away to observe this act with the naked eye and they would deny having done anything wrong.

So I found a notebook in my patrol car and decided to observe these people over a period of time and make notes. Also, I was pleased to see, I could make out their boat license numbers. At any rate, they ate candy bars and I could even identify the brand names. As they caught fish, I noted the time and specie of fish. I could identify each different piece of fishing equipment. In fact, with the aid of the scope, it was almost like sitting in the boat with them.

After about a half hour of making notes and accumulating evidence, I was ready to go home, get my own boat, and go out and contact these people. As I came down the river and under the bridge, I'm sure these men heard my motor or saw my boat. This was confirmed when I pulled up to their boats as everyone was fishing with one line. Their extra poles were in the bottom of the boat. The lines were wet, and the minnows on their hooks were still flopping. I told them they were in violation of the law, which they denied. Because the water was so rough, I told these people to pull up their anchors and come into the quiet water under the bridge. They complied with my instructions. Then I showed these men my notes and they gave up. I made out the summons for the following Tuesday evening. When they appeared before justice of the peace, Clara Quale, on Tuesday evening, one of the men took me aside and said the hardest thing he had to live with was lying to me in front of his son. I was on cloud nine. The spotting scope was a good tool for our trade. Every time I made a case with the use of the spotting scope, I would note this on the bottom of my arrest report hoping to convince the supervisors and the St. Paul office they should purchase one for each man.

A few years went by and one winter day when my area supervisor, Les Borning, came around for his inspection of state equipment, I suggested he come along with me to see how effective the spotting scope could be. We took the state snowmobile on a trailer behind the patrol car, a small portable radio, and we started checking ice fishermen. Finally, I observed one pick-up truck with two fishermen out on the ice a long way from any other fishermen. I got the spotting scope out and hooked it up on the window mount and I started observing.

Supervisor Les Borning and beaver

We were about three-fourths of a mile from them. After some time, I had witnessed the larger of the two people tend and pull fish out using more than the allowable number of lines. I then told my supervisor to take the portable radio, unload our snowmobile, and go out to this individual. I told him to swing in a big arc to the north so he would not get in my line of sight, as I wanted to witness what he did when he removed his extra lines. It took my supervisor about ten minutes to get into his snowmobile suit and gear, stow his portable radio, summons book, etc. All this time, I was recording on my notebook what our fishermen suspects were doing. Finally, I heard our snow machine start up and Les took off staying well out of my line of sight. When he was about a third of the way, one fisherman started hastily pulling out fishing lines and stowing them under what looked like a small blanket or piece of canvas. Then he took a few steps to the north and urinated. About this time, Les appeared in the spotting scope and I could see him check the fishermen's licenses. Then Les got out the portable and announced the men's licenses were good. They didn't have too many fish and everything looked okay. I then told Les, with the aid of my car radio, the larger man had been fishing with too many lines and when he heard or saw you coming, he quickly pulled them out and tucked them under that blanket or object laying there on the ice. Then I said the man took a few paces to the north and urinated just before you showed up. I went on to tell of other things the person had been doing and also that the smaller person was not using more lines than he was allowed.

All the time I was telling Les what happened, I could see the larger person looking in every direction and he appeared to be getting upset. Then I could see Les make out the summons and seizure ticket, picked up all the winter fish lines under the object on the ice, got on his snowmobile, and came back to me. Les was quite enthused and said, "That was the easiest pinch I ever made. That fisherman was so mad at that little black box telling on him. He wasn't mad at me at all."

Eventually, the state did purchase one spotting scope for each man in the field.

Chapter 7/ BEAR MEAT 1962: QUESTIONABLE QUALITIES

A number of state employees met up on Pine Island to discuss input for the coming beaver season. There were people from the Division of Forestry and the Department of Transportation (who, by the way, hated beaver because of the problems they incur). There were people from the Section of Game who would be responsible for setting the future beaver season, the manner of taking, and the number that could be taken.

To this group were added three game wardens; myself, and Gill Keeler, who had only been on the warden force for a few years, then there was Ces Richards, a warden with over thirty years on the force, who was very knowledgeable and a shrewd individual.

Due to the fact one of the members had sighted a bear, the conversation turned in that direction. Bear were unprotected in those days, which was something the game managers were trying to change. Eventually, the conversation got around to the best time of the year to hunt bear so as to get the hide and the meat at the peak of its quality. Some of the men seemed to like the spring when the bear first came out of hibernation. They were lean and usually easy to locate along streams and ditches feeding on fish in their spawning run. There were those that advocated taking them in the summer when they were feeding on berries, etc. Then there were those that liked to take them in the fall when the bear got in the oat fields and acorns.

Through all of this enlightening information, Gill and I kept our mouths shut. Knowing if any comments on the subject were to be forthcoming, it would be from our senior warden. Ces Richards also hadn't said anything. He just looked at one man after another as they poured out their knowledge on the subject.

Then Ces spit a big stream of tobacco juice and spoke up and said, "Boys, if you want my opinion, I think I would rather pay the difference and eat shit."

That concluded the meeting.

Chapter 8/ CLEMENSON STORE ROBBERY

I was mowing the grass at the state home and office where we lived at Waskish. As I remember, it seemed like I mowed grass all summer and shoveled snow all winter. Not only did I perform these tasks, but I also had to furnish the lawn mower and snow shovel.

On this day, my wife came out of the house on the run towards me, motioning for me to shut off the lawn mower. She had heard over the monitor in the house that the dispatcher at Thief River Falls put an all point bulletin out that two young men in a lavender colored Oldsmobile with Wisconsin plates had acquired gasoline at Clemenson, a small town on Highway 11, eight miles east of Baudette. The radio, by the way, was one I had purchased from the state when they updated our car radios. I had the radio man convert it to 110 so we could take power from the house current. The monitor was only a receiver and not a transmitter that received only one frequency, which was all we needed in those days. At any rate, they followed the proprietor into the store. Then, instead of paying for the gasoline, they held him up at gunpoint. They took his money, some cigarettes, candy, and groceries and took off in a westerly direction toward Baudette.

The proprietor of the store got in his car and pursued these thieves to a point two miles east of Baudette where Highway 72 goes south. The thieves turned south on 72 while the proprietor continued on into Baudette to alert the authorities. The authorities in Baudette called the Minnesota Highway Patrol dispatchers' office at Thief River Falls to alert them of the problem.

Waskish is thirty-eight miles south of the point where these men turned onto Highway 72 and as this road comes across the bog with only a couple of offshoot roads, it seemed logical that I could intercept them.

Waskish residence and office

I got into my patrol car, pulled out onto Highway 72, and turned north. About five miles north of Waskish there is a small dirt road going off to the west known as Ditch 14. I pulled onto Ditch 14, parked my car, uncased and loaded my double-barreled 12-gauge shotgun with buckshot. I then took my binoculars and walked back of the patrol car to where I could look north on Highway 72. From Ditch 14, Highway 72 is a straight shot north to the county line, about 15 miles north. However, you can only see about 7 miles because of the high point of land which is known as Ludlow Island.

Within minutes, I saw a car coming over this high point toward me. With the aid of the binoculars, I could see the car, which seemed to be coming at a high rate of speed. It was lavender in color.

I quickly got into my patrol car and backed up a few feet so that I was still out of sight to this oncoming vehicle. When their car was about three-fourths of a mile away, I backed out onto the black top leaving my car as a roadblock. I then jumped out of the car with my double barrel shotgun and ducked behind the hood with just my head and those two black holes of the barrel of my shotgun showing.

The Waskish warden residence, offices, outbuildings, and forestry buildings along the Tamarac River

They had one hell of a time getting stopped and they ended up about fifty feet from me. I'll admit I was pretty excited and I will guess they had no trouble hearing me when I yelled at them, "Get out of the car with your hands in the air, come around to the left side of the car, lean on it and spread your feet." Obviously, they didn't want to argue with my old double barrel shotgun, as they were very cooperative. I patted them down, but no weapons. However, I found five firearms in the car and a bow and arrows.

About the time I got everything under control, another car came from the north. It was the storekeeper and he identified the two men who, by the way, turned out to be juveniles. Eventually, the Minnesota Highway Patrolman, Earl Hendrickson, from Bemidji, showed up.

Using my handcuffs and Earl's, we cuffed the two lads. Then we loaded the two young men, their firearms, and the loot into Earl's squad car and he transported them to International Falls for incarceration because the violation had occurred in Koochiching County.

I went home, got my wife, and brought her back to the scene to drive the robber's car back to the station where it stayed until the courts instructed me what to do with it.

Then I settled down to my endless chore of mowing grass.

Chapter 9/ TRAINEE DURING FISH RUN

This series of incidents occurred in the spring of 1976. It was during that time when fish were moving into shallow areas to lay their eggs to continue their existence on this earth. This was also the time some people took advantage of the fish in their most vulnerable period. These people used spears, gill nets, dip nets, dynamite, unslacked lime, and snag hooks. Most of them operate at night using flashlights because walleye's eyes shine at night under a light and are the easiest to locate. I despise people who take fish in this manner.

While stationed at Waskish, I used to have trainees (new recruits) sent to me for a ten-day period to enlighten them on the ways of the game and fish thieves. Not that I know so much, but more because I lived in and rented a state house that had two cabins at the site where the trainees could bunk down. Unfortunately, my wife got stuck with feeding these men because the only cafe you could depend on was sixteen miles south of Waskish.

After sixteen years, I transferred to the Crosby-Ironton station. I suppose because it was in my records that I had been a trainer of recruits, I again was assigned recruits for a part of their training period.

This particular event was with a young man in his twenties. Me, I'm in my late fifties. There is a culvert that drains from Dahler Lake under state highway Number 6 into Emily Lake. Occasionally, big northern migrate through this culvert on their way to their spawning grounds. I chose this location that night to watch for fish thieves because there was a little trail off of Number 6 southwest of the culvert. From this location, we could sit in the patrol car and had a fairly good view if anyone was to check the culvert for fish. This culvert, by the way, is about five feet in diameter.

Along about eleven o'clock that night, a car came from the north. When it got near the culvert it slowed to about five miles per hour. It did not stop nor did anyone jump out. It had a noisy muffler. The car continued south about a quarter of a mile and pulled into the public access on the east side of Number 6, which is the access for Emily Lake. At first, I thought it could be some customers for us. However, the vehicle sat there for at least fifteen minutes. I assumed it must be lovers.

Then we saw their car lights come on and the car came back north toward us. It was moving very slow and when it just passed over the culvert about twenty feet, it stopped. We could see a shadowy figure get out on the passenger's side and move to the back of the vehicle and open the trunk. The driver opened his door, turned out the car lights, and turned so his feet were on the blacktop. The car motor was running.

A few seconds later, we could see a small light at the far

end of the culvert. I told the trainee I would go down on foot and when he saw me grab the guy at the end of the culvert, he should drive the patrol car down immediately.

I also warned the trainee to not make any noise. I then proceeded down to the road. I sneaked along the ditch on the west side of the road until I came to the culvert. I looked through the culvert and could see our man with his spear and small flashlight watching for fish. I took a deep breath then raised up slowly, getting ready to run. The car driver saw me. He hit his horn and in a flash, both the spearer and I were running. The car was going down the road about the same speed we were running. I had my five-cell flashlight on but never saw the spearer's face. We were both running as hard as we could go. The spearer was about ten feet in front of me. The driver slowed down just a bit. The spearer threw his spear in the trunk, slammed the lid down, jumped into the car and they were gone. I did get the license number. Then I turned, expecting my car to be coming. No way! I ran back to the patrol car. To say the least, I was mad and so winded I couldn't talk.

My trainee was so excited he fairly yelled, "That was just like watching an old cowboy movie. The good guy chasing the bad guy."

I don't think I had a very friendly response because he was very quiet. I called the dispatcher to get the name and address of the car owner. In the mean time, I'm driving every trail and road looking for the car. After almost fifteen minutes, the dispatcher got back to me and said that car license was not on file and even checking the late abandoned numbers they couldn't come up with anything. I kept on looking for at least two hours and finally gave up.

I can assure you before the night was over that trainee was made to realize he was not just an observer.

The next night I picked up the trainee and told him we would try another spot. There was a small dam at the outlet of Lower Mission Lake that could have some fish running in the creek below the dam. This creek drains into the Mississippi River. We drove up County Road 19 to this trail that leads to the dam. I turned off my lights and proceeded down this trail. I noted there were trees close on both sides of the trail that might be a good place to put the patrol car to block any vehicle from escaping. We continued on to within about an eighth of a mile of the dam. I looked to my left in a small opening and there was a pick-up truck backed in there. I told the trainee there might be someone down at the dam already trying to take fish. I backed the patrol car back to that narrow place in the road. I then took the portable radio with me. I told the trainee to stay in the patrol car and not to move it in the event the people that owned the truck came back before I did.

I then took off on foot down to the dam. When I got near the dam, I could hear a lot of hollering and water splashing. I crawled through the bush until I finally got to where all the excitement was. There were four men with hip boots on in the water jabbing with spears. There was a lot of cursing and then once in a while a little jubilation when one of the men would go to shore with a big walleye impaled on the tines of a spear.

I knew I could rush them and catch one, maybe two, but I surely would lose the rest of them. So I backed out, went back to the trainee, and told him what I found. It was my intent to let these men come back to the truck, load up, and then I would step out and tell them they were all under arrest. If they held still and gave up, I would call him on the portable to get down there as fast as he could drive with all the lights on including the red lights. If they got past me, he was to sit tight and I would be there on foot within a couple of minutes. I could see there was a concerned look on my trainee's face. I reassured him that if he followed my instructions everything would turn out okay.

I went back by the truck, checked the ignition and they had taken their keys with them. I then decided to make damn sure nothing would go wrong so I let the air out of one of the front tires.

After about a half hour, I could hear the fish thieves coming. First there were two men dragging a wet gunnysack so full of walleyes you couldn't get another one in. About fifty feet back were the other two men dragging another gunny bag full of fish. I let them load their fish and spears into the back of the truck. Then when all four men were in the cab, I stepped out and yelled, "Game warden. Get out of that truck, turn on the headlights, and get up in front of the lights."

The whole bunch just acted like they were mesmerized. They did exactly what I told them to do. I then asked for their driver's licenses for identification and they all dug them out and gave them to me. Then I remembered my trainee so I called him to come down where I was. He came with lights flashing but when he came around the corner he was coming a little fast and I thought sure he was going to roll the patrol car.

When the trainee got out of the car, I explained everything that happened and what we had to do. He counted the fish but couldn't believe how many and how big they were. Of course, that was because they were all females. There were thousands of fish eggs in and on the gunny bags and all over the fish.

Then I started making out summons and seizure tags. That's when I took the information off the driver's licenses. They were all seventeen years old. That would mean juvenile court, which would boil down to nothing in Crow Wing County.

I know who their parents are. I know I can't prove this but I would bet their parents sent them off to do this. Their parents are among the leading business people in the community.

The boys got their day in court and a gentle tap on the wrist. All I can say is, it stinks.

Chapter 10/ SHINERS

It was on Saturday night of the first day of the deer season. I decided to sit on Highway 72 at Ludlow Island, which is about ten miles north of Waskish. There are no farms within seven miles to the south and no one lives within fifteen miles to the north. It is really a desolate area and I thought it might be a good place to intercept a night hunter. On this particular night, Jim Petrowske, the local commercial minnow dealer, had asked if he could ride along. Being that his dad, Fred Petrowske, had at one time been hired as a predator controller for the Minnesota Section of Game and Fish and who had at times apprehended game and fish violators, I felt Jim might be an asset or at the very least good company through the night.

Along about sundown, we left Waskish with our lunch bags, thermos of coffee, and took up our stakeout position. We had a couple of cars pass our position between sundown and midnight. However, they weren't running a light, driving slow or stopping, so we had reason to believe they were just good citizens.

Around one a.m., we could see a vehicle coming towards us from the south. It was about five miles away. We waited for close onto twenty minutes and the lights seemed to stay in one place. We felt this maybe was something to checkout, however, as long as they were facing us, there was at least a fifty-fifty chance they would come onto us. I had always found that it was best not to expose yourself too early, as long as the party you are observing doesn't know you are there.

Eventually the vehicle in question seemed to be coming toward us and when it was within about a half a mile, we backed our patrol car down a small trail out of sight from the highway. When the car went by out on the highway, I could see a spotlight shining out of the car from the driver's side of the vehicle. Now I was reasonably sure we were in business, so I pulled up on the blacktop without lights. At this point, we were about a quarter of a mile behind them. However, they were driving slowly and even though I was driving without lights, I finally caught up to them. Then we could see they were running a spotlight out on both sides of the car. We followed about a hundred yards behind them. I told Jim now if they find a deer and shoot it right in front of us, we would have a good case.

We followed them like this for about five miles. We were coming to the county line where the highway makes about a quarter of a mile jog to the left to accommodate the correction line then the highway continues on north. At about this point, I could see the glow from headlights of something coming south. Our possible violators saw it also and they turned out their spotlights. I immediately pulled to the shoulder of the road. Jim and I lay down on the seat of the patrol car. When the headlights of the car coming from the north hit our car, they started to flash their lights up and down apparently to alert the car we were following. However, when the car passed us, we started up our car, negotiated the two curves, and we could see our car ahead using two spotlights again. So obviously, the passing car did not alert them.

About five miles north of the county line, the car turned off the road onto an approach of an old homestead. I told Jim I was going to block them right on the approach. The other car made a turn around and when his lights headed back toward the highway there was our car blocking the road. I know our adrenaline was high at this point, but I can bet it wasn't as high as theirs. At any rate, we bailed out—Jim from one side of the car, me from the other. They had two loaded, uncased rifles in the car. There were two men in the front seat and a man and woman in the back seat. The man in the back seat had his gun on the floor and he was stomping on it with both feet. Why, I don't know. We got the key out of the ignition, opened the trunk, and there was a nice little doe all dressed out. The carcass was so warm steam rose from it in the cold air. The passenger in the front seat looked like he had a pair of red gloves on. It was obvious that when we were watching the headlights south of us, when we were sitting at Ludlow Island that is where and when they shot the little doe. The passenger in the front seat had dressed out the deer and did not wash his hands in the ditch. I got IDs from everyone, made out seizure tickets for the two guns, the deer, and the car.

I now had a small problem because the arrest was made in Lake of the Woods county, not in my home county of Beltrami. We had to get these people to Baudette to put them in jail. I asked Jim to drive the outlaw's car with the woman and I would transport the men. We got to Baudette and went to the courthouse. It was locked up. I then went to the municipal building, but no one was there. I hunted all over town for the night cop, but he was nowhere to be found. I was told, later, he had some woman he shacked up with, hiding his patrol car in her garage. Then I went over to Harland Pickett's house, the local game warden. I pounded on the door until I heard someone holler on the inside. The back door was open, so I stepped inside and hollered to Pickett who I was and that I had four shiners out in the car and I didn't know what to do with them. Pickett hollered back, "You damn rookie! Lock them up in jail!"

I explained that I had checked out the whole town before bothering him. He had a key to the courthouse, so he got up, dressed, and went over to the courthouse. He booked them and locked up two of the men. The man and woman, who were husband and wife, had a deer camp and another car south of Baudette so we dropped them off there with instructions they were to be in court Monday morning at 9 a.m.

The following Monday, I was at the Lake of the Woods county court house. All four of the night hunters were there. They all waived the preliminary hearing and plead guilty in district court before District Judge Gordon McRae. The judge had the first man up in front of the bench. The judge removed his glasses, looked the man right in the eye, and said, "Mr. Visner. I sentence you to one year in the county jail."

Then the judge put his glasses back on and started shuffling papers on his desk. After about five minutes, the man couldn't stand it any more, and he spoke up and said, "Mr. Judge you just can't put me in jail for one year."

The judge looked up, removed his glasses and said, " Mr. Visner. I'm not done sentencing you yet."

At this point, I even felt sorry for the poor cuss. Eventually, the judge fined him $250, suspended the one year in jail, put him on probation for one year with the admonition if he was picked up for even going through a stop sign, he would be brought back to Baudette to serve his year in the county jail. The same sentence was given to the other men. The two rifles were sent to St. Paul to be sold at the annual gun auction. I had to auction off the car in front of the Lake of the Woods courthouse the following March.

Chapter 11/ THE KINGBIRDS FROM PONEMAH

This particular night in October of 1963, I elected to watch for night hunters on the range line road about a mile north of the correction line. There are no people living along this stretch of road for about six miles. Also the range road is only two miles from the Red Lake band reservation. Quite often, if the native people can't find a deer on the reservation, they take a little swing off the reservation and down this road because no one lives along here and there won't be any complaints if they do some shooting.

I had been back on an old abandoned township road since

about 7 p.m. It was now about 1 a.m. I had eaten my lunch. I had checked on the radio and there were no neighboring wardens close enough to hear me call on the radio. It was an overcast night and that is good in that you get some reflection from a light further away than on a clear night. It also meant it was warmer and I had mosquitoes to keep me company. I hadn't had a vehicle come past me all evening. I was looking off to the south-southeast when I noticed a glow reflection in the overcast and I thought I might have a potential customer coming. I could see this glow for about three minutes, then total darkness.

About two miles south of the correction line, there is a huge field on the east side of the road and I had a feeling that vehicle turned east on the approach to that field. This field goes back from the road about three-fourths of a mile and is about a half mile wide. Also, out in this field is about a two-acre island of white and red pine and some spruce. The more I thought about it, the more I was sure that vehicle must have turned out on that field.

So I started up the old Ford, switched on my sneak light, and started south on the range line road. I came to the correction where I turned east about a quarter mile then turned south. There were no lights anywhere and it was blacker than the inside of a cow. I'm rolling along about twenty miles per hour with that little bit of a glow out in front of my car, about twenty feet from the sneak light. I finally came to the tree line on the north side of this big field and I started to divide my attention half on the road ahead and half onto the field to my left, when suddenly, there is the shine of a bumper in the middle of the road not fifteen feet from me. I jumped on the brakes but too late. Bam! I hit that vehicle head on. I grabbed for the headlight switch and pulled it to "on" but there was no light. The palms of my hands ached from catching the forward motion of my body, then dead silence. I could hear some moaning coming from the other vehicle and the sound of glass bottles rolling around. Also, I could hear broken pieces of glass from the headlights falling onto the bumpers.

I grabbed my flashlight and ran to the car. The driver was getting out of the car and he seemed dazed. I shown the light into the car and there were about eight occupants. One lady was on the floor rolling around on beer bottles. There were opened beer bottles and two half-gallon wine bottles opened and tipped over with their contents running out. I recognized the driver as one of the Kingbirds. All of the occupants were members of the Red Lake band. The lady on the floor had a bloody nose. About half the people were so inebriated, I don't think they knew what happened. Three of them were snoring. The driver and I checked all the people and outside of the one with a bloody nose, no one appeared to be hurt. By this time, I was starting to get mad at these people for driving until they couldn't stay awake and then stop right in the middle of the road and pass out.

The driver of the car kind of lurched over to me and he said, "Leo, why did you run into us like that?" Now Leo Manthei is my neighbor warden at Blackduck. I did not tell Kingbird I was or wasn't Leo. He just assumed that when he saw the warden patch on my shoulder.

It turned out one of their headlights was not broken. We got their motor started and I told Kingbird not to stop until he got on the reservation or I would call John Cahill, the sheriff, and have them all hauled in.

Then I called the dispatcher at Thief River to call an auto mechanic friend of mine to come out and tow my car into his garage before someone saw me and realized I had no transportation.

To make a long story short, I contacted my supervisor the next morning and got authorization to repair my vehicle. My super wasn't too happy about it, but he used to have a saying, "If you're going to have rail roads, you're going to have wrecks." In fact, he couldn't say too much because he had a similar experience about four years before. In fact, he was nicknamed

"Super Crash."

I heard about two weeks later that the Kingbirds met Leo in Blackduck and they jumped Leo and wanted to know why he ran into them.

Chapter 12/ EARLY NIGHT HUNTERS

It was Thursday morning, two days before the firearm deer season. We (my wife, Patricia, and I) had a visitor from north Minneapolis. It was Cliff Strege, owner of a sporting goods store in north Minneapolis. He had arrived at our home in Waskish the night before. He came up hoping to do a little duck shooting on Blackduck Lake.

Leo Manthei, the conservation officer at Blackduck, had made arrangements for us to use a duck blind on the west side of Blackduck Lake that was on private property. Leo was on four days leave to go to North Dakota to hunt ducks and geese. He planned to be back sometime Friday afternoon as we would be working that night before the deer season.

Cliff and I went down to Blackduck Lake and set ourselves up in this duck blind. We had good shooting. However, I noticed two individuals who were really knocking down the ducks about a quarter of a mile from us. I went to the car and got my binoculars to better observe these two persons. They would knock down three or four ducks out of every flock that came into their decoys. Then they would go out with their boat, pick up the ducks, take them over to a place a hundred or so feet from their blind, place them along side a log and cover them over with leaves. The season, at this time, allowed you to take six blue bills a day and after the second day you could have twelve in possession.

I soon was aware these two persons had more than twelve ducks so I contacted them. They were just in the process of picking up their decoys. I went over to where they had cached their ducks and there were twenty-four blue bills. The hunters claimed they had shot twelve the day before. I knew better but to make my complaint more secure, I took out my thermometer and by inserting it into the rectum of each duck and recording the temperature of each duck, I would have good evidence to submit to the judge in the event they plead not guilty. There was a variance of three degrees in the twenty-four ducks. The duck hunters knew they had been caught up.

Cliff and I went back to Waskish with our twelve ducks. It was our intent to return to Blackduck Lake the following morning hoping to get another good shoot.

That evening about nine o'clock, the phone rang. I answered it and it was Ann Manthei, Leo's wife. She said she had a farmer in her house that lived out east of Blackduck on County Road 13 about halfway to Alvwood on the north side of the road. He heard some shooting west of his house and he could see a vehicle parked on the road with the lights on. He saw a person run in front of the headlights to the north side of the road.

This farmer has a dislike for these kinds of hunters so he got in his pick-up and drove down to the parked car. Before he got to the vehicle, it started moving west at a high rate of speed. He followed it right into Blackduck where he was able to get it stopped. The driver was a young woman and she claimed the car was not operating properly and it tended to backfire. The farmer got her name and the license number of the station wagon.

Ann then said, "Leo is out in North Dakota hunting. Could you come down and check this complaint out?" I took down the name of the farmer and the location of his farm. I told Ann I would be at his farm in about an hour but not to expect too much because so much time would have elapsed.

Cliff offered to accompany me but I told him there was a possibility I would be on this all night. I asked him if he remembered how to get to that place where we shot ducks. He thought he could find it. So I asked my wife if she would set the alarm for about five a.m., wake Cliff up, get him some breakfast, pack him a lunch, and get him on his way. With that, I took off for Blackduck.

On my way east out of Blackduck on County Road 13, I heard Lonnie Schiefert, the conservation officer from Northome, checking in on his radio with the dispatcher from Brainerd. I called Lonnie on the car-to-car channel, gave him my location and told him what I was doing down there. He wasn't too far away, so he said he would come down. The farmer took us out to the approximate location where he thought the station wagon had been parked. We thanked him and he returned to his home. He did tell us he was quite sure that the station wagon hadn't come back nor had he seen any other cars. So it was possible that we had a man out there somewhere. We checked along the road for tracks or empty shell casings. We did find some footprints. Finally, we walked out on the field on the north side of the road. We found where a deer had been dragged almost to the fringe of woods and there laid a nice big buck, a ten pointer with a nice even set of horns. The animal was not dressed out, so I went back to my car, got my knife, and took care of the job. On checking around the drag site, it appeared there were two people pulling the carcass. It would seem the farmer (when he came out with his truck) must have scared the night hunters off. Lonnie and I dragged the deer over to my patrol car and put it up on the trunk. I told Lonnie to pull off the road at some approach, turn out his lights, and sit and watch if someone would come out to the road. I went west about a mile and a half and did the same thing. About two a.m., Lonnie called on the radio and said he was having a hard time staying awake, so he was going to call it a night. I didn't have much hope either so I thanked him, told him good night, and that I would sit around for a while longer and then I, too, would head for home.

A long around 3 a.m., I saw two shadowy figures walking down the road in a westerly direction. I figured these could be our hunters. I decided to let them get way down the road before I started the motor on my car. I also got out and took that deer off the trunk of my car and pulled it into the bush along side my car.

When I was sure these two walkers were about a mile down the road, I started up my patrol car and pulled out on the road with my lights off. Using my binoculars, I could just barely make the people out. One of them went down in the ditch on the north side of the road. He came back and they seemed to continue on west. They disappeared over a slight raise in the road. I backed up about a half a mile without lights. I then turned on my headlights and proceeded west at about forty miles an hour. I came across my two walkers, pulled up and stopped, and asked them if they wanted a ride. They were cold, hungry, tired, and only too eager to get a ride. I had an old jacket over my warden shirt, so at first, they didn't think anything was amiss. Then I told them I was from Waskish and was down here on a complaint from a farmer about some shooting, and was on my way home.

These two were young men (I would guess in their twenties). We were all standing out beside the car when I noticed one man had a knife in a sheath on his belt. I reached over and pulled the knife out and there was dried blood on it. Both of the men said they lived on a farm over northwest of Blackduck and had butchered a beef out early the day before. They had driven to a place east of where we were then north, on a logging road, where they had been cutting pulp. When they quit work the evening before their old pick-up wouldn't start. They fooled around 'til the battery on the truck went dead then the batteries on their flashlight gave out. They offered that up for inspection. I noticed blood spots on their overalls and they said that was from when they butchered out the beef that morning. I asked where the meat was and they both said in the deep freezer at home. I told them I would take them home, but I wanted to see the meat in their freezer.

The two men directed me to their farm about five miles north and west of Blackduck. They took me to the freezer and there was a whole pile of freshly packed meat which wasn't frozen solid yet. The story sounded pretty good, however, I was sure they were my hunters. When I came out of the house, I saw the station wagon and the color was the same as the farmer said.

I went back to pick up the big buck. After I got it loaded, I checked down in the ditch where I saw the one man go. I found a revolver holster, a small bag with a shoulder strap, and a pair of bloody gloves with deer hair on them. It was then I began to believe they had killed another deer before the big buck by the farmer's house. I kept hunting around and just as I could see some light in the east, I found a nice little spike buck all dressed out.

I loaded the two deer onto the trunk of the car and headed back to the farmhouse. I then checked the license out on the station wagon and it jibed with the farmers report. I called the dispatcher at Thief River Falls to tell him where I was and that I was going to wake these two young men up and arrest them. I asked if there were any law enforcement men around to send them up where I was. He couldn't locate anyone right then, but said he would roust someone out. I told him I would call him back within ten minutes if things were okay.

I woke the whole household up and the two young men gave up with no problems. They said they thought I would see through their story sooner or later. I told them when I saw them the first time (when they walked past where I had the car hidden) that I thought they were the hunters.

I hauled them down to Bemidji and put them in jail. Then I went back to Blackduck to tell Ann I had caught the hunters and she should call the farmer and thank him. Ann wasn't up yet so I went over to the cafe to get something to eat. I went in and sat down. The cafe was full of locals and some hunters. I ordered my breakfast and I was about half done eating when some of the patrons that had just left the cafe came bursting back in, mad as hornets. They thought I had killed the deer illegally. I took off my jacket to show I was a game warden.

Then they wanted to know what I was going to do with the deer. I told them I would sell them after I got these two people into municipal court at 10 a.m. Immediately, they wanted to know how much. I told them I had to get as much as possible. That started a bidding war, right then. One guy got up to $75.00 for the big buck and another one got up to $25.00 for the spike buck.

I went back to Bemidji, contacted the county attorney, got the two men out of jail, and up before the judge. They each plead guilty and were fined $300.00 each.

I then went back to Blackduck Lake and found Cliff Strege. He had his six blue bills and wanted to know if I didn't want to shoot my limit. I said, "No way! I just want to go home to bed."

I located the men that wanted to buy the deer and sold them. That $75.00 is the most I ever got for the state for one deer.

Chapter 13/ GET MARRIED

One day in October, Harland Pickett called and told me to come up and work with him that night. He said he had a complaint there was shining activity in the northwest part of Lake of the Woods County.

I arrived at Harland's house in Baudette about 7 p.m. The two of us got in Harland's car and drove to an area southwest of the Piper Farms. There were old abandoned buildings that we parked among and settled down for a night of waiting and watching. It was a very dark, black night with a heavy overcast. Harland told me quite large bunches of deer were coming out on a cutover alfalfa field southeast of where we were positioned. About two hours after we got set up, it started to rain. The rain kept getting a little harder as time went on. Then it started to get humid inside of the patrol car.

Along about midnight, we could see the glow of headlights coming from the east on the gravel road south of the buildings where our vehicle was. When the vehicle got to the north south road, we could see it turned south for about a quarter of a mile, then turned east out on to this alfalfa field. They didn't go a hundred yards when we could see deer in their headlights. Some were standing and some were moving. The vehicle brakes came on and Harland took up his binoculars so he could see well. We cracked our windows about two inches to hear if they shot. Then a moving spotlight came out from the vehicle and it would shine on one standing deer then move to another standing deer. It was beginning to appear that we had some lookers or they were so bold that they were becoming highly selective. Also, we were wondering about the possibility that they could get stuck out on that field. After spending about ten minutes out on the field checking the deer out, the car started to move. It made a "u" turn and headed west off the field to the county road, then the car turned south. At this point Harland said, "I'm going to follow them." He started the car up and by using his sneak light, we got out on the county road and turned south.

The shining car had quite a start on us but Harland was persistent and he was gaining on them. Then the car came to a crossroad and they turned west. This road, according to Harland, was being worked on and he said he didn't think a person could get through on it. We were gaining on the shining car to a point we were about a hundred yards behind them. Harland turned off our sneak light and was driving by their lights. The roadway was getting terrible with ruts and loose gravel.

Then the brake lights came on and it was obvious the shining car was going to turn around. Harland said, "Get ready.

We will have to take them." Just as their car came about and saw us, (we were about fifty feet from them) I was out and running. Harland had trouble getting his headlights on. Their headlights blinded me. I got to the shining car to turn the motor off and pull the keys out. I then saw both the front door and the back door were open on the passenger side of the car. There was a gun case on the back seat. Looking through the car, I could see the tracks of two men in the mud in the ditch headed for the bush. I ran around the car and took off into the bush on the south side of the road. I ran about twenty yards, stopped, and listened. I could hear one man crashing ahead and I took off in his direction and that's the way we went for about a quarter of a mile when I finally caught this one man. He didn't have either the gun or the plug-in light on him. I put a little pressure on the situation and he said just about two minutes before I grabbed him, he threw the gun down along side a log lying on the ground. Using the flashlight, I saw a log about fifty feet away and there was the rifle. This lad, I would guess, was about twenty-five years old.

Both of us sat down on the log to get our wind. We were covered with mud and we were both sopping wet. I asked him why they didn't shoot at a deer on that alfalfa field and he said they were looking for a nice fork horn buck. They figured with the nasty weather they could take their time and pick out just the deer they wanted.

I then felt through my pockets for my compass and either I had lost it or failed to bring it along. The sky was so overcast, we couldn't use the stars to figure out which way was north. I asked the night hunter if he had any idea which way it was back to the road and he had no idea which way he was going. He was just trying to get away from me. The gun barrel was so full of mud, I was reluctant to shoot to get Harland's attention. We sat there about another ten minutes and then Harland assumed we might want something to guide on. He started beeping his horn and we walked out to the sound. When I came out, Harland said, "You only caught one?"

"That's right." But I thought I was fortunate to catch either one. I then told Harland I got the one with the gun and it was loaded. Otherwise we wouldn't have had a case at all.

Then Harland said, "Would you believe we are in Markovich's area?" We ended up in Roseau County. He said he got Mark on the radio and he was on his way over to us.

About a half hour went by when Mark and a deputy sheriff showed up. Mark got out of his patrol car with his flashlight, walked up to my hunter, turned on his flashlight, and shoved it right into the man's face. Then he just screamed, "Not you again! Why don't you get married and stay home?"

Harland then asked Mark if he had any idea who the third man might be. Mark said he was almost positive who it would be. We turned the two men, the car, and the gun over to Mark and the Roseau deputy. They went to some farm near there and eventually the third person was caught.

So Markovich got three good pinches and all Harland and I got was an assist and wet and muddy clothes.

Chapter 14/ A NEW KIND OF LAXATIVE

One night back in the sixties in the middle of the week of the deer rifle season, I had decided to go down into Shotley Township and watch for any night hunting activity. There were a few deer coming out on a cutover alfalfa field southeast of the Dyrhaug farm. I had a good place to hide the car and still be able to observe any outfit trying to shoot any of those deer. I sat there from 7 p.m. to 2:30 in the morning. Two cars came through around midnight and they didn't even slow down. It was a quiet night. I never heard a shot fired. I tried calling Leo Manthei and Lonnie Schiefert on the radio and they never answered, so I decided to go home and go to bed.

I was on the last leg of my trip home. I was on Highway 72 going north. About one mile from Waskish on the west side of the road was a little fawn feeding on the roadside ditch. I thought maybe I should set up somewhere to see if someone would take a shot at this little fellow.

I pulled into Petrowske's minnow station with my lights off. I hoped I wouldn't wake up Jim or any of his family. Apparently, I woke someone up because it wasn't but a few minutes and Jim came out, opened up the passenger side door, and said, "Oh! It's you." I told him why I was there. He wished me good luck and went back in the house.

About four o'clock, a car pulling a trailer with a deer on the trailer went by. When they got to about the area the little fawn was, I saw the brake lights come on, then they went off and the vehicle continued on it's way.

The vehicle got down to the crossroads about four miles south. I saw it turn around and come back. It went rather slow past the area where the little deer was then the car came on at a faster speed, past Petrowske's, and it turned onto the road to the airport. I could see the lights out on the airport then it came back to 72, and headed south again at a much slower pace. When it got near where the deer was, I could see the brake lights come on and go off several times as the vehicle moved slowly south. Then the brake lights came on and stayed on. Then "Pow!"—one shot. The brake lights went off and the vehicle started south at a pretty fair speed. I thought they might have missed the deer. I drove out onto the highway where I could get a better view without my lights. I decided if they went past the crossroad I would chase them down.

When they got to the crossroad, they again turned around and came back towards me. I backed into Petrowske's driveway part way so I could watch to see if they dropped off someone to dress out the deer. When they got near where they had shot, they slowed down. However, they never stopped so I backed in by Petrowske's minnow house. Again they went into the airport to turn around. When they came out this time and headed south, I decided to follow them without lights. As we approached the area where they shot, they pulled to the side of the black top and proceeded very slowly. I was close enough to see with the aid of their headlights that there were three people. Also I could see they were all straining to see down into the ditch. Then the brake lights came on and I was pretty sure we were there. I got out of my patrol car very quietly and having on rubber-soled boots, I did not make any noise running to their vehicle.

All heads were looking down into the ditch when I jerked the driver's car door open and yelled, "Game warden. Get out of the car and up in front of the headlights." At the same time, I was jerking the keys out of the ignition.

At that instant the driver's eyes came around to me and he screamed, "I gotta shit!" The two of us got tangled up in each other's arms for an instant but I got free because this man was tearing at and removing his clothing. As he came out of the car he had a wild moment getting the shoulder straps of his bib overalls loose. He whipped down his overalls and under garments and not a moment too soon. It came out of him like body waste from a schide poke crane. I had to jump to one side to keep it from hitting my boots.

Eventually everything calmed down. All three of these men got the shakes pretty bad. I suppose they figured they were going to lose everything and probably end up in jail.

So I suggested we all go to my home and office and I would make out the paper work there. They were agreeable to that. My home and office was only about three miles away and it would be warm and bright there. While I was sitting at my desk making out the summons and seizure slips the fellow that was the driver said they had been hunting up near Norris Camp and in five days hunting they only saw the one doe deer they had on the trailer. They were farmers from southern Minnesota and they each had spent five dollars for a deer license and they should be allowed to take that little deer and be on their way.

I then told him I figured they were just stupid opportunists and I was seriously thinking about reducing the charge to "taking one fawn deer in closed hours", which will be a misdemeanor and it will cost each of you $100.00 plus $3.00 court costs before a justice of the peace in Kelliher that morning about eight o'clock. Also I wanted the gun that was used to kill that deer. I told them they could get the gun back at the gun auction in St. Paul the next spring if they bid high enough. The driver of the car thought that was too rough a penalty.

So I said, "Okay I will charge you with just what you did. I will charge you with shining. I will seize your car, your trailer, and that deer you have on the trailer. I am going to take you all to Bemidji, put you in jail, and tomorrow morning there will be a hearing in municipal court. You will be bound over to district court sometime next spring. You may have to post bond up to a thousand dollars each. You, no doubt, will have to hire an attorney, and you will have the choice of a jury trial or trial by a district judge. I've got you guys so cold you will lose and the fine will be up to $1000.00 and or a year in the county jail."

Immediately there was pleading by the other two men. "Don't pay any attention to him. We were wrong and we knew it. We want the cheap way out in the morning and we will never pull a dumb stunt like that again as long as we live."

They elected to leave three hundred and nine dollars and the rifle with me as bail for which I gave each of them receipts. I turned the money over to Justice Quale later on that day.

The men left thanking me and I went into the house and went to bed. My wife who was awake asked what that was all about. I told her it was just some shitty outfit from down south.

Chapter 15/ *HOWDALL AND LARSONS*

It was the opening Saturday of the duck season and for some reason Harland Pickett of Baudette was going to be away from his station. He had advised our supervisor, Dick Tarte, that there would be a lot of illegal activity in and around Baudette because everyone knew he was going to be gone. He requested that Tarte send in some men to police his station at least on the opening weekend.

So Supervisor Tarte told Gil Keeler from Littlefork, Gordy Ebel from Orr, Ces Richards from Big Falls, and yours truly from Waskish to go to the Baudette area and watch for illegal activity. Keeler and Ebel worked together and Richards and I worked together. I can't remember just how much activity we got involved in that opening day. That evening we met in Baudette for dinner and as Harland had made reservations of four rooms in the old hotel on main street, we all turned in right after eating because we were all pooped and would have to get up early Sunday morning.

We made arrangements to wake up at 5 a.m., so we hit the sack. This was an old hotel, no phones in the room and one toilet down the hall on each floor.

I woke up to a pounding on the door. I got up, opened the door, and found the hotel owner in his nightshirt. He told me Mrs. Myrtle Pickett had called and she wanted one of us to call her back. I was the only one he could wake up. He took me down to his apartment on the first floor to use the phone. He had the number written down. I made the call and Myrtle answered. She said about fifteen minutes earlier, she had gotten a call from a farmer out east that there were some night hunters shining and shooting at some deer on his fields. I asked her what time it was and how do I find this farm where the shooting was. She told me it was just a little after 3 a.m. Then she went on to say go east out of town on Number 11, across the bridge, over the Rapid River and about a mile beyond take the first county road south. It's a dead end road and she thought the farmer lived at the end of the road.

I went back up to our rooms and no matter how I hollered or pounded on the door, I couldn't wake any of those guys up. I figured it is probably just as well as by the time I got out there everyone would be long gone. I went into my room, got my clothes on, went down to my patrol car, and headed east out of town. It was a black night. The temperature was around forty degrees with no wind.

I crossed the Rapid River bridge and then I was in Koochiching County. I kept going until I came to a gravel road going south. I drove south about two miles then the road turned east. About a mile from where I turned, I could see lights on at a farm and as I got closer I could see people milling around. Also about a half mile down this road, I came across a car parked on the side of the road facing west.

I stopped at the car but there was no one in or around it. There was an empty gun case hanging half out of the car under the passenger side door. Also I noticed the license plates on the car were missing.

I got back in the patrol car and continued on down to the farm where the people were milling around. It turned out they were the people that had called Mrs. Pickett.

They took me down to an area between their farm and the abandoned car. They said this was the place where the men were when they were shooting. I asked if they thought the hunters got a deer. They said they didn't think so because they turned on all their lights and ran outside and started yelling at them. They told me these hunters drove down the road a little way then they stopped their car and about five minutes later another car came and it looked like they all left in the second car.

I looked around on the road and found and picked up about eight empty cartridges. As I remember, it was two different size shell casings. I believe one was a 308 and I think the other was a 3030.

This farmer and I walked out on this field to see if there were any dead or crippled deer. We couldn't find any. However, I asked the farmer if he would check out on the field after sunup.

I then went to the parked car and I found that someone had torn the license plates off. The bolts and the corners of the license plates were still attached to the bracket. I got into the car and got rooting around and found several old envelopes written to someone by the name of Larson in Minneapolis and the return address was a Larson from Clemenson. I went back to the farmer and asked if he knew these people and he said, "Yes, they are probably from a farm over southeast of Clemenson." I asked how I would find this place.

He said, "Go out to Number 11, then turn west back over the Rapid River to Clemenson. Turn south on the blacktop and follow it until you cross the second bridge. The farm on the left hand side of the road is a Larson's."

I followed his directions and I drove into the farmyard. There was a light on in the house. I went up on to the back porch and I could see into the lighted room. In the kitchen there was an older man putting his boots on. I pounded on the door and he came over and opened it up. I told him I was a game warden and I asked him where this one Larson fellow whose name was on the old letters was. The older fellow said they are both in bed. I told him, "They haven't been in bed very long. Go roust them out and bring them down to me."

"All right. I'll get them.", he said. "Now what have those g— d—- punks been up to?"

"A little deer hunting," I told him.

About ten minutes later, two young men in their twenties came into the kitchen. I took them out to the patrol car and I told them I wanted the two rifles that they shot at the deer with. They were pretty groggy and they said they were in the car that was parked at the gas pumps at the resort in Clemenson. We went to Clemenson, unlocked their car, and they turned the two guns over to me. They were the same caliber as the empty brass I had in my pocket. I said if they entered a plea of not guilty, I would have the B.C.A. confirm that the empties I had were fired from these guns. Then they admitted they shot at those deer. Then I asked how come they abandoned the car back near where they had been shooting. They then told me they ran out of gas. I asked who picked them up. They told me one of the Howdall boys was with them and when they were slow coming out on the gravel road another Howdall brother who was sitting out on Number 11 as a look out came in looking for them and that was when they tore off the license plates and got in with him. The Larsons left their guns in the car at Clemenson because they didn't want their folks to know they were out hunting.

I then asked where the Howdalls lived and they directed me to their folks' farm. When I got there, I found an elderly man and his wife eating breakfast. The elderly man opened the door and I asked where the two boys were. "They're up in the loft asleep.", he said.

I told him, "Wake them and get them down here." The old man hollered up to a square hole in the ceiling that had a homemade ladder leading to it. In about five minutes, two men in their twenties came down the ladder. They were pretty groggy and quite ugly. I asked which one was with the Larsons shooting at the deer. Both men denied having anything to do with the Larsons or any deer shooting. I said take a look out in the yard and see who I have in the back seat of my patrol car. They took a look. It was starting to get daylight.

One of them said, "He's got the Larsons." Right at that moment two game wardens cars pulled into the yard and all three of the men got out. One of the Howdalls made the remark that the whole yard was crawling with game wardens. The younger Howdall man then said he was the one with the Larsons. I told him to get the rest of his clothes on and then come out to the car.

I went outside and told my three partners I was glad they showed up then I asked, "How did you find me?" They said they called Mrs. Pickett and she told them about where they might find me. They just drove all over the country until one of them drove by Howdalls and spotted my car.

Ces Richards then took me aside and asked, "What have you got here?" I spelled out the whole story. Then Ces said, "If they get hold of a bog attorney, you ain't got nothing."

As we were in Koochiching County, we would have to take them to either International Falls and put them in jail until court the next day or take them to Littlefork and find the justice of the peace and get this taken care of immediately.

Gil Keeler, who was from Littlefork, said, "I think we will find the justice of the peace in church."

So I said, "Why don't you go on ahead and we will meet you at the community building in Littlefork."

So that is the way we went. Ces followed me in his car. Gil went ahead with Gordy, and found the justice of the peace in church. Then he apparently told the J.P. the whole story. Ces and I had the three hunters in the community building.

When the judge walked into the community room and saw the three men, he said, "So you're the young men hunting deer at night."

The three men just said, "Yeah, we're the ones."

When Pickett came home, I had made out the arrest reports, confiscation reports, and took the guns and the reports for him to sign and turn in. When he saw the name Howdall on the arrest report, he asked if I got a search warrant for the Howdall's farm? I told him, "No, I didn't see where I had any reason to get a search warrant."

I got bawled out for missing a golden opportunity to search the Howdall farm.

Chapter 16/ NIGHT HUNTERS

One afternoon, two days before the deer season was to open, I got a call from my neighboring warden, Leo Manthei at Blackduck, that I was to come down and work with him that night on deer shiners in Cormant Township. Also, he told me our supervisor, Dick Tarte, was going to meet us up there. Dick told Leo to ask if I had some smoked white fish to bring some along.

That evening, after sundown, my wife sent me off with a big lunch and a quart thermos of coffee. I stopped by the smoke house and picked up a half dozen smoked white fish. Eventually, with the aid of our two-way radios, Leo and I got together. It seems Leo had a complaint about night hunting in this area. We thought it might be some of the members of the Red Lake band as we were within a couple of miles of the reservation.

At any rate, we sat there in the dark waiting for someone to come along and take a poke at some deer that were out on a field west of us. Along about eleven o'clock, Dick Tarte called us on the radio and wanted directions to where we were holed up. So, we talked him into us. When he asked if we had any activity, we let him know his car was the only car we had seen since we got there. Dick could smell the smoked fish, so we broke one out and started to nibble on it while we listened to the latest scuttlebutt right from the boss's mouth. Along about midnight, ground fog started to settle in and finally about one a.m. It was so thick you couldn't see ten feet even if you had lights on. So Dick said we were wasting our time here. There would be no shiners out and we would be better off to go home and get some sleep, as there would be little or no sleep for us during the upcoming deer season. Then Dick asked if he could have the rest of the smoked white fish. Just between you and me, I think that was the real reason he came up to be with us.

So we all crawled into our own patrol cars and headed for home. I had about thirty-five miles to go to get home to Waskish and it took me close to an hour to negotiate the trip. About a half a mile south of Waskish I almost hit a small deer right in Jim Petrowske's driveway. I got to thinking I'd better turn around and go back there and chase that deer away from the road or someone might come along and hit it. I soon came to the road that goes to the airport and made a "u" turn. I came back slowly looking for that deer, but it had obviously taken off on its own back into the bush. I had passed Jim's driveway about a hundred yards, when I saw a light wink at me from the west side of the road. I knew right now I had a hunter out there that, no doubt, had been dropped off to dress a deer out and the car had been driven off some place out of sight of the area of the deer kill. This was so that anyone coming along would not get suspicious. Of course that person out in the bush must have mistaken my car for the pickup car.

I stopped immediately, got out of the patrol car, and I believe the man out in the bush realized his mistake because I could hear the brush crack. He was heading back into the bush. So I hollered, "Game warden. Halt." I could still hear him moving to the west away from the road. So with my flashlight, I crossed the ditch and went into the tag alders and high grass. About twenty feet in, I found the deer, a doe. No doubt it was the mother of that small deer I had seen in Jim's driveway.

This man did not use his flashlight and as I was able to follow his trail through the tall grass, eventually in about two hundred yards, I came across the culprit, hiding in the grass. I ordered him to his feet. He had a bloody hunting knife in his hand. I ordered him to drop the knife, which he did. Then I saw there was another man standing behind him with a flashlight. I ordered him to drop the flashlight and then I instructed both men to back up about ten steps.

I gathered up the knife and light and marched them back to the deer. I had them drag the deer to my patrol car and load it up on the trunk. I got some identification from them then asked where their pickup car was. By this time, these two men got the shakes so bad they could hardly talk, but they finally let me know they were three brothers from northeast Minneapolis and the third brother would be along eventually.

It wasn't long before we could hear a car coming. Then we could make out the glow of his headlights through the fog. I flagged the car down and he still had the uncased rifle along side of the driver and the spent shell in the chamber.

I wrote up the two men with possession of a deer in closed season and the driver with transporting an uncased firearm. The three men all plead guilty to their charges in justice court. The two men were fined one hundred dollars each and the third man twenty-five dollars.

Chapter 17/ GLENN LUTGEN

Glenn lives in Hornet Township on the west side of Highway 71 about five miles northeast of Blackduck, Minnesota. His house is easy to find because he is the only one I know who has what looks like a two hundred pound bomb hanging from a homemade frame along side his mail box. There is a sign above the bomb that says "Anti DNR".

On this particular day in the early part of the fall, Leo Manthei asked me to take a ride with him in his patrol car. He told me he thought Glenn might have been doing some pre-season deer hunting and he wanted to drop me off about a half a mile northeast of the Lutgen farm. He told me to take a hike through the woods behind the Lutgen buildings and see if I could find anything suspicious. He said he would pick me up about a half a mile beyond the Lutgen residence. I asked Leo if he knew if any of the Lutgens were home and as I remember he had no knowledge of that. I kind of knew when Leo suggested I do the snooping it might be a bit risky. Glenn is quick with a rifle and he could charge me with trespassing. However, I will admit I use to kind of like to take chances.

Anti-DRN sign by mailbox

Well, Leo did drop me off and I passed down in back of the Lutgen buildings. I had forgotten to ask Leo if Glenn had a dog, so I was exceptionally wary when I was in back of the Lutgen buildings. It was then and there that I came across three fresh deer hides. They couldn't have been more than two days old. Also, I noticed an old station wagon near the deer hides, so I went over to take a look inside. It was full of shoeboxes. All the doors were locked so I couldn't see in the boxes to see if there were shoes in them. I did remember that a shoe store had been broken into in Bemidji a week or so earlier. As I remember, all the thieves took were shoes.

So with all this knowledge, I hurried on out of there and met Leo. I told him all my findings, so we went into Blackduck, contacted the justice of the peace, told him our story, and he gave us a search warrant for all the buildings and property that belonged to Glenn Lutgen. The warrant said we were to pick up all the deer meat and parts thereof.

Leo and I returned to the Lutgen farm only to find no one home. I went out in the woods behind the buildings and picked up the three deer hides. I figured they were one doe and two fawns.

This is the Lutgen farm

About an hour later, Glenn and his family drove into the yard. They saw the deer hides lying on the trunk lid of Leo's car and Glenn knew the jig was up. Leo showed Glenn the warrant and told him we wouldn't go tramping all over their house. They could just bring the venison out but they better come with all of it or we would go in. They brought out a pile of meat all cut and wrapped.

Then Glenn started to quiz us as to who put the finger on

him. "Who squealed on me? I'll bet it was Emmett Carrigan."

I started to say "No" when Leo signaled me to shut up.

Glenn kept bringing up the name of Emmett Carrigan and Leo kept telling Glenn that we couldn't disclose the names of any informer. Finally, Glenn says, "I'll get even with that s.o.b. When he's got some venison over at his folks' farm. I'll blow the whistle on him."

Glenn did get caught up on the shoes by the sheriff. He appeared in justice of the peace court in Blackduck on the deer possession charge.

That following winter, Leo called me to go with him on a search. He said Glenn came in and told him Emmett Carrigan and a man by the name of Carter, who was renting a room from an elderly farm widow that lived south of Emmett's folks' farm on the east side of the road, had an illegal deer. The deer meat was in the buildings of this widow farmwoman.

Leo had acquired the search warrant from the justice of the peace. The two of us drove out to this farm in Leo's car. I believe it was in January. I remember the buildings were at the top of a hill and the wind was blowing. The snow was about two feet on the level. It was cold!!!

When we arrived at this farm, no one was home. We went to the door and knocked and at this location, we could see through the window into the kitchen. There was one hindquarter of venison on the kitchen table. We went back to our vehicle to get warmed up.

There was a double garage along side of the car, so I got out and found the small garage door unlocked. We pushed the door open and the inside of the garage looked like a slaughterhouse. There were seven deer heads. Some were on the floor. The rest were hanging from the rafters on ropes. There were two or three deep freezers and they were just packed with packaged meat.

Eventually, a car pulled in the yard. The occupants were Emmett Carrigan, Carter, and a woman (the owner of the property). She appeared to be about seventy years old. We gave her the search warrant to read. It was made out to her because she was the owner of the property. We did tell her that we were reasonably sure she didn't kill and butcher all those deer. If she would tell us who did bring all those deer carcasses in there, we would relay her co-operation to the county attorney. She elected not to put the finger on anyone. She took the rap and as I remember she was fined $300 or 90 days in jail. The fine was paid.

I did get a chance to tell Emmett that I thought he was the lowest scuzball I had ever met because he let her take the rap.

Chapter 18/ FRANK MARTIN, INDIAN COMMERCIAL FISHERMAN

One day in late September of 1963, Leo Manthei, my neighboring warden from Blackduck, called and asked for assistance to a complaint that the Indians were coming off the east side of the Red Lake Indian Reservation to hunt deer at night. We agreed to meet about 8:00 pm that evening at a farmhouse near Saum that we affectionately referred to as the "pie house." I left my vehicle in behind the barn where it could not be seen from the road and got into Leo's car. We drove south then west on what we called the "Joe Jerome Road." At a point about one mile east of the reservation, there was a small logging trail that went south off the Jerome Road. Leo left me off at that point with a portable radio and he drove south on this trail to where, if we had any spotlighters come out and throw a light in his direction, they would not see him. I cut a couple of branches off a small balsam and brushed out Leo's car tracks where he had turned off the gravel road. I settled down in the ditch to observe and, by the way, furnished a meal for a couple hundred mosquitoes. It was a fairly dark night, overcast and not too cold. Any car that came off the reservation would be a potential customer. We have worked this area before and sometimes there wouldn't be a car all night.

Along about eleven o'clock that night, I could see a pair of headlights coming towards me from the west. I scrunched down in the ditch and alerted Leo via the portable radio. The car went past me going east at a slow speed. However, they were not running a light and I advised Leo of this fact. About a half a mile east of me, I saw the brake lights come on and I could see a light coming from the passenger side of the vehicle. The brake lights went off and I believe the car seemed to continue on east at a very slow pace. However, the spotlight continued to work the south side of the road. This car was not a typical Indian car. It was a late model, four-door car and it could have been a Buick or an Oldsmobile. I advised Leo of this via the portable. It was possible we did not have a hunter but what we referred to as a "looker." In those days, you didn't come out of your hiding place unless a shot was fired. About another quarter mile down the road this vehicle's brake lights came on. I could see the rays of the spotlight pointing in a southerly direction, and then, "pow", they shot. I called Leo and said, "Did you hear that shot? It looks like we are in business." Leo drove down to pick me up with his lights off. I noted our customer sat there with his brake lights on. However, the dome light did not come on nor was there any other indication that anyone got out of the car. This was typical of spotlighters. If the deer didn't drop where they could see it, they never got out to chase any cripples. About the time Leo got to me, the brake light went off and the car seemed to be moving again with the spotlight searching the south side of the road.

I jumped into Leo's car and we started in pursuit of our night hunter with our lights off. Leo was a good driver and his eyes were acclimated to the dark. Eventually, we caught up to the hunting car, and I can assure you that both our hearts were pounding in anticipation of the upcoming activity. We were cruising along about five miles per hour and we could see three persons in the car we were following. We could see the spotlight searching the woods and small openings. I was getting pretty excited and I started to bawl Leo out for not passing and blocking this car so we could get this over. Leo said, "They are driving in the middle of the road and if I try to pass them, we will go in the ditch." The ditch was about two feet deep with an abrupt shoulder.

Finally, the hunters' car moved a bit to the right and Leo took advantage of it. He passed them, snapped on his red light and headlights, and blocked them. I jumped out of the car with a five-cell flashlight in my hand and ran to the car to get the hunters out of it. Instead of sitting there in a shocked state, as most of these hunters do, this guy threw his car in reverse and started backing down the road as fast as I could run. The passenger in the hunting car had a spotlight mounted on the car, and he was shining his light in my eyes. I, in turn, was trying to shine the light from my five-cell flashlight in the driver's eyes. Suddenly, the driver went into a bootlegger turn-around, and as he started to go forward, I hit the side of the car and got the door partially opened. I saw it was Frank Martin, a well-known, illegal, Indian fish-peddler, who was driving. When the dome light came on, there was an Indian passenger in the front seat, who was the spotlight operator, and another Indian in the back seat with a 94 Winchester. I tried to pull the driver out, but he was a big man with both hands clamped to the wheel. My feet were sliding in the gravel and, suddenly, the road went out from under me. I fell in the ditch, losing my hold on Martin and the door handle.

How that man executed that turn-around, without going into the ditch, is a miracle for which I am thankful because the car might have rolled on me. At any rate, there went our violators heading for the reservation, at a high rate of speed, with rocks flying from their spinning wheels.

I then looked around for Leo to engage them in a pursuit

and found him getting out of his car, which was down in the ditch on the north side of the road. It seems when the outlaw car started to back down the road; Leo also tried to pursue him in reverse. However, his back window was fogged up and he was afraid of hitting me when I was chasing the violator's car. He got too close to the edge of the road, lost control, and ended up in the ditch. Nothing to do but chalk one up for the Indians because once they get back to that reservation, they are home free even though I recognized the driver.

We spent the next two hours getting our car back on the road. Now, there is a sequel to this event. The following summer, I drove my patrol car on the north side of Upper Red Lake down to Ditch 30, which is the end of the road and here I came upon a fairly well dressed Indian man and woman standing along side a late model, big, Buick sedan. At this location, the land belongs to the federal government on lease to the state of Minnesota, as part of the Red Lake refuge. About 50 feet south of where our cars are parked is the north shore of Upper Red Lake. Out on the lake are two men in a large open boat. This part of the lake, up to the shoreline, is a part of the Indian reservation.

It was obvious this man by the car was disturbed. I recognized him as Frank Martin and asked him what his problem was. He told me some s.o.b. must have stolen five of his gill nets that his two employees had set the night before.

I told Frank that finally justice had been served. Frank said, "What do you mean?"

I said, "Remember one night last fall when you and two other Indians shot at a deer on the Jerome Road, when a game warden car passed you and blocked you, and a warden tried to pull you out of your car and you got away from them?"

Frank looked more carefully at me then he asked, "Was that you?"

To which I answered, "Yes."
Then Frank came back with, "That wasn't me."

Chapter 19/ WISTRUM AND MICHAUD

On the night of October 24, I, Bill Callies, accompanied by
Warden Harland Pickett of Baudette, was going to work an area
northeast of Kelliher in my assigned district. I had received
information to the effect that there were occasional people
shining for deer in this area.

This was a normal procedure of working arrangements. I
would work with Harland Pickett for five or six days or nights
in the Baudette district, and he would reciprocate for about an
equal number of nights in my district. There was one serious
problem to this arrangement and that was Leo Manthei, the
warden at Blackduck. I also had a similar arrangement with
Leo.

Both of these men were passionate duck and goose hunters
and all of their days off were spent in North Dakota hunting
migratory waterfowl. This would have been fine for me if they
both had gone at the same time. However, it always seemed
when one was gone the other one was always back in his district
calling on me to work with them. Those two damn near killed
me every fall.

Now, I will get back to the above night. I knew how to get
into this area by some back trails and crossing some fields. So
at about 7 p.m., Harland came to my residence. The two of us
got into my assigned patrol vehicle with our lunches, coffee
bottles, and equipment that we might need if we encountered
any spot lighters.

We headed south on Highway 72, about fourteen miles to a
county road about two miles north of Kelliher. We turned east
at that point. There was a family living on the northeast part of

that intersection. It was Forrest Leonhard and his wife and son. He was employed by the county as the motor patrol operator. Forrest was a former heavyweight boxer and a real rugged individual.

We went east to a north-south road then we took some small trails through the woods until we came out on some huge fields. We crossed them until we came to a small wooded area where we could hide the car, and yet we could observe if anyone came on to the fields from the county line road. There we sat drinking coffee, telling lies, eating our lunches, and smoking cigarettes until midnight. No spot lighters showed up. At exactly midnight, Harland announced he was now on time off and he wanted me to take him back to my residence to get his car so he could head back to Baudette. He had planned to leave early the following morning for the Devil's Lake area to hunt ducks.

So we packed up to call it a night. We headed west with our lights off. It was about 12:25 a.m. when we were approaching Highway 72 from the east. We stopped about a hundred yards short of the highway because we could see the lights of two vehicles coming from the north. I backed into Forrest Leonhardt's yard in the event one of those cars turned east. That set Forrest's dog to barking and he wouldn't shut up. Then with a bang, the screen door on the back just flew open and out came Forrest. He was just buckling his belt. He had nothing on his feet or on the upper part of his body and he was looking for trouble. I quickly said to Harland, "Aren't you glad that he is a friend of mine?" With that, I stepped out of the car and called to Forrest and told him who we were. He seemed to look in our direction and then I told him that there were two cars coming from the north and about that time one of them passed through. However, the second one never showed, so we pulled out to the highway just in time to see this vehicle turn around at an approach about a half-mile north of us.

We followed this car without our lights on and because the

car was driving slowly, we gained on him. About two miles down the road, this car angled his car to the left so the headlights shined on the trees, then the brake lights came on. I stopped our car, turned off the motor. We rolled our windows down and stuck our heads out. About thirty seconds later, a shot rang out from the car ahead. It sounded like a high-powered rifle.

Immediately after the shot was fired, their car lights were off. There was about two-thirds of a moon that night and the sky was clear. I could see with my naked eyes. One person got out of the right side of the car, came around the car and proceeded toward the ditch on the west side of the road. The driver also got out of his car and stood at the side of his car on the road.

This stretch of Highway 72 is 3.6 miles long and unobstructed by curves or hills. We were 800 feet behind them. I was afraid we were too close and that they might see our car. Then, too, we were concerned that a car might come along and expose us which could cause us to lose the man out in the brush on the west side. These kinds of people do run on you given the opportunity. They are usually people well familiar with the bush.

Warden Pickett took my binoculars and watched them. He whispered a running account of their activities to me. We could hear brush cracking on the west side of the road. We could also hear the men talking but we could not make out what they were saying. After about ten minutes, the man standing near the car went toward the ditch on the west side of the road.

Warden Pickett asked if I could see the four popple trees in a clump on the west side of the road. I assured him I could see them. He told me to remember them as he had seen the man go into the brush this side or south of this clump of trees.

A few minutes later both men returned to the car, but they did not have anything with them. They got in their car and I heard their motor start. I started our car. Their car proceeded north without lights. We decided to pursue and apprehend them.

They had moved about three-tenths of a mile when we overtook them. Warden Pickett shined his five-cell flashlight in the driver's eyes when we came along side. I turned on our headlights at this same instant. We commanded them to halt and they complied. We instructed the men to get out of the car and get up in front of the headlights. I turned on the headlights of their car.

Warden Pickett found a gun in their car. He examined it and it was unloaded and in a case. We also saw a hunting knife lying on the front seat. There was a sheath for the knife and a two-cell flashlight on the front seat also. The knife was clean and wet.

I then inquired of the two men what their names were and where they were from. One man, the driver, identified himself as Art Wistrum of Bemidji. The other man identified himself as Myron Michaud of Minneapolis.

Warden Pickett noticed the back seat of the car was loose and underneath were newspapers neatly laid out under the back seat. When we asked why the newspapers were there we were told that the car was drafty and the papers were there to reduce the draft.

I then examined both men's hands for blood. Both men's hands were clean. However, Michaud's were wet and fine, wet sand was visible in the hairs on the back of his hands. I then examined his pants and boots and found quite a lot of wet blood on his boots and also some green substance.

I then instructed Michaud to get in the patrol car with me and Warden Pickett drove their car with Wistrum as a passenger. We turned the cars around and returned to the area where the clump of popple trees was on the west side of the road.

Warden Pickett told me to stay with the two men while he searched the brush in the west side of the road. Within a couple of minutes, he hollered that he had found the entrails and within seconds he shouted, "Here is a deer, a small doe." They had spread her legs out belly down so the blood would drain out.

I then made out seizure receipts for the rifle, a 94 Winchester 30-30 caliber, which Wistrum signed and I gave him a copy. I then made out a seizure receipt for the car, a 1960 Ford Galaxy. He then advised us that the car belonged to Luella Beck of Bemidji and neither man would sign the receipt. I then made out a receipt for the deer and neither man would sign that.

We loaded the deer on the patrol car that Pickett drove accompanied by Michaud. I drove the 1960 Ford accompanied by Wistrum to Kelliher where we located the town constable, Keith Dingman, and stored the Ford in the Kelliher garage. Then all four of us drove in the patrol car to the Bemidji city jail. Enroute both men denied any knowledge of any shooting of any deer.

At the police station, I asked Michaud to remove his boots for evidence. I offered him a receipt, which he refused to sign. We also enlisted the aid of several policemen at the station to examine the pants on Michaud. There were several spots and smears of blood on his pants. The policemen corroborated this. The two violators were turned over to the custody of the Bemidji police about 3 a.m. on October 25, 1964.

These two men were bound over to district court to be tried on a gross misdemeanor. The men were allowed to post bail and be released from jail until their case would come up in district court.

On the 12th of November, at the county attorney's suggestion, I sent Michaud's boots down to the bureau of criminal apprehension to have the blood and green vegetation analyzed. Eventually, the boots were returned to me from a W. Fong with the B.C.A. His analysis was that the blood was from a member of the deer family. The green stuff was ground-up vegetation.

Eventually, I was notified to appear in district court to testify on two different shining cases before Honorable Judge McRae of the Ninth District in Bemidji.

The first case was three Indians from the Red Lake reservation who had shot a deer on the Battle River road at night in closed season about ten miles from the reservation. I had them held in the county jail under Sheriff John Cahill.

The three men went before the judge. The judge read the complaint and asked them how they plead. They all pled guilty. The judge had them tell all the details of what happened that night. The judge let them know the minimum on a gross misdemeanor was, as a minimum, $100 and/or 90 days in jail with a maximum of $1000 and/or a year in jail. Then he told the Indians he would accept their plea of guilty. At this point, the judge inquired of John Cahill, "How long have you had these men in your hotel?"

John responded with "Nine days, your Honor."

Then the judge returned to the Indians and said, "Your penalty is 90 days in the county jail and I will suspend 81 days." Then the judge turned to me and told me to return their car to them. All the state got was an old beat-up rifle and the dead deer.

I went back and sat down behind Michaud and Wistrum. They were whispering back and forth during another trial and I heard one of them say, "This judge is easy. Let's just go up and plead guilty and get this over with."

Finally the bailiff called for Wistrum and Michaud to approach the bench. After all the preliminaries were over the judge read the complaint, "Did take one deer in closed season with the aid of the headlights of the car." Both men pleaded guilty. They were instructed to tell just what they had done and the wardens' part in the apprehension. The judge accepted their plea of guilty and fined each one of them $250 or 90 days in the county jail.

They elected to pay the fine. Then they told the judge that the car we had seized belonged to Luella Beck of Bemidji. It was their claim that Luella Beck didn't know they were going spotlighting with her car. Luella Beck was in court and she swore that she had no knowledge that these men were going out to shoot a deer. The judge believed her and instructed me to return the car to her, which was done.

Chapter 20/ TROUBLE ON THE WICKHAM FARM

I received a telephone call from someone at the Wickham farm located on the Battle River Road west of Kelliher, Minnesota. This call was about some trespassers on their pasture during the 1962 deer rifle season.

My brother-in-law, Jerry Liemandt, who was in charge of the firearm youth training division had stopped off at my station in Waskish, Minnesota. He told me he had just delivered supplies to Warden Markovich and was on his way back to St. Paul. I suggested if he was not in a hurry I would like to have him accompany me to be a possible witness.

It took us roughly thirty minutes to make the trip. On the way I gave him a rough background of these people, as I knew them. They moved into this area from somewhere in Missouri. Mrs. Wickham who seemed to be the one in charge in this family was a substitute teacher at the Kelliher School. Rumor had it she was not very popular with the students. Mr. Wickham was a very quiet figure who was supposed to have some kind of a heart condition. Then there is one boy and one girl, both of them quite brash and bold compared to the average students in this community.

When we pulled into their driveway, we were met by the wildest unkempt woman you would ever want to meet. Her hair stuck out straight and filthy from her head. Her clothing was covered with mud, deer hair and blood. I introduced her to Jerry as Mrs. Wickham. Then I asked her "What ever happened to you?"

She just screamed, "I want you to arrest those two men, Silver Anderson, the cattle buyer and Norman Florhang, the bartender at the Kelliher Municipal Liquor Store."

I asked her, "What happened, what did they do to you?" She started to calm down some and started to relate her complaint. It seems she and her husband were up on the roof of their house patching their roof before winter set in. They heard some big rifle shots northeast of their farm in the wooded area on the east side of County Road 23. Shortly, from their vantage point on the roof, they saw a buck deer cross County Road 23, jumped the barbwire fence on their pasture, ran about two hundred yards out on to the field and fell down dead.

The Wickhams climbed down the ladder from the roof, looked out on the pasture and saw two men climbing their barbwire fence and started walking toward the deer. Mrs. Wickham jumped in her old pick-up truck and drove out to where the deer lay just ahead of Norm and Silver. They told her that was their deer, they had shot it across the road and it had ran across the road and piled up in her pasture.

She then told them that the deer fell dead on her property and that they were trespassing, and that they had not come to her to ask permission to walk on her land. That deer was hers and they should just get themselves back across the fence.

Florhang said to her, "We shot the deer. We were on his trail."

So with that, he grabbed one horn of the deer, instructed Silver Anderson to grab the other horn to drag the deer back to the road. Then Mrs. Wickham threw herself onto the deer and wrapped her arms real tight around the neck. Anderson and Florhang started off dragging the deer with Mrs. Wickham hanging on and screaming at the men.

When the men stopped to take a breather, Silver asked Florhang, "What are we going to do to get her off the deer when we get out on the road?"

Florhang said, "I will go get the car and drive it to where

the deer and Mrs. Wickham are. I've got a tire iron in the trunk, if she is still hanging on I will hit her over the head with the iron."

That was too much for Mrs. Wickham. She let go of the deer, ran back to her pick-up, drove home and called the game warden.

After listening to her tale of what had transpired, I told Mrs. Wickham those men actually did nothing wrong. It would have been nice if one of them came to you and asked permission to trespass. Your property is not posted for no trespassing. These men had to stay on the trail of the deer in order to claim it. Also, they should not have dragged you but you gave them no choice. I will speak to Mr. Florhang about his threatening you with a tire iron.

Mrs. Wickham was upset that I had no intention of charging the men with trespassing. Then she spoke up and said, "What are you going to do about my prize Angus cow in calf that they shot?"

I asked, "Where is this cow and when was it shot?"

"It's right over here by the barn and it happened when all that shooting was going on while we were up on the roof," she answered.

I told her, "Well that could have been an accident but let's see this carcass."

She took us over by the barn and there laid a big Black Angus cow bloated to the point where it looked like it could blow up. I told her, "That cow has been dead for some time — at least a day or two or three — and I don't see any bullet hole."

With that, she grabbed the tail and jerked it up exposing the anus. There were a few drops of blood on the anus. Then she announced, "That's where the bullet went in."

I had a hard time to keep from laughing. She kind of jumped at me and shouted, "What's so damn funny!"

I said, "If that's where the bullet went in, the shooter had to be a good shot and the tail would have been shot off."

About that time, one of her neighbors came around the barn with a couple of large knives and a bone saw. I asked him, "What are you going to do?"

He responded with, "Butcher that beef."

I told him, "That meat is not fit for human consumption. However, Mrs. Wickham insists the animal was recently shot. The bullet obviously did not go through the animal, there is no exit hole – so if you find the pellet, I will compare it with pellets fired through Anderson's and Florhang's rifles – that will clear or convict them."

Then I told him, "You give us two minutes to get in our car and get out of here before you cut that hide. It's going to stink something awful around here. I'll be back this evening to pick up the pellet if you find one."

That evening I stopped again at the Wickham residence. Mrs.Wickham said they did not find the pellet but they did find the exit hole in the center of the brisket right where they split the hide.

I told Mrs. Wickham, "There is no exit hole anywhere in that area and if you subpoena me to testify, I will only tell the truth. That angus cow was not shot."

Chapter 21/ FISH SNAGGERS

One day in early fall, I had to appear in Municipal Court in Bemidji on some arrests I had made. When I arrived in the courtroom I found Leo Manthei, the warden from Blackduck and Jim Hinz, the "new" warden at Bemidji.

After we all got done with our various cases, Jim came to me and said he had about thirty fresh white fish. He had been advised that I had a large smoke house at Waskish and that I smoked a lot of white fish in the fall. He asked if I would take the fish home and smoke them for half the fish.

I agreed to this, and then I asked, "Where did you get these white fish?"

"I took them away from a couple of men that were using snagging equipment on the Mississippi River below the dam," he replied.

I asked, "Have you had these men in court yet?"

Jim said, "No. I didn't even charge these men because I was not sure if it was a violation or not." I then told him he had no right to take their fish if he hadn't written a summons or given these men a seizure receipt. I went on to ask if he might know who these men were or where they were staying. He had no knowledge on either query.

I then asked if there was any more of this snagging activity out on the river.

"Every day for the past three days, I have seen from one to half a dozen men with fishing poles, fishing below the dam," he said.

I said, "Let's all go down there and clean this up."

When we arrived at the dam, there were at least half a dozen men. Some were in the river with waders and some were on shore casting weighted, large treble hooks then retrieving in hard jerking movements. It seemed at least one person had a fish on all the time we watched.

I then said we have to do a little planning here. The next day, we were scheduled to go to a regional supervisor's meeting at Fosston. These meetings are usually boring and now we all have an opportunity to get out of this meeting. We would write all these fishermen up and schedule them into Municipal Court the next day. Then Leo and I told Jim to call the regional supervisor, Dick Tarte, the next morning and tell him we may be needed to testify at the hearings.

So we went to work with a vengeance, wrote up all these people that were snagging, seized their equipment and fish, and in twenty minutes we were the only ones on the river. I suggested we leave the area for a couple of hours and maybe there would be some more snaggers to show up.

Sure enough, when we came back there were a couple of more snaggers. We kept this up until about nine p.m. when we finally went to our respective stations.

The next morning, I picked up Leo and we headed for Municipal Court in Bemidji. About the time we got to Bemidji, Supervisor Dick Tarte was calling us on the radio to let us know our little plan wasn't going to work, and that Jim could take care of running the fishermen through court. He also advised that we better get our bodies up to Fosston and attend that meeting. I guess that is how Dick Tarte got to be regional supervisor. He saw through our plan.

At the meeting, around noon, Jim Hinz showed up and we saw him sit and whisper to a couple of the wardens at the far end of the table.

About fifteen minutes later there was some laughter and one of the men stood up and said he wanted to read a poem one of the men had just written. Following is a typed copy of the ditty:

MR. POPULARITY COMES TO TOWN

Mr. Popularity came to town.
Wrote everyone up and hauled them down.
He had the court calendar filled up thick
Then wondered why everyone called him a dick.
He wrote up his mother, father and his brother
Then looked around to find any other.
He had two partners named Leo and Bill,
They with bullshit, poor little Jim, did fill.
They wrote them up and passed them down
Then got their asses out of town.
They left poor Jim holding the bag
And took all the fish the outlaws did snag.

Chapter 22/ VIRGINIA RANGERS

It was early winter. The ice was about four to six inches thick—not thick enough to drive a car or pickup on. The walleyes were really hitting in Upper Red Lake and the word was out. I was down at Dyrhaug's farm or landing. This is a place that later on will have an access out onto the lake. Melvin Dyrhaug always keeps a well-plowed and maintained road out onto the lake and charges a reasonable fee.

There were at least forty cars and trucks parked in his yard. The fishermen would walk out about a quarter of a mile usually with a small sled to carry their ice chisels, fishing sticks, minnow pails, or whatever each person thinks he needs to catch six walleyes.

I drove in to Dyrhaug's yard with my patrol car and maneuvered around to get up as close to the lake as possible in an area where there were no trees or brush. I hooked up my spotting scope on my window mount and settled down to see what I could see. In those days, only one line was allowed to be used at a time. So basically, I was looking for fishermen using more than one line.

Usually people that angle with more than one line try to get away from the other fishermen so I looked for those fishermen that were off by themselves. There were two men off to the west at least three hundred yards from the main mass of fishermen. They had a sled with a small box on it. There were two men together so I concentrated on them. They were very active pulling out walleyes. In fact, I believed they had the limit or close to it lying on the ice.

One of the men pulled up his line and wrapped it on his fishing stick. Then he started picking up the fish and putting them in the box on the sled. I assumed they had their twelve walleyes and would be coming in to their car. The one man took the rope to pull the sled and started to head for shore. He came to the shore about a quarter of a mile west of me and disappeared into the woods. About ten minutes later, he came back out of the woods still pulling the sled and went back and joined his partner. He unwound his line, put on a minnow, and went back to fishing. Within twenty minutes they had about a dozen more fish lying on the ice. Again, the same man loaded the fish in the box, took up the rope on the sled, started walking toward the shore, and disappeared into the woods at about the same place as the first time I saw him do this.

About this same time Leo Manthei, the warden from Blackduck, called me on the radio. He wanted to know if the walleyes were biting on Red Lake. I told him everyone was catching fish and right at that moment I had two men under surveillance that I was sure had too many fish and I was just waiting for them to come to me. Leo said he was at Saum and would come right up and give me a hand. I told him it wasn't necessary for these two men, but if he didn't have anything else to do, come on up as we might find some more people that thought the limits did not apply to them.

A few minutes later, the man came out of the woods with the sled, headed out to his partner, and went back to fishing. Eventually, they had what looked like another limit lying on the ice. As Leo had arrived, I told him to take a look through my spotting scope at the two men. Again the man made a repeat performance towing the sled to the woods and disappearing. I told Leo I would bet the two men had at least thirty-six walleyes stashed in the woods, and maybe more.

The man reappeared and went back to his partner on the lake. Again they caught what looked like twelve more walleyes. However, this time both men wrapped up their equipment, put all the fish and their gear into the sled on the box, and headed straight into shore. When they got to the edge of the woods the two men stopped and talked. One of the men was waving his arms and then the two men split up. One man followed the shoreline pulling the sled, the other disappeared into the woods.

Leo and I started walking west, paralleling the shoreline. There was an inch or two of snow in the woods, not enough to make it hard walking. When we came to the area where the man was pulling the sled, we came out of the woods. I checked the man's angling license. He had a resident angling license and his residence was Virginia, Minnesota. I then counted his fish and he had twelve walleyes. I told him you have six walleyes over your legal limit. Then he told me he had a partner that had gone into the woods a way back because he had to have a bowel movement.

I told Leo I would go on down and find this man but Leo spoke up and said he thought he was a better tracker. He would check on this man's story. I told Leo I would take this man back to our patrol cars. As this man from Virginia had their car parked in Dyrhaug's yard, I would wait for him there. The two of us went east to my patrol car and sat and waited.

About forty-five minutes later, Leo came back along the shoreline and said he couldn't find any tracks of any man going into the woods.

I was quite a bit upset with Leo because I was reasonably sure the man would walk straight south through the woods about a half a mile with a sack of fish then turn east on the south end of Dyrhaug's pasture and come to the county road where he would be picked up by his partner. Leo was positive that no one walked south into the woods. I knew different and about that time I saw our man coming toward us walking on the county road.

I said to Leo, "There is our man. Go pick him up in your patrol car, then go back south of where you pick him up and watch on the west side of the road in the snow. Back track him and you will find the fish."

Leo was a bit putout but he did what I told him. We could see him pick up the man. He drove south to where he saw his tracks cross the ditch, walked in there, and within minutes came out with a sack on his back.

He brought the man and the fish back to me. Some of the walleyes were still kicking. I wrote them up and we took the men into the justice of the peace, Clara Quale, in Kelliher. They had thirty-six walleyes over their legal limit. The fine was thirty dollars or thirty days each.

Chapter 23/ FISH PACKERS

Leo Manthei, the warden from Blackduck, and I used to kind of coordinate our working periods so that if either needed assistance, the other person would usually be available. Most of our working periods were between 6 a.m. and midnight except in the fall when we used to work all night. There would be periods when it would seem there were no game and fish violations and we were in such a dry period this particular August. We couldn't buy a pinch so I suggested we go to work at midnight and see what we could find.

This particular night, I drove out to Highway 72 just about midnight. I called Leo on the radio. He was up, but said he had to gas up at the forestry gas pump and would be available in about fifteen minutes. I could see a pair of car lights coming from the north and as I did not have my lights on and being of a curious nature, I backed up to let this vehicle go by. In those earlier years, it was almost a novelty to see anyone driving in this country after 10 p.m. When the car went by, I noticed it was pulling a boat on a trailer, so now I can assume they are probably fishermen. I pulled out onto the highway without lights and eventually caught up to them and then I could see the trailer license was from Iowa. About five minutes later, Leo was on the radio and said he was gassed up and leaving Blackduck heading north on 72.

I told him I was following a car south on 72 that was towing a boat and trailer and the vehicles had Iowa licenses. I also advised him I was driving without lights and we were about half way to Kelliher. I also told Leo I planned to stop this vehicle in Kelliher under the streetlights, right along side the Mercantile Store and that is where he would find me.

Leo Manthei and Bill Callies

When we came to the town limits, I turned on my lights and just when we were coming to the Mercantile Store, I turned on my red light and brought them to a stop. There was a man and woman in the vehicle and I identified myself. I told him I wanted to check his fishing license and his fish. He was very cooperative with the licenses. He had a combination husband and wife license non-resident for Minnesota. Then he said the fish were in a cooler in the boat. He showed me the boat had a tarp cover and at least fifty feet of rope lashing it down and it had taken him a long time to get everything tied down for his trip home. Also, he said the fish had been packed by a licensed fish packer that his card was right inside the cooler with a list of all the fish and their species.

So I told him I still wanted to check the fish and that I would untie the ropes and if everything was okay I would retie the cover and ropes. When the lady heard this, she spoke up and said that they had been fishing at Lake of the Woods and stayed at one of the resorts. She had run out of some very special heart pills she had to have and that was why they started home in the middle of the night and that if I delayed them by insisting on uncovering the boat, they would hold me responsible for her well-being. She looked pretty healthy to me, so I kept on untying knots and eventually got down to the canvas. I removed the cover and when I got inside the boat, I found a huge metal cooler. When I opened it, the box was solid with fish filets and I knew there were too many for two people. There was a fish packer's card on top that was filled out with twelve walleye pike, sixteen saugers, and six northern pike. I got a piece of cardboard out of my car to lay the fillets on as I counted. They should have sixty-eight individual fillets according to the fish packer's card.

Well, I counted out sixty-eight fillets and I hadn't made a dent in the number of fish in that box. Both the man and woman insisted the fish packer put those fish in there and they had absolutely no knowledge that anything was wrong. I assured these people the fish packer had his name printed on the card plus his signature as to the contents and I would deal with him later. In the meantime, I would charge them with possession of too many fish. I don't have the confiscation report handy, but it seems they were about one hundred and twenty over their limit.

About this time Leo pulled up and as this woman was in the process of putting on quite a show about her heart and lack of pills, Leo and I decided we had best try to wake up some justice of the peace and run them through court so they could be on their way. Otherwise, we would have to take them to jail in Bemidji and have them in Municipal Court in the morning.

We couldn't seem to arouse Justice Quale in Kelliher, so we proceeded to Blackduck where Leo got the justice of peace up and brought him down to the town hall. This justice was a schoolteacher and he was not too happy about being awakened. I only wrote a complaint against the man and he pleads guilty. His fine was one hundred dollars or thirty days. He elected to pay the fine.

On the way down the hall from the court room, I told this man I was going to go up to Baudette, locate this commercial fish packer, put a charge against him, and that I would probably have to subpoena this man to have him testify that the packer put the fish in the box. In the event he was found guilty, I would cancel his fish packer's license.

At this point the culprit said, "Don't do that. I'm the one who put all those fish in that box. The packer knows nothing about what I did."

I told this fellow I was reasonably sure he was lying when he came up with that story because when the fish packer signs his name to that card and it doesn't match with the contents, he knows he can be penalized and lose his license.

Chapter 24/ SOUTHERN MINNESOTA FISHERMEN

One winter day, I was checking ice fishermen on Upper Red Lake. Usually most of the fishermen would be out in front of one of the many resorts. This was on a Monday and I was curious to know if there was anyone fishing west of the Rocky Point Resort, which is the last resort on the north side of the lake. I drove west on Ditch 14 to the Nieber Trail, which lead to the Heulien Ditch grade. There wasn't much snow that year so I was able to drive down close enough to see the lake. I could see two small portable fish houses and about two hundred yards from the fish houses was an airplane on skis. There was also a car near the fish houses.

There were two men fishing out in the open near the airplane. I got my spotting scope out and hooked it up on my window mount so I could get the numbers off the airplane to call it into the dispatcher to see who the plane belonged to. The dispatcher called me back in about ten minutes and told me the owner was Erickson, a Minnesota state patrolman that lived at Bagley. I was told a couple of days later that Erickson got mad as hell when he found out I was checking on him.

Also, with the aid of the scope, I was able to read the license number on the car next to the fish houses. The car was from some farmer that lived down near the Iowa border. The two men with the fish houses each had a line outside of their house. Every once in a while a man would come out of his fish house and check this outside line. Occasionally, they would lift this line to see if the minnow was still on the hook and sometimes they would come out of the house, grab their fish stick and lift out a walleye.

I became aware the men were using the fish houses for spearing northern because on two occasions I saw one man come out of the house with a huge northern impaled on the tines of a spear.

That evening I drove into Hudec's resort and found their vehicle parked beside one the rental cabins. I knew from past experience that Ed Hudec would not be cooperative with me as to where these men were keeping their fish or how long they planned to stay at the resort. All Ed, who was typical of most resorters in that area, cared about was the revenue that could be garnished from these fishermen.

The next day I went back to the area where the two spear houses were and I could see their car parked next to the houses.

The lake had very little snow on it so obviously the men were able to drive the nine miles from Hudec's resort to their fishing site on the ice.

This situation was repeated every day all week so I had reason to believe they had accumulated too many fish. Not knowing where their fish were being stored, it was my hope and intent to try to intercept them when they were leaving for home.

Saturday morning I started out in my patrol car to make another check as to the location of these two fishermen. I received a call from Leo Manthei, my neighboring warden from Blackduck. He said he was on his way up to Waskish to work with me. From past experience, he was really more interested in catching a mess of walleyes.

So I went back to my residence and waited for him. When he arrived, I told him of my suspicions and that I didn't want to do anything that day but keep these two men under observation. It was my feeling they would pack it all in and head for home. Leo knew if he stuck with me there would be no time for fishing. He did agree to accompany me up to Heulien to see the operation. When we arrived there it was a repeat of the previous five days. We sat there for a couple of hours watching these two men. Leo was getting real bored and kept suggesting we go check fishermen on other parts of the lake, and incidentally, we could stop in my fish house and pull out a few fish for him to take home.

He suggested we could make occasional trips up to check on these southern fishermen. I finally gave up and we did go down to the east end of the lake, checked some fishermen, stopped at my fish house, caught six walleyes for Leo, and took Leo back to my house where he got in his car and left.

I immediately drove back to the Heulien Ditch and my major concern had happened. The fish houses were gone. I immediately turned around and went to Hudec's resort. The car was not there either.

I was beside myself for letting someone con me out of my

intended plans. I went into the house and told my wife how stupid I had been. She too was upset because she knew how badly I wanted to check these men out. Then she said this isn't the first time something like this has happened. You have to be firmer with Leo and just say no. I came back with a weak excuse that he was my neighbor and there could be a time I might really want help.

Then my wife started to think along a more positive track. She suggested as long as I had a description of the car, the license number, and the possible destination of these men that I should call the dispatcher at Thief River Falls to put the message out state wide to watch for this vehicle, stop it, and check for the number of fish. I did this. However, there would not be the satisfaction that I had looked forward to.

The next day was Sunday and I was still upset with myself. I searched all around the lake but to no avail. I checked with the dispatcher and he had no news for me.

Monday morning, I got up to a new layer of snow (about ten or twelve inches deep). I shoveled the snow from the walk and in front of the garage. I could hear the snowplow way off to the northwest heading for Waskish. I wanted to go to the store and post office, so I plowed through the snow with my patrol car out to Highway 72. I could see the plow coming so I waited for it. The plow passed me in a swirl of snow and there, about two hundred yards behind the plow, was the car with the two men and their portable fish houses on top. I couldn't believe my luck. All I could think of was my wife must have made a pact with the Lord because she knew how much I wanted to check these people out.

Down the highway we went, snowplow, fishermen, and yours truly. I would follow them to Kelliher, fifteen miles south, because there was a justice of the peace there. I was on cloud nine when we pulled into Kelliher. I pulled along side of them, gave them the red light, and a hand signal to pull over. They complied. I parked behind them, walked up to their car, told them I was the local warden, and asked them how fishing was. They said it was real good so I told them I wanted to check their licenses and fish. They were extremely cooperative and relaxed. I began to think they might have disposed of any overage with wherever they had been Saturday and Sunday night or maybe these were good honest sportsmen. Actually, I hoped so, but I wanted confirmation. I asked them to open the trunk and there were six humongous northern pike as long as the trunk was wide. They were all frozen in the round, as were twelve walleyes and about fifteen perch. I looked in the back seat and all I could see were suitcases, packsacks, and heavy clothing. I went back to the trunk to admire those big northern. Underneath all these fish was a pair of hip boots with the top of one boot into the top of the other boot. I reached in and felt the boot and something was in it. I pulled it out and here was another big northern.

I then told them you have one northern too many. They admitted they had taken one too many but it was not intentional. It seems they had five and each was in their individual spear house. They needed one more to fill out and they each had a big northern show up in the hole in their spear house. When they came outside to shake the fish off their spear was when they became aware they had taken one too many. The fish were so tore up they wouldn't survive if they put one of them back in the water. Also, they didn't want to be wasteful so they took it.

Now I've never pinched anyone for one or two over. So I told these men I would take the largest northern and give it to the local nursing home and they could make muyacka out of it. Then I asked, "Are you sure if I dig around in the car I won't find some more fish?" They said that was the only extra fish they had.

I got into the back seat and felt into the packsacks. Then I got hold of a large suitcase and it was heavy. I opened it up and it was full of walleye fillets (a total of around seventy fish).

I was elated that I was so fortunate as to find these men

after I was sure I had lost them. I escorted them over to the newspaper office where Mrs. Clara Quale was the owner and operator. She was also one of two elected justice of the peace. I submitted the court copies of the summons and the seizure receipts for the fish. She accepted their guilty plea and fined each of them one hundred dollars and three dollars costs or thirty days in jail. They had the money so they paid the fine. Then they asked if they could at least keep the limit of walleyes and northern. I told them no. I did tell them if they wanted to stay over until the next day they could take and have a limit of fish. Then one of them said, "What are we going to tell our wives when we get home after one week with no fish and no money?" I told them to show their wives their copy of the summons and the receipt from Beltrami County made out by the justice of the peace.

I took all the fish over to the nursing home and gave the fish to them after they signed the confiscation book.

One of the employees weighed the seven northern and the total weight was one hundred and sixty three pounds.

When I got home my wife and I were on cloud nine. We took the rest of the day off.

Chapter 25/ RED LAKE FISHERMEN

It was the first Sunday in February. The annual Red Lake fishing derby was scheduled for that afternoon from 2 to 4 p.m. The Red Lake Sportsman's Club sponsors this annual event. The different members are assigned specific jobs to make the event as enjoyable to the paying guests as possible. Prizes are given out all through the contest. Then there are cash prizes for the largest, second, and third walleye, northern, perch and burbot.

It was always my assignment to weigh and tabulate the fish

to determine who would win the first, second, or third cash prize in each category.

The fishing derby was over and all the members of the club were closing the operation. The sun had just gone down when Anne Manthei, the warden's wife from Blackduck, came running up to me and told me a big man over where she was fishing had just fallen down and seemed to be having a heart attack. Could I do anything to help?

About an hour earlier, I had seen Doctor Reed and his wife fishing at the derby. I looked over where he had been and he was still there. I told Anne I would enlist his help and she should go back to where the man was down. I jumped in my patrol car, drove to the doctor, and told him of the emergency. He had his doctor's bag in his car. He grabbed the bag and he and his wife, who was a nurse, got in my patrol car and rushed over to the victim. The doctor and his wife did everything in their power to bring the man back. There were several people nearby fishing. One man and woman said this man had come up with them from Grand Rapids. They kept on fishing while I was questioning these people as to the man's identity (his name, address and next of kin). These people pulled out two or three walleyes. They had their twelve walleyes.

The doctor finally announced the man passed away and that I should call on my radio for the coroner, who was also the undertaker, to come and pick up the body. While we were waiting for the undertaker, the man that came up with the dead man, came over to me and asked if he and his wife could keep on fishing and catch and take home the dead man's limit of walleyes. How about that?

Chapter 26/ DUCK HUNTERS

Leo Manthei, my neighboring game warden at Blackduck, called me over one day in the fall before the duck season. He had a hot tip on some illegal duck hunters in his area and he wondered if I would plan on coming down to assist him on the opening day, which was a Saturday.

So on the day in question, I showed up at his house about 7:00 a.m. The season didn't open until noon of that day and the limit was a total of four ducks.

We took Leo's patrol car with a 15-foot canoe on the top rack, two push poles, and two paddles and proceeded to his informer's home. We were advised that a group had come up from the cities the year before and had a field day on a small bay located on this small river that ran past this man's farm. According to this informant, the bay was full of wild rice. There were a fair number of ducks around and if these big city hunters came back, we should have a field day.

Leo and I unloaded the canoe and then we put push poles, paddles, our shotguns, and a summons book and seizure book into the canoe, and shoved off. Both of us were dressed like duck hunters. About two miles down stream, we came to this bay off to the right side of the river and found it to be occupied on all sides by hunters. It seemed to be about ten men and they rose up to let us know, in no uncertain terms, that no other hunters were welcome. We continued on past them around the bend and out of their sight, and then we pulled into shore. It was about 10:30 a.m. And as they seemed to be set up for shooting, we thought we might also get them for early shooting. We crawled and sneaked through the brush and got close enough to the hunters, that we could hear their conversation. We kept them under observation until noon and not one shot was fired before noon. However, we started hearing shooting off in the distance.

We could see small flocks of ducks flying and then they started to come into this bay where the hunters we were watching were. It seemed as though the whole bunch started shooting at once. They knocked down a few ducks every time a flock came in. There was a lot of cursing every once in a while and admonishing about, "Watch where you are shooting."

It seems when a flock came in too low, and as there were shooters on all sides, some of the men were having shot come real close to them. On a couple of occasions, I could hear shot swoosh through weeds and grass near me. However, it was not intentional, as they did not know we were there. These men were poor shots. They should have knocked down at least five for every one they did get. They were having fun and the shooting was almost constant.

Along about 2:30, they were talking about running out of shells, so they appointed one man to go to town and purchase more. We could hear a motor start off to the west and in about forty-five minutes we could hear the vehicle return. The man apparently came back with more shells because the shooting seemed to increase. The daily shooting was to cease at 4 p.m. So Leo suggested I slip up through the woods and locate their vehicles and if no one was around, get the license numbers. I located their vehicles and while I was writing down the license numbers, one of the hunters came up to the vehicles. It was about 4 o'clock and this man removed his waders, unloaded his shotgun, and put it in a case. Then he put the waders and his gun in a pick-up truck. All the time he seemed to be looking for someone. However, he did not see me as I was well hidden.

Then came a blood-curdling yell, "Bill, Bill!" from down where the hunting had been going on. I took off as fast as I could run, without the hunter by the vehicle seeing me, to get to Leo's side. I found him in a brushy area near the water with a number of the duck hunters milling about. I noticed three of the hunters had their shotguns in their hands pointing in the general direction of Leo's legs. Leo asked me if the rest of our men had the road blocked. I told Leo the road was blocked and no one could get any cars out until we showed up and okayed it. Then, we instructed all of the men to lay their shotguns down and back away from them. There were eight men in this group. Leo advised me he had gotten close enough to this group to hear them counting their ducks and as I remember it, he said their count was eighty-seven. He also heard a couple of the men make remarks to the effect that what they had done was shameful and they had really abused a privilege. After hearing this, Leo told me he stepped out and announced who he was and that they were all under arrest. At this point, five of the men submitted and laid down their shotguns. However, three of them hung onto their guns and pointed them in Leo's general direction. This prompted the outcry for me from Leo.

We herded the group up to their parked vehicles, carried up the shotguns and sacks of ducks, and proceeded to make out seizure tags, summons, and advised these people of their rights. They could legally take thirty-six ducks for the nine men. However, they had eighty-seven, so they were fifty-one ducks over.

We told these men we should take them to Duluth and run them through federal court. However, that would also tie us up and if they all felt they were guilty as charged, we could run them through justice of the peace court that evening at the local justice of the peace court. They all were anxious to get it over and they all pleaded guilty and paid a fine of $50.00 each and they lost all their shotguns.

The next morning, I came back to Blackduck at Leo's request and we returned to the area of the day before. We picked up about a dozen more ducks that they had missed. Also, as Leo and I reloaded our own ammunition, we made a nice haul of empty shotgun shells (one of the side benefits of the job).

The following Tuesday when I came home, my wife confronted me with, "Where were you last Saturday from 6:30 a.m. to 10:30 p.m.?"

I told her I was working with Leo all day.

"Not according to the Bemidji newspaper", she said. I read the article in the Bemidji newspaper written by Anne Manthei about how Leo captured these nine duck hunters from Minneapolis with eighty-seven ducks.

The next day, I drove to Blackduck to Leo's house. When I had Leo and Anne together in the kitchen, I told Leo he was going to have come to Waskish and tell my wife that I was with you all day Saturday. Anne seemed surprised, so evidently, Leo didn't include me in his narration of what happened on the opening day of the duck season.

Chapter 27/ PAGE AND KEEHR

One day during the deer season in 1963, I got a call from a local resident to the effect he thought there was trespassing on his property at night on his hay fields about seven miles southwest of Waskish. These fields were on the old Highway 72 and were known as the Tweeten Fields. I told this landowner I would spend some time down there starting that night. He then asked if he could ride along. I told him I would enjoy his company but warned him that usually these stakeouts were monotonous and boring but if he still wanted to go to bring a big lunch and plenty of coffee. He was still game to go and I was glad because he would be a good backup person in the event there was a problem.

I picked him up about 7 p.m. and we headed down to Tweeten's Field. Upon arrival, I couldn't find a really good place to hide our car and still have a good observation of the field. I noticed a big hay stack on the field about fifty feet long, twelve feet wide, and about twelve feet high. It was parallel to the old road just across the ditch and about fifty feet north of the approach from the road. I decided to park the car up tight to about the middle of the haystack on the side away from the road. No one could see us from the road, however, if they drove out on the field, we would be exposed. That would be okay because I would have reason to stop and check them.

There we sat, trying to out-do one another with our past hunting and fishing experiences. There was no traffic at all until about a quarter to midnight when a car came from the north. They drove rather slow. We could see the glow of their headlights. At one time, I thought I saw a light hit the backside of the field, but I wasn't sure. We could see the glow of their headlights and hear their wheels as they passed on the other side of the haystack. Then within seconds, I saw in the rear vision mirror, the lights of their car facing west coming out onto the field behind us at the approach. The car hesitated and we didn't know if they were going to come on or back up to turn around. The car started to move again out onto the field in a westerly direction, then it turned north. It was driving very slow and at this point I figured they hadn't seen us.

In those days, we had to get them with a loaded, uncased firearm in the act of shining a light on a field or woodland in order to have a shining case. I told my partner I would try to catch up to them on foot, jump in the back seat, and if they had a loaded uncased gun, I would have a better chance to surprise them than if I went after them with our car. I could see from the other car's lights there were two people in the front seat. I told my partner to get behind the wheel and if he saw me pull this off, he should come immediately with our car.

So I took off on a dead run, caught up to this car, jerked the back door open, and jumped in. I had two really surprised men on my hands. I told them I was a Minnesota game warden. With the aid of my flashlight, I could see no gun in the car and then they told me they were just looking. About this time, my partner drove up with the state car. When the two men realized I had nothing on them, they became a bit belligerent. Then, I let them know they were trespassing. I informed them that I had the landowner in the state car and if he wanted me to charge them with trespassing, I would do that. That took the wind out of their sails.

I noticed both men were dressed in red clothing, so I asked to see their deer licenses for identification. The older man was Mike Page. I vaguely remember him as having a cabin on Sunny Beach on Red Lake about two miles from where we were. His home was in Bemidji.

The other man was Ray Keehr, Page's son-in-law. His home address was East Grand Forks, Minnesota. I used to get suspicious of people that lived along the border so I asked to see his driver's license. He said he didn't see any reason to bring his billfold along as his father-in-law was doing the driving. He said his billfold was at the cabin so I told him I wanted to see his driver's license. We went back to the cabin but he was unable to find his billfold there. He said that he must have left it at his father-in-law's house in Bemidji. I had him sit in the patrol car while I called the dispatcher at Thief River Falls to call the police at East Grand Forks to see where Ray Keehr lived. The East Grand Forks police were the first to answer and they said there was no Ray Keehr in east Grand Forks. By then, Ray knew the jig was up so he admitted to purchasing a resident deer license instead of non-resident license. So I wrote him up.

The property owner thought that was enough penalty, so he told Page and Keehr he would not have me charge them this time, but he told me if I ever caught them on his property again, I should charge them.

One year later, on the first Saturday of the deer season, Harland Pickett of Baudette wanted a work party in the southern part of Lake Of The Woods County. That was November 7, 1964. John Parker was to fly with the super cub. Dick Tarte, our supervisor, was coming up from Bemidji to fly observer with

Parker. They were to meet and take off from the Baudette airport. J.C. Richards came over from Big Falls to ride with me. Pickett had Al Markovich to ride with him. Tarte brought a new trainee, Gene Pierson, up to Waskish. Leo Manthei of Blackduck was to come up and take Pierson with him. Pierson had been on about a month. So we would end up with three two-man teams on the ground and two men in the air in a super cub. We were strung out along Highway 72, which is a forty-mile stretch of highway between Waskish and Baudette. Pickett and Mark were to be by the big rock about twelve miles south of Baudette. Richards and I were to be near the Shortly Castle road and Manthei was to be at Ludlow Island with the trainee. We were to be at our stations by 8:30 p.m.

As usual, Manthei was late. So Richards, Pierson, and I started out driving slow. When we got to Ludlow Island we would wait there for Manthei.

About two miles out of Waskish, we came upon a little fawn on the west side of the road. Its mother had been killed about five weeks earlier by a car. In the past, I used to run that little fellow back in the bush when I caught it out grazing along side on the road. It didn't have the fear of man it should have although it had survived the opening day. I said to Richards, "The first car that comes along is going to poach that deer." I drove about an eighth of a mile on up the road turned around in Irv Davidson's driveway and came back past the little deer. It was still grazing down in the ditch. I went on to Annie Newill's driveway about one hundred yards from the deer. I backed into her driveway. Annie didn't live there any more. I turned off the motor. It was a black night—no moon. It was rather warm for this time of year so we rolled our windows down. Richards of course was chewing his snuss, he spit, then said, "You know Tarte and Pickett are going to be p.o'ed at us if we're not on our station on time." I reminded him we had an excuse. Manthei was late and we had to wait to turn Pierson over to him. We had no problem.

Within ten minutes, a car came from the north at fairly slow speed. We could hear the wheels on the road and we could see the headlights through the brush. The car came to a stop about where the deer was. Then a small light came out the side and "pow" a shot from a high power rifle. We could even see the flash from the rifle. This occurred at 8:20 p.m.

Richards hollered, "Get up there. Drive the car right up against theirs." I was already rolling out of the drive and drove up against their car. It was a 1955 Chevrolet, four-door sedan. I jumped out and ran to the driver's side of the car, turned off the motor, and took the keys.

I instructed the two men to get out of the car and get up in front of the headlights. They both complied with my instructions. When they got in front of the lights I could see both men had red coats and hats on. I then asked the two men to give me their deer-hunting license. The older man gave me his license. It was made out to Mike Page of Bemidji. Mike, by the way, was the driver of the car, so obviously the other man was the one that shot the deer.

About this time my partner said, "I've got the gun. They must have thrown it in the back seat when we jumped them." Then Richards commented the barrel was warm and he offered the gun to me to feel the barrel. It was warm.

I asked the other man for his deer license, and he said he didn't have one. Then he went on saying, "Remember me? Last year you arrested me for having a resident deer license when I was supposed to have a non-resident license on me." Then he went on to say he received a letter from the DNR that he would not be allowed to purchase any non-resident hunting license in the year 1964.

About that time, Richards said he had found the empty rifle shell and that too was warm. Also about that time, a Volkswagen, one of those little beetle types, came down the highway and pulled up behind Mike Page's car. The driver, an older woman with no hat on and a severe hair style (it was parted in the middle and the hair was drawn real straight back and down her head), came running out of the car at me yelling, "You've got the wrong ones, they didn't do it." I asked this lady what her problem was and she said again, "Those aren't the ones. They didn't do it." (They, meaning Mike Page and Keehr.)

So I assured her we had the right ones, but just for the record, "What is your name and are you related to these two men?" She gave her name as Mrs. Chris Johnson. She denied knowing either Page or Keehr. I assured her that we had witnessed the shooting and not for a second were the two men or their car out of our sight. Mrs. Johnson got back in her vehicle and continued on toward Waskish.

I asked the trainee, Gene Pierson, if he knew how to field dress a deer. The deer was lying in the ditch along side of my car. Gene said he knew how to do that but he didn't have a knife. I went around to the driver's side of the car to get my knife that I always kept under the seat on the floor. Just as I bent over to reach under the seat I saw someone in a red coat move in on me real quick. I whirled around, grabbed him, threw him to the ground, and then pounced on top of him. The guy started hollering, "I ain't one of them, I ain't one of them." I really felt bad. Of course Page and Keehr thought that was real funny. I had forgotten that Pierson hadn't been issued any warden clothing. I apologized several times. Fortunately, I didn't hurt him. I finally dug out the knife and he dressed out the deer. We loaded the two night hunters into the back seat of my patrol car. Gene Pierson drove their 1955 Chevrolet. We all went to the fish hatchery on the north end of Waskish. I made out seizure slips for the car, the rifle, the deer, and the empty shell. I had the night hunters sign them and they got copies. We locked the car up in the Minnesota fish hatchery garage.

About this time Manthei showed up and we turned Gene Pierson over to him. Also I told Manthei to take Page and Keehr back to Kelliher and lock them up in the jail until later when I would see they got transported to the jailhouse at the county seat in Bemidji. Leo wasn't to enthused about my unloading this chore onto him and his new found trainee, however, he did do it. I told him I would explain to Pickett why he was late to his assigned work area.

To say the least, it was a wild night and I'm not going to enumerate on all the arrests we made that night. On one occasion, when we hauled some night hunting big game hunters into jail, it was around 2 a.m.. Parker and Tarte had just landed at the Baudette airport because they were low on fuel. I suggested they go up and locate some more night hunters for us. Supervisor Tarte said, "No way. We have had it. Parker is taking the plane back to Warroad and I'm going to pick up Pierson and head back to Bemidji." I did talk him into stopping at the Kelliher jail to pick up Page and Keehr and transport them to the Bemidji jail. Ces Richards got sick and went to Waskish and crawled into a bunk. Markovich and Manthei went back to their respective districts. Pickett and I kept messing around and we made several more big game arrests. In fact, when the sun came up, Harland Pickett's front yard looked like a used car lot. The local people, when they drove by Pickett's house, knew we had been out working the night before.

The following Monday, I had to go to Bemidji Municipal Court to testify and get the violators bound over for a gross misdemeanor in district court. Page and Keehr were allowed to post bail of five hundred dollars each pending the time to set a date for their trial in district court.

Page and Keehr hired Whitney Tarutus to represent them in court. Tarutus, no doubt, got statements I had made in municipal court and started to weave a story similar to what actually happened to present to the jury. Tarutus was good at this sort of thing and I can vouch for that from previous experiences. Tarutus requested that Page and Keehr be separated and each have a trial of their own and the court approved this.

Page's trial came up first and I testified to the facts of the case. Page was put on the stand and to say the least, he had been well schooled. He claimed he had his car recently overhauled, which was a true statement. Then he went on to say he was driving south on Highway 72 when he wanted to spit. He chewed tobacco and so as not to get any tobacco juice on the side of the car he brought the car to a halt so he could spit. In stopping the car and because the car was not properly tuned up, it backfired with a big bang and a flash. His son-in-law noticed something in the ditch and he used his small two-cell flashlight to shine on the object. It was a small deer and it was dead, obviously shot during the daylight hours in season and it finally dropped dead right there in the ditch along side of their car. The men complained of rough treatment at the site and added that one of us hit him in the head when he was getting in the patrol car. Also they complained about being locked up in a bear cage in Kelliher. The jury saw through the whole facade and found Page guilty as charged. The judge fined him $350 and 90 days in the county jail.

To this day, I do not know if Ray Keehr plead guilty or if he ever was brought to court or if the court just decided to take his bail in lieu of a fine. I made many requests to the court as to the final disposition of Keehr. After all, he had to be the one who did the actual shooting.

I forgot to mention the new trainee, Gene Pierson, resigned from being a game warden at 8 a.m. on November 9, 1964. It seems he thought it was too rough an occupation.

Also, about seven months after the incident, I was finally notified to auction Page's car off in front of the Beltrami County courthouse in Bemidji. Page was the high bidder.

Chapter 28/ SOUTH FORK OF THE BATTLE RIVER

It was the spring of the year 1963. The ice was going out and the fish were making their spawning run up the various streams that drain into Upper Red Lake.

This particular morning, I decided to walk the edge of the south fork of the Battle River from the county road north of Saum to the Red Lake Reservation line.

There was still three of four inches of snow on the ground. I was looking for fish traps, gill nets, and persons spearing or dip-netting fish. The season for taking walleyes and northern was closed. The season for taking rough fish was over a month away if you used spears or dip nets.

About three miles on this stream, I came across a gill net that was stretched from bank to bank on the stream. There were some tracks in the snow on my side of the stream but there were lots of man tracks on the other side. About a hundred feet down stream, I found a tree that had fallen across the stream. According to the tracks in the snow, the operators of the gill net had used the tree to negotiate crossing the stream.

When I got to the other side, I could see quite a trail in the snow that lead through a pasture to a set of farm buildings about a quarter of a mile away.

I pulled the net out of the water. There were a couple of small walleyes in the net. I worked the net off of them and released them back into the stream.

The tracks in the snow were fresh. It appeared someone had been there within the past two hours. The freshest tracks headed off to the southwest towards the farm building.

I rolled up the net and headed for the farmhouse on the trail in the snow. The tracks led to the first building. It looked like it might have been an old garage with a dirt floor. There was no door and when I looked inside it was literally covered with walleye heads, backbones, and skins. A bunch of chickens were picking around the fish guts. It looked like they had taken a couple hundred fish.

The people saw me and the lady and one teenage boy came out to where I was. I recognized the boy because I had him in firearm safety class about four years before. He said, "I'm glad you caught us." He said he kept telling his dad that this was wrong but his dad kept making him go to the net every morning and evening to get the fish, clean them, and store them in plastic containers in the deep freeze. The mother confirmed the lad's statement.

I asked where and how many containers of fish they had. The mother said about one hundred square one quart plastic containers. They invited me in and showed me. I counted them out and there were eighty-four one-quart containers of frozen fish.

I had to leave the fish there because I couldn't begin to carry all those containers back to my patrol car. It was almost four miles. I did carry one container and the gill net in the event they made the other eighty-three disappear before I got back with my patrol car. I asked the lady where her husband was because I wanted to make the summons and seizure tickets out to him. She said he was out in the bush cutting pulp like always.

I got back to the farm with the car and all the containers were there. I made out the summons to the husband. I was on squeaky ground because I didn't have a search warrant for the fish.

I had a talk with the justice of the peace about these people's living conditions and finances. She fined them the full amount according to the bail schedule, but she suspended most of it.

I did advise these people if I caught them doing anything like this in the future, they would be liable for the full amount of the fine.

Chapter 29/ PLEAD NOT GUILTY

This incident started on the Tamarac River in Waskish, Minnesota in May of 1963. A family from St. Paul purchased a summer cabin on the Tamarac River. The house was on the highest piece of ground on the whole lot and that was only about two feet above the normal river level. The front yard was about two inches above the river level and the road in was impossible.

A church college in St. Paul employed this man. I believe he was a professor and a pastor. He was a very pleasant nice man.

I heard that he was looking for someone in the community to haul in fill to create a good drivable access road to his property and to haul in fill for his yard. Also I heard he had contacted Ben Koisti in Kelliher who did this type of work.

I stopped over and talked to this person about the proper procedure and also brought an application from the Division of Waters for him to fill out. The Section of Game and the Section of Fisheries would check the area, however, I could see no problem in his acquiring a permit. He did say he had hired Ben Koisti. So I advised him Ben Koisti could do the work, however, Ben was a shortcut artist and not inclined to follow the law if he thought he could get by with it. I told him after he submitted his application the people from the Division of Waters would, after approval, issue him a permit. Also, he would receive a large cardboard sign with his permit number on it, the starting date and the date the work must be completed. The man said he understood and I thought there would be no problem.

About two weeks later, I stopped by and found a road had been created by digging dirt from one side and piling it on the road there by creating a borrow pit or ditch that led right out into the river. Also, the dragline cat tracks around the cabin led me to believe the fill in the front and backyard was pulled up from the bottom of the river. Also, there was no permit sign displayed.

That following weekend, the man and his family came up to their cabin. I made it a point to contact him and he admitted he had not applied for a permit. He also said he took the application to Koisti to fill out. Koisti told him the state would take three weeks or more to approve the permit. Also, he had time right then to do this job. A month down the line, he had other contracts to fill. He told the man he would take care of everything and not to worry about all that paper work. Just have the money ready when the work was completed.

I told the man that Ben Koisti had no right to tell him that. I asked him if he had paid Ben. He said he had stopped in Kelliher the evening before and paid Ben the full amount. Then, I told this fellow "You've got a problem now." At that, he said Ben Koisti told him the work was all done and the state would just have to accept that fact.

I told him "No it doesn't end there. I am charging you with having all this work done. Because there has been digging in the river, Koisti had changed the cross section of the bed of public waters. That is the charge, here is the summons to appear in municipal court in Bemidji." In those days, this was a gross misdemeanor with a possible fine of up to $1000.00 and/or up to a year in jail.

This poor fellow went back to St. Paul and retained a lawyer. He appeared on the scheduled date. Judge Reed was sitting on the bench. The county attorney was in attendance to prosecute the case. The complaint was read.

I was called to testify. After being sworn in, I told the court

I had contacted the man and brought him an application. He failed to fill it out and wait for his permit. The work was all done. I explained where the fill came from, etc.

Then this man was called before the bench and asked if he wanted to plead guilty or not guilty. He told the judge he had hired an attorney from St. Paul. The attorney had a prior commitment on that day but he told him to plead not guilty and ask for a twelve-man jury trial. His lawyer said "The judge would set up a trial date and they would argue it out at that time."

The judge then, said, "You want to enter a plea of not guilty?" The poor fellow was obviously disturbed and he told the judge he really was guilty and everything occurred just as the game warden said but his attorney told him to plead not guilty. Then, the judge asked, "Are you pleading guilty or not guilty?" The fellow stood there a while then finally, he said, "I am guilty and I want to get this over."

So, the judge said, "I accept your plea of guilty and the fine is $300.00." I then whispered to the county attorney that he should have the man put everything back exactly the way it was. The county attorney stood up and made that suggestion to Judge Reed.

The judge said, "I was about to make that very issue as a part of the penalty and if it isn't done within thirty days, I will have the violator picked up and remanded to the county jail in Bemidji for ninety days."

The next day, this man came to my home in Waskish and asked "Does the judge mean every grain of dirt and sand be put back the way it was?" I told him "No, just return every yard of sand and gravel to about where it was." Then, I told him to make Ben Koisti do the work for no charge or I will put a complaint against him for doing all the work before a permit was posted on the work site. I also suggested he should sue Ben to return the money he was paid. I don't know if that was ever done.

Chapter 30/ IOWA FARMERS

One winter day, while stationed at Baudette and checking fishermen on Lake of the Woods, I noticed a winter fish house with smoke coming out of the chimney. There was no car or snowmobile anywhere around to have transferred any fishermen from the resort to the fish house.

So being a curious person, I stopped my snow sled and opened the door. There were two husky young men inside fishing. There were seven or eight nice sized walleyes lying in the snow by the house. I asked the men for their licenses and they just laughed and said, "We don't have any licenses."

I asked where they were from and they told me they were farmers from Iowa. So, I told them I would have to write a summons on each of them. They would have to post $50.00 cash each for bail or I would take them to Baudette and put them in jail until the county judge came over. That was no problem and they dug in their pocket books and came up with one hundred dollars. Then, I told them I was going to seize their winter fishing gear and I would give them a receipt for the fishing gear and another county receipt for the hundred dollars. Then, I asked, "Are those fish outside the house yours?"

They both smiled and said, "Yep, we caught them." I told them I would not write a complaint on the fish but I was going to seize them and I would give them a seizure receipt for the fish.

The smile came off their faces and they said, "We caught those fish and they are ours."

I told them, "Boys, those fish belong to the State of Minnesota. If you want to make an issue out of it I'll write a summons for taking fish illegally, then, I will finish this seizure receipt for the fish and I will put you two in jail until the county judge comes to Baudette next Wednesday."

I guess the thought of having to sit in jail a few days didn't appeal to them so they denied ownership of the fish.

I did spend a few minutes telling them their options on how to do things legally in Minnesota. They even thanked me. I told them I would tell the operator of the Cyrus Resort to go out with his Bombardier and bring these men back to camp.

Chapter 31/ COMPLAINTS FROM SOUTH OF SAUM

It was one day during the deer season, Jerry Liemandt, the head of the state firearm training system, stopped at the state house at Waskish, Minnesota that I rented from the state. Also, Jerry was my brother-in-law—we married sisters.

We knew he hoped to put his feet under our table and have a bed for the night. He was always welcome. Jerry was on his way back to St. Paul.

Late that afternoon, Leo Manthei called and said he had a complaint from some farmer south of Saum that there had been shining and shooting down near his farm the night before. Leo wanted to know if I would come down that evening and work with him. I told him I would be there; I asked him where we should meet and what time. He gave me the name of the farmer and suggested we meet there around 8:00 p.m.

I told him that was O.K. Also, I told him Jerry Liemandt had stopped in and I would bring him along.

After dinner that evening, Patricia packed a big lunch for later on and filled two-quart thermos with coffee. About 7:00 p.m., we started out as we had roughly thirty-five minutes to go. We went down through Shotley and for most of the way we drove without lights. We never saw another car after we left

Highway 72. We slipped quietly through Saum. Slim Wolden's store was closed and locked up for the night.

A few miles south of Saum we turned into this farmer's yard. Leo wasn't there yet. However, it was only about 7:45 p.m.

Just before 8:00 p.m. a car came from the west on the Joe Jerome Road, then turned north pass us headed for Saum. It looked like a car full of Indians and they weren't driving too slowly or shining a spotlight. Right after they passed us, Leo showed up from the south.

Leo pulled into this farmer's yard where Jerry and I were. We all got out of the car. So, Leo got a chance to talk to Jerry and shake hands. Then Leo said, "As long as Jerry is here why don't you two go on south where you can watch down the Joe Jerome Road." He went on to say, "I am going to talk to the farmer who called me."

With that Jerry and I drove south to where we could watch down the Joe Jerome Road. There was an old approach where we could pull off and yet we could see if we had any activity.

Jerry inquired as to where that Indian car could have gone. I told him he might have stopped at the Saum Store. Slim Wolden would open up if he knew the customer and it was a substantial cash deal like maybe a case of beer or a carton of cigarettes. Or, the car may have gone into Kelliher via the Battle River Road.

Anyway we sat there for ten or fifteen minutes. Then Jerry said, "I wonder why we haven't heard from Leo?"

I said, "Leo is probably doing his P.R. work telling the farmer about the long hours he puts in that he doesn't get paid for it. Also, he probably is telling the farmer he has two of his men staked out to watch for any illegal activity."

I remember Jerry chuckling and saying, "He probably hasn't changed from the days when I was stationed at Thief River and worked with him."

Sometime shortly after we noticed a pair of headlights coming from the north. Jerry commented, "Here comes Leo now."

I told Jerry, "That's not Leo. That car is north of the farmer's place. Leo would come with his lights off and he would call us on the radio before he pulled out of the farmer's yard. That may be that car full of Indians or some other car."

This car, when it passed us, turned west on the Joe Jerome Road. I said to Jerry, "That looks like the car that passed us earlier before Leo arrived."

The car no more than made the corner, when the brake lights came on. I can't say for sure if it came to a dead stop but it proceeded west at a very slow speed. Also, two spotlights came out, one on either side of the vehicle. They were hand-held lights but very bright so they must have been hooked up to the car's electrical system.

I started up our car immediately and took after this car without lights. We got to about a hundred feet of this car and it was comfortable to drive by their lights. Both spotlights were really searching carefully on both sides of the road.

About two miles down the road, the brake lights came on. I brought our car to a stop. Then we could see the driver of the car held his light over the top of the car shining to the north, the same as the passenger's spotlight. Then we could see what looked like the barrel of a rifle come poking out the window on the right side of the car. It held there for about ten seconds then "Pow!" the gun went off with a big flash of fire from the barrel.

I quickly pulled up to within twenty feet of the car. We each bailed out. I jerked the door of the driver's side open, grabbed the keys, shut off the motor, and ordered him out of the car while I reached in the window of the back seat. A man in the middle had retracted the firearm and the barrel was pointed up to the roof. I grabbed the barrel just above the forearm and jerked the gun out of his hands. The man hollered, "Watch out, the gun is loaded!" The gun turned out to be a Remington, semi-automatic, 30/06 rifle.

We ordered all the people out of the car and demanded identification from each one—preferably driver's licenses. At this point, we noted both spotlights had wires from the lights directly to the battery under the hood—a crude but effective hook-up.

We were all standing out on this gravel road in front of the Indians' car headlights. There were Jerry and I with three Indian men and two Indian women.

Either Jerry or I got on he radio and called Leo to come down where we were. I told him over the radio we had an airtight case of spotlighting. It was his district so he should get on down here, now!

A few minutes later, Leo showed up. We turned over the gun, shells, drivers' licenses, and car keys to Leo. We told him what happened and that he should write them up and we would help him transport them to jail in Bemidji.

I told Jerry and Leo I would go back in the brush to find the deer. The shooter had told us he was not sure if he hit the deer.

I got back in the brush with a five-cell flashlight. I searched everywhere but could not find the deer or any blood. I could smell the scent of the deer odor that they give off when thoroughly scared. I began to assume the deer might be gut shot and he could run a long way before going down. After fifteen or twenty minutes of searching, I gave up and came out to the road.

The Indians were in their car and headed back to the Reservation. I asked, "What is going on?"

Leo said, "I know who they all are and they will come into court voluntarily the next day."

Leo said, "No use hanging around here anymore. When that car full of Indians get back on the Reservation, they will warn everyone on the Reservation where we were working." This was Leo's district, so Jerry and I headed back to Waskish.

On the way, Jerry told me he thought Leo made a deal with the violators while I was looking for the deer. He said he wasn't sure but he thought that Leo was going to charge the driver with transporting a loaded, uncased gun. I never did find out.

Chapter 32/ CARRIGANS

One night during the firearms deer season, I was staked out near Tom McCarthy's farm, which is about eight miles north west of Kelliher, Minnesota. It was around ten o'clock when I heard Lonnie Shiefert, the warden from Northome, call on his radio for assistance. He gave his location as being a couple of miles north east of Funkley on Highway 71.

He had just witnessed a car shine a light on a field and he heard a shot from a firearm. Then the car took off towards Funkley on Highway 71. I think he had hopes Leo Manthei was working because he was not too far from Blackduck. He called several times and got no response. So I called Lonnie and told him I was over thirty miles away but I was on my way.

Lonnie answered and said he had the car stopped. There were four men in the car and he would try to hold the vehicle until I got there. He said he didn't know if they got a deer or not. He figured they might have missed. I came back with, "If you've got Emmet Carrigan in the car and you know which field he shot on, when we go back there, we will find a dead deer. That's the way the Carrigan's operate." They never pick the deer up until some time later in the night when they are reasonably sure there is no law enforcement around.

Just before I got to where the two cars were on 71, about three quarters of a mile northeast of Funkley, the occupants started to get a little ugly about being detained. I pulled up behind their car and got out and had Lonnie tell me again what transpired. I then walked over to the car, opened the back door, and there was Emmet Carrigan. He had a small caliber rifle on the floor. He usually used a 22 Magnum, a 25-20 or a 32-20. I don't remember the caliber as it was Lonnie's pinch and he made out the paper work.

Emmet started claiming that Lonnie didn't see them shoot any deer and this was a poor arrest on our part. I mentioned another time he was caught cold and he acknowledged that. Then I told him, "Lonnie has you better than that this time."

Leo showed up about this time and two of us took the four men to Bemidji and locked them up in the county jail. Then the three of us went back to the field and we found the deer just about where Lonnie thought the shot came from. We noted the time of the shooting, the time we found the deer, the outside temperature, and the approximate weight of the deer. We made a slice into one of the hindquarters, inserted a thermometer, and noted the temperature of the carcass.

The federal fish and wildlife have run studies on the time versus temperature on various sized carcasses and one can assess the length of time elapsed from the instant of death to the time of contact. This was noted in the event of a not guilty plea and we would have to prove to a judge or jury that we had what we said we had.

Another freak thing was the deer was killed in Itasca County. The car was stopped in Beltrami County. If the violation occurs within a hundred yards of a county line, you can take the violators to either county. However, the county attorney of Beltrami County said don't take any chances with Emmet or anyone with him. So someone transported them to Grand Rapids where the men were brought up before a municipal judge and bound over to a gross misdemeanor. The trial would come up the following spring in the Grand Rapids courthouse.

I was called to testify at the trial along with Lonnie Shiefert. The district judge was Judge Spellacy and there was a twelve-person jury. The testimony was all in and it went to the jury about 4:30 p.m. It seemed to me the jury went to dinner, came back to the courthouse, and retired to the jury room. About an hour later, the jury came out and the verdict was guilty for all four men. It turned out that two of the men had agreed to pay Emmet Carrigan and Emmet's girl friend's brother money to kill some deer for them. They all met at the bar in Funkley.

The judge decided to hand down sentencing that evening. He called Emmet up first, and he told him the maximum he could penalize him was one thousand dollars and one year in the county jail and said, "That, Mr. Emmet Carrigan, is your fine. I'm sorry I can't give you more".

Then the judge turned to me and he instructed me to take Mr. Carrigan down to the sheriff's office on the next floor and put him in jail.

Emmet Carrigan's girl friend, who by the way was younger than any of Emmet's children, tagged along as we walked down this long empty hallway. Emmet pulled out his billfold and gave her two dollars. She was walking along bawling all the way with tears running down her face. Then she looked up at me and she said, "You big shit ass!"

from the MINNESOTA DEPARTMENT 2820
of NATURAL RESOURCES

BUREAU OF INFORMATION and EDUCATION   Room 350 Centennial Office Building   ST. PAUL, 55

No. 11   Clarke Anderson, News Editor   March 19, 1975
Contents:

FOUR DEER SHINERS RECEIVE FINES,   HEAVY RUN OFF SEEN AS SAFETY
JAIL SENTENCES   PROBLEM

HERBST TO SPEAK AT ENDANGERED   DNR ISSUES BOAT LICENSE
SPECIES MEET   REMINDER

DEEP SNOW, "CRUSTING" CAUSING
DEER-DOG PROBLEMS

IMMEDIATE RELEASE   Four Deer Shiners Receive Fines,
                                     Jail Sentences

    Four deer shiners arrested by state conservation officers in Itasca county last fall received stiff fines and jail sentences when their cases came up for trial in Grand Rapids last month.

    Emmett Carrigan, 46, of Blackduck was fined $1,000 and sentenced to one year in jail. John W. Week, 19, also of Blackduck was fined $500 and given 90 days.

    Their two companions, Joseph T. Newman, 44, Minneapolis and Donnie G. Young, 34, of Spring Lake Park, were fined $500 and given suspended sentences of 30 days each.

    In addition to the fines and jail sentences, Magistrate John Spillacy canceled all of Carrigan's hunting priveleges through 1976, noting that the defendent had a record of repeated game violations.

    The suspension of Young's jail sentence was conditioned upon his payment of the fine within 30 days.

    Conservation officers also confiscated a deer and a rifle and spotlight used by the men.   /   /   /

DNR communication about the Carrigans

Chapter 33/ FRENZELS

It was Saturday, November 11, 1963. My son, Frederic, who was a student in the Kelliher High School, and his friend Ron Waldo asked if they could ride along with me in the state vehicle when I went out to work at night. They both wanted to know what a Game Warden did all night.

I told them basically it was a monotonous job. I would go out some place where I knew deer were coming out to graze and that some opportunist might come along and try to shoot them. I told them sometime I would sit out at night for two or three weeks straight and never see a violation. But, I had the satisfaction of knowing no one killed a deer where I was sitting.

You don't catch deer shiners in the coffee shop or at home in bed.

Also, I was very emphatic that they both ride in the back seat and that under no circumstances were they to get involved if I got on the trail of a night hunter. Just sit in the back seat and observe.

We all had our lunches and we started out from our home and office in Waskish, Minnesota, at about 6:00 p.m. We drove south on Highway 72 past Eland Island. There was a doe and two fawns grazing out in a small opening on the west side of Highway 72. There were no real good places to hide a car on Eland Island. There was a small-time farmer and logger with his family that lived in a little shack on the east side of Highway 72 on Eland Island. At that time I was not really sure of this party, Bill Lindquist, if he would kill a deer out of season or not. As I got to know him later on, I felt sure he wouldn't pull a stunt like that. They were poor, hard working, high caliber people.

I continued on south a short piece to a ditch grade that crossed through a big culvert under Highway 72. I checked out the grade on either side and decided the west side of Highway 72 was the safest to back down on to. I backed off the highway about one hundred feet. It wasn't too cold so I left my window open so I could hear.

Several cars went by. No one was driving slowly nor was anyone running a spotlight. Around 9:00 p.m. a car came from the north turned east onto the same ditch grade we were on, then backed up and turned back to the north.

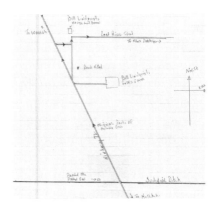

Map drawn by Bill Callies

I told the boys something is up. I quickly started the motor and pulled onto the blacktop without lights and started after this vehicle. We caught up within a hundred yards of this car when it turned right, or to the east. It came to a T, at which point it jogged north for about fifty yards, then east again.

When we got to the T, I saw a car to our right, apparently stopped. It was facing the other way. There was a small hole in the brush to our right. I drove our car into that, out of sight of the road.

I told the boys, "I'm going to see what is going on down there." I was running down this road when I realized this car was backing up. When I got to the car, I opened up the door on the passenger side and jumped in. There was a man with a small flashlight in the brush about ten feet dragging something parallel to the road.

I said to the driver who was looking to the back, out his left side, as he was backing up. "What the hell's going on here?"

The driver just said, "Oh, where did you come from?"

I recognized him as Hans Dahlberg, an old Scandinavian that lived about four miles east of there. I then asked who is that out in the bush and what is he dragging. He said that is Bill Lindquist and he is dragging that deer so those night hunters can't get it.

Then he went on to say he and his Mrs. came down to play cards with Bill Lindquist and his Mrs. when they heard this shot south of the house. He and Bill ran out of the house and could see the taillights of a car stopped about four hundred yards down this dirt road.

They jumped in Hans' car and drove down there and when they got almost to this car it took off fast. Then they could see two fellows out in the brush on the east side of the road. They had a small flashlight. Then the light went out and Bill jumped out of the car with his two cell flashlights and ran into the woods and there he came across this little dead fawn deer.

Hans went on to say he didn't know who they were but they decided they wouldn't let those guys get that deer. Bill had said, "I'll just drag the deer back to the house to dress it out. I didn't want to put it in my car and get blood all over the car."

At that I told Hans, "Just stop right here."

I got out of Hans' car and ran down the road a ways, then into the bush to intercept Bill Lindquist dragging the deer. I stopped Bill. He recognized me. I asked him what his story was.

He too said that he and his Mrs. were playing cards with the Dahlbergs when they heard this shot south of the place. He and Hans came out of the house and saw the taillights of this car stopped. So he and Hans got in Hans' car and drove down to this parked car but before they got close enough to see whom it was or get the license number the car took off. Also, he told me he was almost positive there were two guys that ran east into the woods.

They were out by the deer to either drag it back to the car or dress it out and when he and Hans drove down there the hunters got scared and took off on foot.

Bill went on to say that he and Hans decided to take the deer back to his place so those night hunters couldn't come back and pick up the deer. Bill went on to say they intended to contact me in the morning so I could come and pick the deer up.

I told Bill, "I accept your story for the time being, however, let's take the deer back where it was and I'll sit in the brush and wait. These guys might be dumb enough to come back."

Bill and I dragged the deer back to where he had found it and then Bill and Hans got out of there. I crawled into a little thicket of spruce and sat down to wait.

About fifteen minutes later this car that we originally followed, came back driving real slow. It didn't stop but continued on south to the blacktop and disappeared. About ten minutes later the car came back from the south past the site where the deer was. It drove slow but never stopped, then turned east on the Lost River Truck Trail.

I decided to pull the deer just to the edge of the road and see if the car came back. They might stop and pick it up. I did that, got myself hid across the road. About twenty minutes later the car did come from the east then turned south toward me. I can't say for sure if the car stopped or was moving so slow, I opened the passenger side door, crossed over the passenger turned off the motor and pulled out the keys.

The driver was Melvin Frenzel and his younger brother, a juvenile. I had had the young fellow in a firearm safety class in Kelliher when he was in sixth grade.

I told these two Frenzels I was sure they were a part of the crew that killed that deer and I wanted to know who was out in the bush. I separated the two. I had one inside the car with me and took down a statement had it signed and gave the party a copy. Then I took the other one in the car while the first brother was outside and took a statement.

The statements were so far apart but I kept working on interrogating them and it finally, reluctantly came out, Wesley Frenzel was the one that shot the deer and he and their cousin from Alaska were out in the bush. I was sure I had the people who killed that deer, however, if they hired some high-powered attorney, on a not guilty plea, I might have a problem to convince a judge or a jury that I had the right people.

So, I had them follow me to my home and office in Waskish where I made a call to my area supervisor for a little advice. This was around 1:30 a.m. He told me to seize their car and hold it at Waskish with the gun in the trunk that was used to kill the deer. Make out a summons against Wesley and Melvin of "Take one deer in closed hours" and tell the two Frenzels to walk home and that I would sort this all out in the morning.

I made out the summons; however, I took Melvin and his younger brother home in the patrol car because they lived almost twenty-five miles from Waskish.

When we got by Wesley's house near Shooks, I told Melvin to take the summons into Wesley's house and leave it on the kitchen table. I was reasonably sure Wesley and his cousin were walking home through the woods.

Then I took Melvin and his younger brother to their folks' home and I went back to Waskish and called it a night.

I don't remember if Ron Waldo had a way to get home or if he stayed over with Fred.

The next morning, Sunday, I went back to the place the deer was killed and I could see the trail in the high grass where the two violators ran. This area was part of an old abandoned farm and there were old wire fences in the high grass. One of the deer poachers had hit one of those wires; obviously, at full speed the way the wire was pulled up and bent. Then, about ten feet beyond you could see where a body had piled up in the brush and grass. Whoever it was had to be hurting. I followed their trail for a little way. Then I returned to my patrol car and drove to Lindquist's house to let them know that it was a couple of Roy Frenzels' boys. I thanked Bill Lindquist and asked him to convey my thanks to Hans Dahlberg.

Bill Callies (right) working for DNR meeting with his son, Fred Callies, working for the Minnesota Highway Patrol

I went back to my home about 11:30 a.m., I got a telephone call from Melvin Frenzel that Wesley and his cousin hadn't gotten home yet. I told Melvin to give them a little more time. I knew Wesley was at home in the woods and he would show up eventually. He had to travel about fifteen miles through the woods and his cousin might not be too good a woods traveler. They did show up shortly after the call was made.

The decision was made to charge them with a misdemeanor, which is what I had done on the original summons, "Take one deer in closed hours."

The trial could be heard before the local justice of the peace and the maximum penalty could only be $100.00 and/or ninety days in jail. Melvin would get his car back. Their three or four guns were in gun cases in the trunk and the only way I knew which gun was used was that the juvenile pointed it out.

I never did find out the name of the cousin or get him into court. He beat it back to Alaska.

Later on my son, Fred, came to me and said, "Dad, I don't ever want to be a Game Warden." Now, thirty years later, he is flying for the Minnesota State Patrol.

Chapter 34/ BEAR

One evening I was driving in an area known as Sunny Beach. It is an area on the southeast end of Upper Red Lake. The original owner had subdivided the lakeshore property into seventy-five foot lots and the owners had either built cabins or brought in mobile homes.

This was Saturday evening of a long Memorial Day weekend and all of the cabins seemed to be occupied. I was just on patrol, nothing special. About halfway past the row of cabins, a man ran out from in back of one of the cabins and motioned for me to stop. He came around to my side of the patrol car and asked if I was the game warden. I told him I was. He said, "Good. I was hoping you would show up."

"Why?" I asked.

"Well," he said, "there is a big mother bear with two cubs around here and I want you to kill them."

Bear photo taken by Bill Callies

I said, "Why? Are they doing damage around here?"

He said, "No, not yet." He admitted he hadn't seen them but a neighbor had and he had two little children. He wanted those bears killed. I asked him if that cabin was his. He said no, that the owner had to work that weekend and told them to go up to his cabin and enjoy themselves but there was no way they could enjoy themselves with those bear around.

By this time I was getting a bit disturbed so I asked this individual where he was from. "St. Paul," he responded.

So I said, "This is the bears' home. You pack up your gear and go back to your home in St. Paul and everyone will be happy."

His last remark was, "I will report you to your superiors."

Chapter 35/ PAUL JANSEN

Paul Jansen of Kelliher, and formally from Iowa, was one of the most active fisherman on Upper Red Lake during the time I was stationed there. I know he despised Game Wardens or maybe I was the only one he hated. I checked him every year for his angling license and he always had one. I never knew him to have over his limit. I've known him to catch his limit of walleyes every day for a week or ten days straight. I couldn't believe he and his wife could eat that many fish and I never heard of him giving any fish to anyone.

He was born and raised in Iowa and so was I, and every Iowa fisherman I ever knew was a fish hog.

Paul did have one little stunt he would get great satisfaction doing and he caught me up on it three times and nothing could please him more.

In those days of early sixties, a fisherman could only angle with one line with one hook attached to the end of the line except when false bait is used.

The first time he got me in his web was when he became aware I had acquired a spotting scope. I picked up many fishermen angling with more than one line. The most lines I ever caught someone with were seven being used by a man from Minneapolis.

This particular day, I found Paul sitting in his boat and he had four poles sticking out of his boat and each line had a bobber attached to it. I watched him and he did pull in a couple of walleyes on one line so I thought I had him for angling with more than one line. I went and got my boat and came out to see what Mr. Jansen had to say. When I pulled up to his boat he didn't make a move to pull the extra lines out. I had a feeling I had been had. I lifted the poles up. Three of them had only a sinker and a bobber on. Only one pole had a hook on the end. I didn't say anything nor did Paul, but I'm sure he was pleased with himself.

That following winter, I watched him fish with fishing sticks in three different holes. The holes were within ten or twelve-feet of one another. Two of the sticks were lying on the ice. One was stuck straight up on the ice. It was cold that day,

15 to 20 degrees below zero, so he was busy scooping the ice out of all three holes so the bobbers wouldn't freeze in. He was a good quarter-of-a-mile out on the lake with his back to the wind and me. I started walking when I got within a hundred yards. He heard me and he started to grab for his sticks. I was running and I hollered, "Just leave them be." So he dropped the stick. Well wouldn't you know he did it to me again? Two of the lines did not have any hooks on them.

The following summer on July 12, 1964, the worm started to turn. I was out on the lake and I saw a boat ahead of me trolling. There were two men, a woman, and a small girl in the boat. Only the two men had poles in their hands and they were trolling with a small motor. All of a sudden I realized it was Paul running the motor. He had his back to me. He turned and saw me pulling up to them. He turned to the other man and apparently told him to reel in his line fast because he was doing that. Paul wouldn't stop his boat until this other man had reeled in his line and laid the pole down in the bottom of the boat.

I asked to see Paul's license and he dug it out and showed it to me. Then I asked the other man for his license and both men said, "He wasn't fishing."

I told him, "You were. Give me some identification."

Paul spoke up and said, "He is my son-in-law and this is my daughter and granddaughter. They just wanted to go out fishing for just a little while and he won't pick up the pole again."

Again, I asked for identification. Then Paul started to beg and plead. I told Paul, "Either I get some identification or I'll take and put him in jail." They finally told me his name was Michael Collesides from Athens, New York. He was a non-resident on top of it all. I told him he would have to post $30.00 bail and that his court date was the following day before the Justice of the Peace in Kelliher.

Both of the men said they had no money. I told Michael I would have to put him in jail because he was a non-resident. His wife and daughter started to bawl. I told Paul Jansen if he would be responsible and see to it Michael appeared in court, I would release Michael to him. Paul assured me he would have him in the Justice of the Peace Court the next day. I told Paul if he wasn't there, I would take Paul to Bemidji and sign a complaint against him.

The next day Michael and Paul appeared before the Justice of the Peace Clara Quale. She read the complaint and he plead guilty. She told him the fine was $30.00 or fifteen days. Michael said he didn't have the money. She said, "If you can't pay, you go to jail in Bemidji."

About then Paul's daughter came in and begged her dad to pay the fine. He just said, "No way" and walked out. The woman started to bawl while the Justice of the Peace made out the commitment papers. I hauled Michael down to Bemidji and they locked him up.

I returned to my station in Waskish. Paul Jansen called me on the average of three times a day for the next week. From what I could gather, he was living a life of hell at home. His wife, daughter, and granddaughter were on his back 24 hours a day. Paul had plenty of money but he was as tight as the bark on a tree. Almost every time he called me he would start in with "I hope you're satisfied," then he would moan and groan about not being fed at home and his wife wouldn't let him sleep in the bed nor would they wash his clothes.

Finally, he could take it no longer and he went to Mrs. Quale. At first she told him she still wanted the whole $30.00. Paul countered with he should get something for time served. Mrs. Quale relented and said she would reduce the fine to $10.00 and $5.00 costs providing he pay the $15.00 right now or the deal was off and Paul's son-in-law would have to complete his jail time.

Paul obviously had his back against the wall because that was the end of the bargaining. He came up with the $15.00, right now.

Things remained pretty quiet for the balance of that year. That winter, I had been sent a new trainee so I was obligated for ten days to try to show him how to conduct himself, and teach him what the job position expected of him.

As I remember, it was the last part of January. There was very little snow on the ice so the fishermen could drive almost anywhere they chose. Occasionally, there would be cracks that would open up in the ice, and they sometimes would be a foot wide and three or four hundred feet long. Often when this type of condition would exist, the fisherman would take advantage of it if the crack were out where the water was six or more feet deep.

I had this trainee in the patrol car with me. I had maneuvered the patrol car to a point where the brush pretty well covered our car. I then hooked up my spotting scope and started checking fishermen. It was this day I came across Paul Jansen again sitting on a stool close to his car. He was fishing in one of these open fissures in the ice. He was up to his old tricks again. He had four fishing sticks that I could see and they all had bobbers on the lines. He would go from stick to stick, pick it up, and jiggle it a little then go to the next stick and repeat this performance.

I unhooked the spotting scope from the window mount started the motor of the car, and backed up to a place I could turn around. Then I backed up so my trainee could look out his window and check fishermen with my spotting scope in the same place I had been looking. I did not tell him anything about what I had seen or Paul Jansen's idea of fun.

I handed the trainee the spotting scope, told him to hook it up on his door window and start checking the fishermen.

He was quite eager to check this piece of equipment out. He asked a couple of questions about clearing up the picture when he increased or decreased the power. Finally he seemed to settle down and move the glass from one fisherman to the next. Then I noticed some tenseness at the same time the scope was pointed toward Jansen. He concentrated on him for a good five minutes then he got pretty excited. He announced he was sure he had one guy fishing with three poles and maybe four. He pointed him out but all you could see with the naked eye was one man sitting by a vehicle.

So I asked this young trainee how he thought he would handle the situation. He responded with, "Just get this car out there. I've got that man handling three of those lines. There is a fourth line there that I think is his but I've got him dead to right on three lines and I know which ones they are. Go fast before he pulls those extra lines."

I had to go up to Hudecs to get on the ice and be on the other side of that crack. That young fellow had the enthusiasm of a young dog chasing a jackrabbit.

I came in on Paul fast. I think I slid the last hundred-feet when I hit the brakes. The trainee bailed out of the car and ran to Paul to tell him he could not angle for fish with more than one line. He got Paul's license, stuck it in his pocket and started in winding up the lines. It was then he became aware only one line had a hook on it. He was quite upset; he did check how many fish he had before he returned the fishing license. Paul did absolutely nothing. The young man came back to the car a little bit ugly. He said, "You set me up with that guy."

I told him, "In a way I did, but don't feel bad. Paul got me twice on that a few years ago. I just thought when I saw Paul out there that this might be that one chance in a million to make you realize you have to be more patient." I told the young man I did get Paul in a backhand sort of way.

The following year Paul bought some raffle tickets in Northome and won the prize of a twelve-foot aluminum boat, a trailer, and a five-horse outboard motor. I was checking him that following summer and when I came up to his boat I realized how close water was to coming over the transom. Paul was a heavy person and that coupled with an outboard motor and a narrow transom was a disaster in the making. When I checked his license, I told Paul of my concern and I suggested he get a life jacket and wear it when he was in that boat.

He laughed at me and said, "I've got a boat cushion for flotation and that's all the law requires. You're just jealous because I won this outfit. Anyway, I was always a good swimmer."

A period of time went by. I believe it was late on into the summer. I got a telephone call from the Sunset Resort that they could hear someone out in the mouth of the Tamarac River hollering for help.

I ran out in back of our house onto the dock where I had my state boat on the Tamarac River. I went out to the area that the caller said the pleas for help were coming from. When I arrived, I found two or three other boats with fishermen. They were near a boat that only had about two feet of its bow sticking above the water. There was an anchor rope tied to the bow but the anchor was gone, apparently, on the bottom. On close examination of that part of the boat, I realized it was Paul Jansen's boat or one like it.

One of the boatloads of fishermen said they witnessed this boat and it seemed to sink by the transom. All of these men could see this person thrashing in the water. They couldn't hear anything because they had their motors running, and by the time they wound up their lines, and their fish stringer and started to go to see if they could help this fellow, he just disappeared and they weren't too sure just where he was in relation to the bow of this boat sticking up.

There was just nothing to do but go get my drag hooks. I talked Pete Olson into coming to either drive the boat or hold the dragline.

As word got out, many other local people came out to drag with anything they could come up with that might hook the party that was in that boat. Pete and I worked the water between the boat bow and shore and we were the ones that hooked him. It was Paul Jansen on his final day of fishing on Red Lake. We noted when he came up on our hooks his glasses were still on. Paul was so big and heavy we couldn't get him into our boat alone.

Other boaters gave us a hand to get Paul into the state boat. We then ran the boat into the state boathouse next to the fish hatchery until the coroner came.

Chapter 36/ BAPTIST PREACHER

One morning, I was mowing the grass at the Waskish station. The residence and office are located on the Tamarac River, which in turn, drains into Upper Red Lake. From my headquarters, I could observe 80% of the fishermen going to and from Red Lake to their cabins or their resorts. The walleyes were biting real good and even a poor fishermen could catch his legal limit in a half hour.

As I progressed around the yard following that cursed lawnmower, I noted various boats going out to the lake and eventually, I would observe those boats returning to their base.

One of the boats that went out had two men wearing bib overalls and several cane poles protruding from the bow of the boat. About a half hour later, I noticed these two men returning upstream. About another half hour went by and I noted these same two men going back out to the lake. Curiosity, getting the better of me, I shut off the mower, got in the patrol car, and drove to a location where I might observe these fishermen. Using my spotting scope, I finally located these two men. Of all things, they were fishing with too many lines. However, the fish were biting so fast they were unable to land any fish. They finally settled down to using one pole each and I counted as they boated their fish. Within fifteen minutes, they had landed and put on a stringer their limit of walleyes, a couple of northern, and three perch. Then they pulled up the anchor, started their motor, and headed for the Tamarac River.

By driving down the back road, which parallels the river, I was finally able to observe that they were renting a cabin from the Waskish Grocery Store. I left the patrol car and slipped up behind a small building where I observed these two men tie their boat up to a dock, pick up their stringer of fish, and come up to a cabin. They pulled a large cooler out from under this cabin, took the fish off the stringer, and put them in the cooler. Then they sat down and drank what looked like a bottle of pop. After that, they went back down to their boat and took off downstream towards the lake.

I came out of my little hiding place, went to the cabin, and pulled the cooler out. There were twenty-four walleyes, five northern, and several perch. It would appear they had twice as many walleyes in their possession than the allowable limit.

I went back to my station and started mowing grass again. Eventually, I noted these two men heading back to their cabin, so I drove the patrol car back to their resort. I watched these men tie up their boat and bring another stringer full of walleyes up to the cooler. When they put them in the cooler, I stepped out, advised these men who I was, and asked to see their licenses. Their licenses had been issued on that date. Both men were from Sioux City, Iowa. I counted their fish. Now they had thirty-six walleyes, three times their allowable possession limit, so I advised them I was going to make out summons charging each of them with twelve walleye pike over their legal possession limit. Next, I made out seizure tickets for the fish. I instructed the men to get in the patrol car as I was going to take them to the justice of the peace in Kelliher. The smaller man started to give me some static, however, we all ended up in the car and made the trip to Kelliher. The justice of the peace is a woman, Mrs. Clara Quale. She owns and operates the Kelliher Independent newspaper. On this day, she and her assistant were in the process of getting out the weekly newspaper and both of them had ink on their hands and arms up to their elbows.

When Mrs. Quale saw me enter the office with my customers, she shut down the press and came up to her desk to see what I wanted. I gave her the judge's copy of the summons and the seizure slips. She commented on how good the fish must be biting. I then introduced her to the two men I had with me. At this point, the smaller man said, "Mrs. Justice of the Peace, will you tell this would-be game warden he cannot arrest me?"

"What makes you say that?" asked the judge.

"Because I am a minister in the Baptist church and my partner here is the church deacon," he said.

"Not a good enough excuse," she said, and with that, she sat down to her old typewriter and filled in the blank places on the complaint form. After I had sworn to the facts and signed the complaint, the judge proceeded to read the complaint to the minister. When the judge asked for a plea, the man pled not guilty. Then the judge asked if the man had $35.00 he could post for bail until the trial would be held. She also asked him if he wanted a trial by judge or if he wanted a jury trial. He said he had no money for the likes of her and he started for the door. The judge told me to stop that man which I did. Then she sat down to her old typewriter and started filling in the blank places on a much larger form.

Finally, the man asked, "What are you doing now?"

"I am making out commitment papers. You are going to jail down in Bemidji until court, which will be at 9 a.m. on this coming Friday."

The man thought that over for a minute then he asked, "How much will it cost if I plead guilty now?" The judge then inquired if he was sure he wanted to change his plea. He responded with, "I am guilty. How much does it cost?" She told him $35.00 and he paid the judge.

The other man spoke up and said, "I'm guilty, also, but I want to throw myself on the mercy of the court. My money comes hard."

"All our money comes hard," responded the judge, "but the fine is still $35.00."

While transporting the two men back to Waskish, the small man announced, "I'm getting out of here and I'm never coming back."

Ten days later, I was looking over the fishermen and out on the lake and in one of the boats was the Baptist minister hauling in some fish. A check later on him confirmed that he now knows when to quit.

Chapter 37/ CUB BEAR

Late one summer day, I got a telephone call from Ole Roe, a local beef farmer and a man that trapped predators for bounty. He said he was calling from Ingvar Renemo's house. He said he would like to meet at the gravel pit on Eland Island. He said he had a serious problem. Eland Island is a higher piece of land about halfway between Kelliher and Waskish and the gravel pit area is on the west side of Highway 72.

When I arrived, I found Bill Lindquist and Ole Roe standing near their trucks about halfway into the gravel pit. I asked Ole Roe, "What is the problem here?" Ole took me over to a place where some animal had made lots of tracks in the sand and they looked like large and small bear tracks. Then Ole started to explain he had made a trap-set here for a timber wolf, however, a cub bear got in the trap. The trap was not staked down because he had a drag on the trap. Ole said he could hear the cub whimpering back in the brush about a couple hundred yards. Now the brush north of the gravel pit is so thick you have a hard time pushing your way through. At no place can you see more than ten feet. Then, to top it off, that old mother bear had to be somewhere around.

Neither Bill Lindquist nor Ole Roe had any stomach for

going in there to try to get that trap off the cub. Bill Lindquist lived near there so he offered to go home and get his 30/30 Winchester, which he did. I knew I couldn't handle the rifle and get that trap off the cub, so I got on the radio and called for my neighboring warden, Leo Manthei. Leo answered, so I told him I had a little problem and I needed help. Also, I gave him my location, but I didn't go into any detail about the problem.

Eventually, Leo showed up and I explained the situation to him. Leo said, "I had a hunch I shouldn't answer you when you called. We could both get mauled if that old she-bear decides we are hurting her cub." I knew Leo was a good, fast shot with any kind of a gun, so I finally talked him into carrying the rifle and covering me while I tried to get that trap off the cub. Well, we started back through that brush and believe me, we were both on edge so bad if someone hollered, "boo", we would have been up the nearest tree right now.

We could hear scratching ahead and the trap chain rattling, and occasionally, a pathetic little whimper. Eventually, we came on the little cub. He must have weighed about 35 pounds. The old sow was not with the cub.

Leo hollered, "Get that trap off him quick!" I finally got my foot across his head so he couldn't bite me then I grabbed one spring of that double, spring trap in each hand and squeezed. That little cub's foot came out. I took my foot off his head and in a flash that little fellow was gone. I unhooked the drag and Leo and I got out of there as fast as we could.

When Leo and I got back with Ole Roe and Bill Lindquist, I was so drained I felt as though I had done a whole day at hard labor. I examined the trap before giving it back to Ole and I saw it was a number 14 double spring. I tried to squeeze those springs down but I couldn't do it. I even tried to do it over my knee the way I usually set double spring traps, but no way. It must have been Leo's screaming at me that gave me that extra strength.

Anyway, Ole was glad to get that trap back and we were sure that little bear was happy to be out of it.

Chapter 38/ BUM

That was the name we (our family) hung on a little brown and white Springer pup in 1959. This dog turned out to be one of the most intelligent dogs I ever had. I could write an entire book about this animal and even then I wouldn't get all of his qualities, abilities, and his accomplishments across to the reader. He did have one failing fault—female dogs at certain times of the year. Then he was almost impossible to control. However, I will give you one example of his involvement with my work as a game warden.

This incident occurred one night in October of 1964. I had been babysitting various bunches of deer on a route traveled by members of the Red Lake band. The Indians had been having poor luck trying to find a deer with the aid of a spotlight on the reservation because they had their deer herd pretty well killed off. These people would try to make a quick kill and get back to the reservation without getting caught. These people would never come off with their super equipment, which would be a platform on top of the car, an old mattress to sit on with a guardrail in front to hang onto, and usually with one super hi-powered spotlight. There were usually two men on the platform, one with the light, and the other with a high-powered rifle. Often, if it were a four-door sedan, there would be two men in the back seat, each armed with a rifle.

However, when they came off the reservation, they would try to conceal their intentions. They would usually have only one gun in the hands of one or two men in the back seat. Sometimes, the passenger in the front seat would have a hand-held spotlight. Occasionally, they would have women or children along to make it look like a family outing.

Their usual route was to come east off the reservation, on what we called "The Joe Jerome Road," about five miles then they would turn north on the range line road. They would go through Saum, which is only one store, two homes, and an abandoned schoolhouse. This north-south road is about twelve miles long with one jog in it due to a correction line. Eventually, you come to an east-west crossroad and, at this point, these people would turn west and in about five miles they would be back on the reservation.

On this entire roadway, there are six families living, mostly farmers, with fields along the road. Also, there are a number of abandoned farms with open areas. It is on these fields and open areas the deer like to come out on at night. Occasionally, I have caught white men spotlighting in this area, but usually it is residents from the reservation.

By the way, these people don't kill these deer to eat. It's mostly a sport for the young bucks. They sell the deer to the great white hunter.

I had been spending a lot of nights down here with my dog. Bum was satisfied to come along with me and he usually spent the whole night sleeping on the floor on the passenger side. Sometime, during the night, he would help me eat my lunch that my wife always packed. There were many nights we never saw a car and that brings us down to the big night that really brought me closer to this dog than any other.

I had parked in an abandoned borrow pit about a half mile north of a field where there were some deer. I pulled in here about a half hour after sunset (7 p.m.), moved the car behind some brush, went back to the approach road, and with the aid of a small branch, brushed out tracks into the abandoned pit so that any hunter would not be aware of my presence.

I was about three miles north of the Saum store. I had a little portable radio and I spent most of the night listening to WBBM out of Chicago or KOA out of Denver. These were talk shows.

About 1:30 that morning, I could see the glow of headlights to the south of us heading north. Just seeing a car moving in this country at that time of night could get the old adrenaline going. I have been known to get so excited I would start to shake.

The car drove past my approach at a very slow pace, maybe about ten miles per hour. I started up my patrol car and eased out onto the range line road. The car was about a quarter of a mile ahead by then. I was driving without lights and I had to be careful not to go in the ditch until I could get up close enough to them to drive by their lights. When I got up behind them, I could see there were four people. They did not use a hand held light. However, a lot of these hunters just drove slowly and with their headlights could see a deer along side of the road. They were driving so slow I began to believe they were hunting and my game plan was to stick with them and if they saw a deer, stopped their car and shot, then I had a customer.

The car continued on north to the crossroad then turned

west toward the reservation. There is only one farmer along here, Wistrom, and this car was not his, so it had to be some people from the reservation.

I have stopped cars and found deer in the trunk that I had not seen them shoot, and I let that work on my brain. Finally, curiosity got the upper hand. We were about a mile from the reservation and once they cross that line, I have no jurisdiction. I've got to act now or forget it, so I turned on my headlights and my red light, passed their vehicle, and turned my car so as to block their car. I bailed out of the patrol car leaving my engine running, lights on, door opened. Bum never moved. He was used to me doing things like this. I ran to the drivers side of the car, shined my light inside, and all I could see was four, stout Ponemah residents, all with an open bottle of beer in their hands. I made the query to the driver "No gun?"

The driver answered, "No guns." So I asked him to give me the keys so I could check the trunk. He told me, "You don't need a key. The trunk is unlocked." I went to the back of the car, lifted up the trunk lid and all there was in the trunk was two old dirty spare tires and one beat up five-gallon gas can.

About the time I started to lower the trunk lid, I looked up and saw all four doors of the car open up and all four men got out and started to move slowly toward me.

I started to back up down the road. I knew what these men had in mind. Game wardens are not their best friend and here these men had a golden opportunity to really beat the day lights out of one. I had witnessed the aftermath of such an encounter of an elderly white man on Highway 89. Three young buck Indians had worked him over so badly that he was bleeding from every opening in his body.

Also, I was aware this was the kind of odds and location to their liking. I had a revolver, but to pull it out and point it at an Indian doesn't scare them a bit. The only firearm they respect is a shotgun or a high power rifle.

As we were slowly moving back down the road I was busy trying to figure a way out of this mess. I knew I could turn and run or dive into the woods on either side, as I was sure they wouldn't follow. Looking past these four men, I could see our two vehicles in the road, lights on, motors running, doors open. I knew if I abandoned my patrol car they would drive it onto the reservation, play with the radio (two way), strip the car, and either smash it up or burn it up, and I would be making out reports on this incident for the next six months.

Then it hit me. The car door was open for Bum! Well, let me tell you, I yelled, "Bum!" I yelled loud enough to startle the whole Chippewa nation. Even these four men stopped for about a minute.

Then I saw my brown and white Springer pop out of the car and come on a dead run towards us. He passed in back of the two men on the south side of the road and I heard a low growl. He came around in back of me and leaned his left shoulder against the calf of my right leg. He pressed so hard that he almost tipped me over. He seemed to sense we had a problem.

One of the four men announced, "He's got a dog."
Another one asked, "Will he bite?"
I told them, "He will if I tell him to." Then I said, "You men turn around and walk back and stand in front of your car headlights." They did as they were told.

Bum and I walked slowly past them to the patrol car. Bum jumped in and lay down on the floor where he always rode. I put the car in gear and drove down to Wistrom's approach, turned in, waited 'til their car went by, backed out, and headed for home. I was still shaking a half hour later when we got home.

Chapter 39/ THE LAUSNICK BROTHERS

Two bachelors, the Lausnick brothers, lived southeast of Waskish back in the bush. The rumor was they were born in the Baltic Republic. They migrated to the United States. One of them supposedly worked for the Ford Motor Company. The other one worked for some glass manufacturer. They apparently heard of the land the United States Government was giving away in Beltrami County. So they came into the Red Lake area and settled on a quarter section about three miles south and a mile and a half east of Waskish. All the squatters had to do was to improve the land, maintain residency for five years, and then start paying taxes.

When they came to this new home, they came with two new Model T Fords. They still had them and drove them when I first showed up in the area as a game warden in 1960.

I never had a problem with them and consequently I knew very little about them until one day in late August of 1966. I came back to my station to have lunch around noon on this day to find these two small men standing in our driveway. The way they were talking in some strange language and gesturing with their hands, I thought they were having one big argument. It looked like they were coming to blows.

After I got out of the state car and asked what I could do for them, both of them doubled up their little fists and shook them at me. I finally made out they were saying "Them G__ D__ Bivers," I had to have them repeat it about three times before I realized they were having beaver problems. I told them to give me a minute. I wanted to talk to my wife.

When I went into the house to ask my wife what she had for lunch, she told me she had made a big kettle of soup. Then she told me these two men had been there for an hour. She couldn't understand them so she told them I should be home soon. I told Patricia they seem to have some kind of beaver problem. Then I asked Patricia if she had enough soup for all four of us. She thought she did. So I said to her, "They look clean and if it's okay with you could I invite them in for lunch?" She agreed.

I went back outside and found them looking at a huge bush of high bush cranberries we had in the yard. The berries were large and dead ripe. These two men said they would go home, get some pails and come back and pick the berries to make jelly.

I told them, "You leave those berries alone. We have partridges that come in every day and feed on them."

These men couldn't believe what I told them. They responded with, "Those partridges can go find their own berries out in the woods."

I told them, "My wife likes to see the partridge come in and feed on them." I also told them, "My wife has a big kettle of good homemade soup, she said you could come in and eat lunch with us. Don't tell her you even thought of picking those berries or I will throw you out on your ears."

These two brothers were hard to understand and when they talked with each other, they always were arguing. They came in and sat at the table and the chatter between them during lunch was almost unbearable. To top it off, they were the loudest soup slurpers that my wife or I had ever heard.

After lunch, I went outside with the two brothers. At the mention of beaver their fists doubled up and they both talked simultaneously and I couldn't understand a word they said. Finally I hollered at them to shut up and take me to where the problem was so I could figure out how to solve it.

They finally got across to me that I should bring along rubber boots. I always had a pair of hip boots in the trunk of the patrol car and I showed that to them. That seemed to meet with their approval.

The two of them went over to their Model T Ford. One got behind the wheel to control the choke and spark levers, while the other one went up front to crank the motor. It started on about the third pull and they took off with me behind in the patrol car. They went south to the first ditch grade that led east. The grade was on the north side of the judicial ditch. We went east on the ditch grade that was a poor excuse for a road. About three-quarters of a mile in on this grade, I could see water on the north side of the grade that shouldn't be there.

Eventually, we came to the clearing where their house and small outbuildings were. It was like a huge lake and it was obvious there had to be water in the house.

They absolutely insisted I should put on my boots and follow them down to the house. I really couldn't see how that was going to solve any problems. However, they were insistent and I couldn't really understand their jabbering.

We had to walk about a hundred yards from the ditch grade to the house. The water was about a foot deep. We got inside their one room house and some of their jabbering started to make sense. There was an old iron double bed they slept on. They had to put about six inch blocks of wood under the legs to keep the springs out of the water. The main problem was the small wood cook stove. They had blocked it up about four inches but the water had come up to the bottom of the oven and they would be unable to bake their bread. They told me they could cut six inches off the stovepipe and raise the stove high enough to bake bread, but, when the water went down, they would have to buy a new piece of stovepipe when they lowered the stove.

All I can say is you would have to see it to believe it. I asked them how long they had put up with this. They said about two weeks. I asked if they had any idea where the beaver dam was that was causing this problem. The oldest was John. He told me it was over east on a north, south judicial ditch about three miles.

I told John, "I will take County Road 110 to the T, then go north until I locate the dams."

Then John told me, "The closest way to the dams is to continue east on the grade that we have our cars on."

I asked him, "Has anyone driven east on the grade recently?"

He said, "To the best of my knowledge no one has driven on the grade, but, I walked the grade about five years ago."

So I told the boys I would come back in the morning with the state jeep. I would bring plenty of dynamite and see if I could locate and remove the dams causing the trouble. Then John wanted to know if he could ride along and watch. I said, "That would be okay. I will be back about 9:00 a.m."

The following morning I came back, picked up John, and we started east on the old ditch grade in the jeep. There were popple trees growing on the ditch grade that had trunks up to ten inches in diameter. We had to maneuver around and the weeds were higher than the hood on the jeep. It was nerve wracking to drive when you can't see the road under your wheels. I was afraid of falling into some big hole created for an animal den.

About a mile on the grade we hit a huge bump. John flew out of his seat and his whole body came down on my arms holding the wheel. We didn't have seatbelts in those old jeeps. I stopped to see what we had driven over. It was what was left of a fair sized tree trunk that had fallen across the grade.

I told John to reach between his legs and hang on to the bottom edge of his seat in case we hit another bump. I had the steering wheel to hang onto. We drove about five miles per hour from there on. We hit at least six more bumps like that.

We eventually came to the north south ditch. There were three dams north of us. Two of them were small but the third was humongous. This last dam was full of a hundred inch pulp sticks that some one had cut to sell for pulp. Why that pile of pulp sticks was never hauled and sold only the cutter knows.

Those beavers had used many of those sticks in the construction of this big dam. I would guess there could have been a hundred pulp sticks in that dam, along with limbs and mud.

I blew the small dams out with about five sticks of dynamite each. Then I went to work on the big dam. I punched about six holes, four or five feet deep. I dropped five or six sticks in each hole. Then I rigged one with a cap and fuse. I cut the fuse so we would have about two minutes to make our getaway.

When the smaller dams blew, we only had to get about a hundred yards away to be safe. For the big one, I knew we should run as far as possible in the two minutes I had cut the fuse for. I got out my wooden kitchen matches and struck it on the seat of my pants. (My wife always bitched about that because it always left a white streak on my right butt). I lit the fuse and hollered, "Fire in the hole" and ran off the dam, only to find John hiding behind a big old popple tree at the end of the dam. I hollered, "Get out of there or you will be killed." I was running and suddenly I was passed up by that little old man. He really could pick them up and lay them down. When she blew, there were eight-foot pulp sticks flying in every direction. A couple of them, we heard came down back in the bush beyond the jeep. John Lausnick was really impressed. I asked him why he was hiding behind that popple tree. He said he wanted to be where he could see the action. That blast really turned loose a wall of water.

We got the jeep turned around and started back. By the time we got back to their house the water had already dropped about three inches. I told the boys, "Don't ever put up with a problem like that in the future." Then they told me they hadn't paid their real estate taxes for years and the property had reverted to the state. They were afraid I might turn them in and they would be forced to move.

Eventually, they did move into Waskish and rented a little cabin from Olga Warren. I would stop and visit with them on occasion. They still baked their bread in that little old wood cook stove. Also, they still had their old gramophone. It stood about four feet high. It still had that old high water mark on the wood about fourteen inches up from the floor.

Chapter 40/ BIG WHITE MERCURY MOTOR

One fall day back in 1966, Harland Pickett, the game warden from Baudette, paid me a visit at my station at Waskish. He came to tell me that some person that lived along the Rainy River had witnessed two men operating a nice runabout boat with a big white Mercury motor on the back. (That was a big motor in those days.) At any rate, they were chasing and shooting ducks from this boat. The witnesses saw these men make several kills. Of course, we have two things wrong here. First of all, it is against the law to shoot migratory waterfowl from a motorboat in open water while underway. The second thing is, the season isn't open in Minnesota. However, the season is open on the Ontario side of the river.

Harland wanted to know if I had a fast boat that we could use to try to catch these dudes. The state had issued me a model

"K" Alumacraft, which is a 16-foot aluminum boat, and also a 35-horse power Johnson. This combination, although not deluxe accommodations, could skip across the water at a fare clip. We also had a trailer to move this equipment around. As this was the best equipment we had between us, it was decided that is what we would use. Harland then said, "You come up to Baudette tomorrow morning and be here at 5:00 a.m. on the nose, and I will have breakfast ready. We will eat, put the boat in the water, and stake out in some hiding place near where these people have been operating." Now for the benefit of you people who do not know Harland Pickett, let me tell you when Harland says 5:00 a.m. he does not mean 5:01 a.m. Nor does he mean 4:59 a.m. I screwed up with him once and he hung the nickname "Rookie" on me and that is my calling card to this very day.

In the course of the conversation, I suggested that he tow the boat and motor up to his place that afternoon. He was obviously disturbed at having to perform this task, but as he was the party asking for assistance he reluctantly agreed to do so.

I went to bed early that evening. I set two alarm clocks for 3:30 a.m., which should give me plenty of time to get up, get dressed, and drive the forty miles to Baudette. I woke up about 2:30 a.m. I was slept out and also a little excited about the task before us so I decided to get up. I shut off the alarms, got dressed, loaded my gear in the patrol car, and took leave of my station about 3 a.m. It was my intention to drive slowly with my lights off and possibly I would run across a spot lighter.

At any rate, I finally arrived within sight of Baudette. I put my lights on, checked my watch, and noted the time at 4:40 a.m. I came on into town where I met my first vehicle. A big 98 Oldsmobile, four door car with four men in it. They were towing a runabout boat on a boat trailer with a big white Mercury motor on the transom of the boat.

My first thought was if they are the dudes we were going to be sitting out in our little boat, freezing our butts off, waiting for them, and they are in a nice warm car headed for home, this would be a revolting situation. I checked my watch and I had eighteen minutes with nothing to do. I made a U-turn and caught up to them about two miles out of town. I gave them the red light and after we stopped, I went to their car, identified myself, and told them I would like to check their licenses and their bag.

All four men were well dressed in business suits and were very cooperative. They opened the trunk of their car and I saw ruffed grouse, sharp tail grouse, and some fish. I counted their game and they were short of what they could possess. I then climbed into the boat where there were a number of suitcases, cartons, and old sailor sea bags. As I opened up each container they gave me an accurate account of the contents. Eventually, I pulled out one sea bag and one of the men said that it was full of dirty laundry and I may not choose to shove my hands in there. He was right, but as my hand probed down into the bag I felt what I knew to be a duck. They were pretty well picked and drawn. I don't remember at this date exactly how many, but it was in the neighborhood of a dozen. At any rate, I had our hunters I thought.

Then I asked them if they had Ontario hunting licenses and they didn't have any Ontario licenses. I told them to turn that rig around and follow me back into town. I told them I would lead them to a home and when we got there they should drive in and I would drive my patrol car in behind their trailer.

They cooperated all the way. I got out of my patrol car, locked it up, and checked my pocket watch. It was 5:00 a.m. straight up when I came through the door. Here was the scene in Harland's kitchen. The table was set for two people. All four burners were going on the stove. There were pancakes on a griddle, four eggs in a frying pan, bacon sizzling in another pan, and the coffee pot was perking on the fourth burner. There was toast popping out of the toaster on the counter.

Then I told Harland "I've got your duck hunters out in the driveway."

Harland gave me a strange look, shut off two of the burners, and then said, "What did you say?"

I came back with, "I've got your duck hunters out in the driveway."

He turned to the stove, shut off the other two burners, slapped his hat on his head and out he went. He had a long talk with the men advising them of their rights. He convinced them we could charge all four men with illegal possession of waterfowl. However, he let them know only two men had been observed shooting from a motorboat and if they would come forward and admit they were the ones shooting from the motorboat and turn over the gun they were using we would just charge the two men. That was agreed all around so Harland made out the summons and seizure tags. Then, because these men were from southern Minnesota and anxious to be on their way, we started to try to find someone to take their bail.

We waited until 8:00 a.m. to call the municipal judge's home only to find out from his wife he had gone to his office located upstairs over the bank. Harland and I went up to see him to see if he wanted to have court or just take bail. He let us know it was Saturday and no way was he going over to the courthouse. Then he asked what the story was and Harland explained it all to him. The judge then said, "Have them post $25.00 a piece, which will be the amount of the fine if they fail to appear for court."

To which I said, "Judge, they will laugh at us. Down where they come from, they get fines of $100.00 for one pheasant."

The judge was a bit miffed at my contesting his decision. Then he asked what kind of a car they had. I told him they had a big new 98 Oldsmobile, towing a big nice runabout boat with a 60 hp Mercury motor on the back. The judge came back with, "Oh, they're men of means. Make them post $50.00 a piece. You are right."

I'm sure, those men left town laughing at us.

Chapter 41/ BEAR AND BEAR PROBLEMS

Every station I was assigned to I had bear complaints or problems. These complaints usually occurred in years when we would be experiencing poor berry crops. Also, the bear became aware that where there were people there was food and or garbage. Wasted food and fish cleanings were to be found at every resort and private home in garbage cans. All the bear had to do was tip over these cans or barrels, pull out the contents and make a selection for his meal—much to the chagrin of the property owner that had to clean up the mess.

Three cubs

When I went to work for the Department of Conservation in 1960, bear were not a protected animal. They could be killed at any time, except at night with the aid of a light.

My first station was Waskish and the local people would take care of their own problems. Occasionally, I would be called to remove the problem. I would either chase them away with the aid of my dog, "Bum", or I would live trap them and haul them away. I never did shoot one. However, I usually had a big rifle handy.

One typical problem while at Waskish was when a fair-size bear came into the forestry campgrounds on the Tamarac River. It was on a weekend. The forest ranger alerted me to the problem. There were a mass of people in the camping area and the campers—men, women, and children—were feeding the bear and at times had the animal completely surrounded. I heard some children ask their mother, "How come Smokey doesn't have his hat on?"

My future son-in-law, Herb Hanson, had come up to visit us from Bemidji where he and my daughter attended Bemidji State College and he had asked if he could accompany my dog and me. I told him that would be O.K., but, just as an observer. I had a big rifle in my hand.

When the people feeding the bear saw me, some thought I came to kill him. I just told them, "That's the last thing I want to do." I let these people know that the bear was a wild animal and could be unpredictable. He could hurt someone severely and their weekend could become a disaster.

I told the people to go to their cars and I would have my dog try to move the bear out of the community. The people complied. Bum was at my side shaking with excitement. I had decided to move the bear south, if possible. So Herb and I, with Bum, moved to the north side of the bear.

Then I told Bum to move him. Bears seem to have a natural fear of dogs. However, bear have been known to kill dogs. Bum, in his excitement, was a bit too enthusiastic. He tried to move the bear too fast and the bear elected to go up a big Norway tree on the north side of the forestry buildings.

So, I called Bum back and we all sat down about fifty yards

from the tree. The bear kept his eyes on us and after about fifteen minutes came down from the tree. He stood at the base of the tree for a few minutes and then slowly moved off to the south. We got up and followed him for about a quarter-of-a-mile. Both the bear and Bum were trotting along until we just got past the log cabin that belonged to the Section of Game.

Apparently Bum got a little too close and the bear went up another Norway tree about a hundred yards south of the log cabin. So Herb, Bum, and I sat down about twenty-five yards from the tree. At any rate, the bear finally elected to come down out of the tree and started to move south. He had gone about ten or fifteen yards and he was keeping his eye on us. Then I told Bum again to move him easy. Bum got up and started with a growl.

That bear evidently thought it was too far to the safety of the next big tree and he came back running toward us but actually he had that last tree in mind for safety. My gun came to my shoulder, but the bear elected to go back up the tree he had just vacated.

So I called Bum to back off and we moved back to give the bear ample room to come down. Then I realized Herb was missing. I called his name and when he answered I located him up on the roof of the log cabin. To this day Herb, who by the way is quite an athlete, doesn't know just how he ended up on that roof. He said at one point he was nose to nose with the bear and the next moment he was on the roof. There was no way to get there except straight up. It must have been quite a leap!

Bear and cub

In another instance on a nice summer day I had taken my patrol car down to Kelliher for some minor adjustments. My wife followed me the fifteen miles to Kelliher to do some shopping. I found out it would be at least four hours before the garage could take care of the state car. So I prevailed on my wife to take me home. I had a room to paint in the state house and I could do that instead of sitting in that garage for half of a day.

I had opened up the can of paint, took a mixing stick, and spent a good ten minutes mixing the paint. Then I selected a paintbrush. At this point the telephone rang. I laid down my brush and answered the phone. It was a pretty excited voice on the other end. It was obviously a man. He said he was the party that owned a cabin south of the Kansas City Resort. I had met the man sometime before. He was a dentist from the metropolitan area with a large family.

His problem was that he and his family came in from fishing and when they approached their cabin they found a huge black bear digging up their lawn and there was no way they could get in their cabin. His question was, would I please come down and chase the bear away or shoot him if it was necessary?

His cabin is about seven miles away from my home and headquarters and I was temporarily without a vehicle. I explained that to him, but no way was he going to let me off the hook. I told him I would have to come down by boat and it would take at least a half hour.

Then I suggested that he borrow a metal pail or a small tub from the Kansas City Resort and a substantial stick or club like a baseball bat. He should go back down to his cabin and walk in until he saw the bear. Then he should rush the bear while pounding on the bottom of the pail and yelling his lungs out. That would chase the bear away.

There was dead silence on the telephone for a good minute. Finally I inquired, "Are you still there?"

Then he came back, "Officer, I'm just a city boy. Chasing that bear is not in my life for things to do."

So I finally gave up and told him I'll be down by boat and it will be at least a half hour.

I gathered up a water pail and my shillelagh, got in the boat and headed down the lake. I found the doctor and his family waiting in his boat a hundred yards off shore. The whole family followed me in and to my surprise the bear was still there. I gave him the "Bum's rush", pounding on my pail and yelling and away went Mr. Bear.

I noticed the bear had been rooting around in the yard and there were odds and ends of fish cleanings everywhere. I told the doctor, "You can't just throw your fish guts around, that will attract bear."

Then he told me, "Someone told me fish cleanings made good fertilizer."

I granted him, "That's true but it will also attract bear,

skunks, and coyote. In the future, you should haul the fish cleanings over to the dump and you won't have anymore problems."

With that taken care of I went to my boat. The doctor thanked me and I returned to my headquarters to do my painting.

On another instance while stationed at Orr, Minnesota, I got a call from a resort owner at Crane Lake that I best come down to his resort to observe what had happened and to pick up a bear carcass. There was no emergency but he would like to have me down there within the hour so they could start cleaning up the mess. Crane Lake is about a forty-five minute drive from Orr.

I located the caller, who in turn took me to a fairly new "A" frame cabin. There I met several people that were enthusiastically waiting to tell me what had happened as it was told to them by the occupant, the wife, and daughter.

I don't guarantee that my version is absolutely correct but it is my understanding that this is what happened.

The cabin was rented by a family of three. The man was a policeman from Ohio with his wife and teenage daughter. I was told they immediately packed up and left after the incident even though it was pitch dark outside.

It seems this cabin or "A" frame had a living room, dining room, kitchen, bath, and one bedroom on the first floor and a single bedroom in the loft with a set of stairs from the living room to a balcony that led into the single bedroom.

The father and mother slept downstairs while the teenage daughter slept in the loft overlooking the living room.

These people had a pork roast dinner the evening before and had deposited the bones and scraps in their wastebasket in the kitchen. One of the sliding windows that had a screen on it had been opened and a stick had been placed under the window to keep it open.

It was obvious that the bear had made his entry there

because there were bear tracks in the dirt under the window and the screening had been torn out of the frame. Apparently, the bear knocked the stick out from under the window and the window slid down too close. The stick was on the living room floor under the closed window. The contents of the wastebasket were scattered all over the kitchen floor.

We have to assume the bear tried to leave by the way he came in and found the window closed. At any rate, he went up the stairs into the daughter's bedroom. She woke up, saw the bear and started screaming. The bear panicked went onto the balcony and was looking down into the living room.

The screaming awakened the father and mother. The father ran out into the living room with his policeman's thirty-eight special revolver in hand. He looked up and saw the bears head and neck stuck out over the balcony. He fired one shot into the bear's neck and, apparently, hit a big artery. The bear panicked and leapt from the balcony to the living room trying to find a way out of there, while the Ohio policeman shot the rest of the bullets out of his six shooter at the bear. All this time the blood was spurting out of the bear's neck until he finally collapsed and died from loss of blood.

The cabin was pretty much in shambles with bear blood all over the walls, floor, and furniture.

Of course the whole camp was woke up with the screaming and shooting. I got a little different version from everyone that related the story. They said that family from Ohio couldn't get out of there fast enough. They even left some of their stuff behind.

On another occasion while at Ironton, I had arrested a man for a minor fishing violation on a small lake east of the Green Roof Store on Highway #6. Sometime after this altercation he called me to make a complaint regarding bear damage. He demanded that I come immediately to his small farm that was located north of the Green Roof Store.

When I got to his house he came out and told me to follow

him a couple hundred yards where he pointed to several beehives that had been knocked down. A couple of the super boxes were broken and there were at least a dozen combs of honey scattered in every direction.

The air around the broken hives was full of bees and they were obviously mad.

This farmer beekeeper insisted I go out to the hives where the bees were boiling around. I told him I could see the damage he had sustained from where we were standing.

When I was a young lad in Iowa my dad had eleven swarms of bees. On many occasions he had me help. I had been stung many times and although I didn't like it, I wasn't afraid to be stung.

This farmer absolutely insisted that I go out to the hives and observe a bear track in one of the honeycombs lying on the ground. So to make him happy I went out there. One bee stung me on the lobe of my ear and another one got me on the forearm. That pleased this farmer to no end.

I was able to flick the stinger off my forearm but the one on my earlobe managed to get most of the poison into my ear before I got the stinger out of me.

Later that day I brought a live trap out and set it. The bear did not come back so after a few days, I removed the trap.

This just shows you what a game warden will put up with to make the customer happy.

While at the Orr Station, I ran into the greatest amount of bear problems in the summer of 1978. I had two homemade bear traps made out of two fifty-five gallon metal barrels with the ends cut out and welded together. A sliding metal door on one end hooked up to a simple, but ingenious, and effective trigger.

There were many nights I had both traps set and ended up with a bear in each one, come morning.

I had a pick up truck to haul away the trap with the bear in it. I usually hauled them some place where no one lived fifteen or twenty miles from the catch site and released the animal.

For a bear that would weigh up to about a hundred-and-fifty pounds, I could load the trap onto the pick-up myself. Once in a while I would seek help. One time I got a bear so big I had to have three other men help me load the trap onto my pick-up. I couldn't believe how that bear could or would squeeze himself in there to get the bait. (If I have time and space later on I will relate the circumstances when I released him.)

I began to realize from markings, usually a white patch of fur on the bear's chest, that I was catching the same bear twice and one bear three times. I had to take more drastic methods and locations on releasing these problems. I didn't want to shoot them if I could possibly avoid it.

I decided to take them through the Nett Lake Indian Reservation and release them over west of Orr. So for the next month I hauled them over to State Highway #65 where I had located a convenient little trail to release the bear. Also, it seemed I was doing something right. I wasn't having any of these bears returning to their old haunts. My dad would occasionally ride along with me. On a couple of occasions, I even took pictures of the released bear running away after being released.

One day when I was coming back to Orr after releasing a bear, I met one of the Nett Lake Indian Game Wardens, Wendell Drift. He stopped me to check on what I was doing on the Reservation when he realized I was the State Warden from Orr. He asked me, "What is that barrel device on the back of your pick-up?"

I told him, "It's a homemade live trap to catch and remove problem bear."

Then Wendell made the remark, "We are having a lot of bear coming into the Nett Lake garbage dump site."

I asked him, "Are you having any problems with the bear?"

He responded, "No, we just shoot them."

I'm sure those were bear I had released heading back to

their old haunts around the resorts in the Orr district.

Bear are not a protected animal on the Nett Lake Indian Reservation.

E. L. Callies (father of Bill) with bear trap containing a bear

That is My Dad who Chose to
Ride Along with me one day to
Release the Bear inside
I use to have to Lift the Trap onto
the Truck or Trailer.
I had one Bear so Big I dont Know
how he Squeezed in.
Took three other Men And Myself to
get the Trap on the Truck
Orr minn

Notes on the back of the above picture written by Bill Callies

That was the end of my problem on bear at the Orr Station.

To get back to the huge bear I had in the trap. He was so big he couldn't reverse himself inside the live trap. I backed into that small trail where I had been releasing bear. I climbed up on the back of the truck and then up on to the live trap. I stood on top of the trap and lifted up the iron door. The bear would have to slide out backward but he didn't seem to want to try. So I shifted my weight to one foot and holding the trap door with both hands, I started to bang on the trap with my free foot. Finally, after several minutes of this approach, one of the bears back feet came out and felt up, down, and sideways. It could not feel anything solid so he drew his foot back in.

My arms, hands, and back were starting to ache, so I slid the door back down, moved up and sat down on the roof of the cab of the truck.

Bear running after being released from trap

After a few minutes rest, I resumed my attempt to get the bear out of the trap. There I stood holding the sliding iron door with my two hands while standing on one foot on top of the trap and kicking the trap with my free foot. This time it worked. This big pile of black fur just seemed to ooze out of that barrel down onto the ground in a big pile. Then this pile started to straighten up on to his back feet and there he stood standing on his back feet looking me in the face not two feet away. I let go of the trap door and it came down with a loud bang. I jumped up on top of the cab of the truck looking back over my shoulder to see the bear was just as scared as I was. His feet were throwing up dust dirt and small rocks as we went running down this little trail out of sight.

I suppose that bear was wondering what that was all about. He never came back around the resorts on Pelican Lake, so it's possible he ended up on somebody's table on the reservation.

Chapter 42/ THREE MEN RESCUED AT RED LAKE

It was late in the afternoon of June 20, 1968 when two little children — 8-year-old Bradley and 6-year-old DeeAnn Kosbau thought they could hear someone out on Upper Red Lake holler for help. The wind was blowing strong and toward the children. The lake was wild and I didn't think anyone would be out on the water.

These two youngsters ran up to the Upper Red Lake Lodge, owned by their grandparents, and told their mother of the cries for help. The mother told them what they heard was probably herring gulls — no one would be out on the lake that day. Then she thought maybe she had better call the game warden just in case there was someone out there.

When I got the call from Mrs. Franklin Kosbau, I ran over to the Forestry Headquarters and alerted Roger Anderson that I probably could use some help if there was someone out there.

We grabbed our life jackets and some floating cushions and went into the state boat, a 16-foot Lund with a fifty-horse power Mercury motor on it, and out to the mouth of the Tamarac River.

That old lake was wild. We stopped, stood up, and had to hang onto the windshield. We took a good look north and west. We could only see raging white cap water. We moved about a third of a mile out into this pounding water. Then we stopped again to take another look. I believe this was when we could see a waving seat cushion about a half a mile further on. In fact, we weren't sure if we really had seen anything. However, we headed out in that direction. Sitting down we couldn't see anything but these pounding white caps. Even Roger and I didn't feel too safe out there in this sixteen-foot aluminum boat.

Eventually, we did come upon the overturned boat. It was one of those glass fiber boats. There were two small men straddling the keel. The transom of the boat apparently was held on the bottom by a heavy outboard motor. The bow of the boat had apparently trapped some air as about one-third of the front bottom of the boat was out of the water. Down in the water, hanging on to a rope that was attached to a screw eye on the bow was Dallas Reed who owned and operated a small resort on the Tamarac River. He was the only one that seemed to have any life in him. The two laying on the keel I was sure had already succumbed to hypothermia.

I told Roger we had a real mess on our hands to get all three of these men into our boat without tipping our boat over or losing our grip on these men when we grabbed them. It would be necessary to get our boat motor into neutral or shut off so the prop wouldn't cut them up.

I told Roger I was going to maneuver our boat at a right angle to their boat just up wind of them. I told Roger then to try to grab the bottom man on the keel and pull him into our boat. This was an iffy thing because Roger's arms and hands were torn up so badly from World War II injuries. The man he was to grab laid there on the keel like so much dead meat. He was absolutely no help at all.

I would be just finished controlling the boat and shutting down the engine when I should jump and grab the other man so our boat would not come down on him and flip him into our boat.

I maneuvered around where I could holler at Dallas Reed how we were going to attempt to pick these men off. I asked Dallas if he could hang onto that eyebolt as our boat pushes your boat completely under as we passed over them. I told him I would have our motor shut down so the prop would not hit him. The bow on the other boat should come up after we passed, however, and hopefully had these two small men in our boat. Then we could pick Dallas out of the lake with two of us and Dallas was alert could help himself a little also.

We put the plan in motion, however, our boat almost rolled over from the weight of Roger and I and the two men we were lifting off the over-turned boat on the same side. A big wave hit us from behind. Fortunately, the air in the bow of the upside down boat gave us a bit of a push back. Then we had slid with a lot of grinding sounds passing over and beyond the overturned boat.

I was about to start the motor to get some control of our boat when I noted Dallas didn't pop back to the surface hanging on to the eyebolt. I thought he might have been knocked cold. I hollered to Roger, "Look for Dallas."

Then I heard a welcome sound, he was hanging on to our starboard gunnel hollering, "Here I am."

I grabbed him by the shoulders and started to lift him when he got hit by another wave and almost rolled over again. We are getting more weight in the boat with four bodies plus water from the breaking waves.

So with Dallas being let down to again hang on to the gunnel, Roger, and I shifted the two bodies to the other side of the boat as counter weight. Both Roger and I grabbed Dallas (he was well over two hundred pounds) and with Dallas helping, we flopped him on to the floor of the boat.

All of us were sopping wet. Dallas made a query; "Should we try to tie on to the over turned boat and tow it in to the river?"

I just said, "No way. We are lucky to have pulled this off without losing one of you and not turning our own boat over. You can come out and salvage the boat when the winds calm down."

Then Dallas had concerns, "Some other boat might run into it."

I told him, "No one else is dumb enough to come out into this mess. Also, we've got to get these young men in where it's warm and dry. They could die on us yet." We were at least 45 minutes running time into calm water in the river.

Chapter 43/ THIEF LAKE GOOSE BLINDS

One fall day in the late 60's, Dick Tarte, our supervisor, called Leo Manthei, the warden at Blackduck, and me into the office. He gave us instructions to go to the Thief Lake Game Refuge the next day. We were to contact the game manager and have him show us what his problem was and see if we could be of any help to straighten things out.

Leo and I left early the next morning and arrived at the Thief Lake Game Refuge headquarters about 11 a.m. We checked in with the head game manager. He said he was short-handed and did not have the manpower to police the goose blinds on the west side of Thief Lake. We asked him to take us over to this area and show us what his problem was.

The Thief Lake game managers had created a goose-shooting zone by clearing an area about three hundred yards wide and two miles long with a huge parking area on the southeast end. The blinds were constructed on posts that were driven into the ground surrounded by snow fencing with brush leaning up against the fencing. Each blind was about six feet wide and twelve feet long. The blinds are in the center of the three hundred yard area and spaced about a hundred yards apart forming a neat straight row for about two miles.

The rules for the goose-shooting zone were posted all over the camp and in the parking lot. These rules were copied from a commissioner's order that stated that the blinds cannot be occupied before 5 a.m. and must be vacated by 10 p.m. Some blinds are better in that they are located in the flyways the geese use the most when they fly from the lake out to the grain fields to feed. Some of the local hunters have made a study of the better blinds to shoot from and are reluctant to give up possession of these choice sites. They also choose to ignore the commissioner's ruling to vacate the blinds after 10 p.m.

In fact, eighty percent of the blinds had permanent residents. They had sleeping bags, air mattresses, and apple and orange crates set up to store canned goods. They had twenty-pound bottles of gas, two and three burner gas plates, and tarpaulins to put over the top if it rained or snowed. There was always one member of the family or hunting group that occupied the blind twenty-four hours a day, seven days a week.

We all returned to the headquarters where it was planned that Leo and I would get up about 2 a.m., go down to the blinds, and create a mass evacuation of all the blinds.

At 2 a.m., Leo and I were awakened by an alarm clock. We got up, dressed, and headed for the goose blinds. We started by a nudge on the sleeping bag. If that didn't get their attention, we increased the velocity of our boot until we got their attention. Then we told them who we were and to get themselves and their gear out of the blind and up to the parking lot. Most of them were cooperative. We gave them the option of getting up now and moving out or we would write them up and bodily throw them out. Also, we warned them that the next night we would write them up first and then kick them out. I can assure you there was a lot of groaning and a few belligerent hunters.

We managed to clear out about the first mile in an hour and a half. I suggested to Leo one of us should go back to see that they had in fact cleared out and were up in the parking lot and see to it they stayed there until 5 a.m. Leo elected to go back while I continued on to the end of the line. About half of the blinds in the second mile were vacant so I assumed that part of the zone was not in the goose flyway.

I started back and when I got within about a half a mile of the parking lot, I could hear what sounded like a thundering herd coming my way. I looked up and I could see what looked like the light of at least a hundred flashlights. You could even feel a vibration in the ground through your feet. I looked at my watch and it was just 5 o'clock. So Leo must have just turned them loose. The pounding got louder as this herd of human flesh passed me and as they passed an empty blind one man would try to take and retain possession until his partners showed up in the second wave carrying guns, shells, and gear. As near as we knew, word must have got around because we were never called back.

About a half hour before shooting time a small flock of honkers went over us about thirty feet in the air going west over a small freshly plowed field. The plowed field and everything west was private land. When the geese passed over the far edge of the plowing someone fired three shots. I did not see a goose fall. I kept my eyes glued on that spot the shots came from and I started across that plowed field. A third of the way into that plowing, I knew I had made a big mistake. My boots had so much of that gumbo on them I could hardly lift them. I really struggled to get to that pit these shooters were in. When I got there, I found two men and one woman all dressed in hunting clothes and each person had a shotgun. When I asked which person did the shooting, they told me they had no knowledge of any shooting. So I said, "I heard three shots come from this pit as the geese flew over so I will write up all three of you, that way I will get the shooter."

Then the woman spoke up and said she was the one that shot. However, she didn't hit any of the geese. She went on to say it was still so dark she could hardly see them. I told her from where I was when I heard the shooting and saw the gun flashes I, too, did not see anything fall out. I told her other hunters hear shooting before legal shooting hours and it makes good sportsman mad at illegal shooters. Also, it could well start everyone shooting. However, because she didn't seem to hit a goose and it didn't precipitate any other shooting, I would only write her up for shooting before legal shooting time and I would not seize her gun.

And you can believe me, when I said I took the long way around that plowed field on the way back. We all learned something on this morning.

Chapter 44/ CHARLIE HERMAN'S ACCIDENT

It was around 9 p.m. on a Sunday evening in Waskish, Minnesota, on September 22, 1968. My wife and I were sitting in the living room. I had removed my boots and we were both thinking of going to bed. The telephone started ringing, so my wife said, "I'll answer it." After she said, "Hello", I realized from the conversation that she was taking directions. She was much better at that than I was. I assumed it was another car that killed a deer or a moose. We used to have to go immediately to pick them up. If they were salvageable, we would dress them out and sell them. If not, we would drag them back in the bush and leave the carcass for the ravens and animals to feed on.

I started putting my boots on when Patricia hung up. She said, "That call came from Hudec's Resort. Annie Herman and her sister came in there screaming that Charlie Herman had been run over on Highway 72, right by Cole Herman's mailbox." Hudec's beer joint was full of local people and it seemed that Roger Anderson, the forest ranger, told them to call the game warden.

I finished with the boots, grabbed a jacket, and ran out and jumped in my patrol car. It is about four miles to Cole's house and mailbox. I would pass Hudec's Resort about three miles from Waskish. I hoped and assumed that a lot of the people from Hudec's had gone immediately to help Charlie.

Charlie Herman operated Rocky Point Resort on the north side of Upper Red Lake. He was not too popular among his neighbors because he had married Annie who was a member of the Red Lake Band of Indians and they had a reputation for catering to game and fish violators.

On the way to the accident scene, I called the dispatcher at Thief River Falls to advise him of my problem. The closest ambulance, hospital, and doctor were forty miles north at Baudette. I asked him to call up there and have the ambulance stand by and I would update him on the seriousness of the accident when I got there.

It was misting out and the clouds were low overhead. I was amazed when I got to Cole's mailbox. There was one car and one man standing along side it. I came out of the patrol car and asked, "Where is Charlie? Where is everybody?"

The man spoke up and said, "The guy I hit is down in the ditch and I'm afraid he is dead. There were two women in a car in that driveway across the road. I never even saw what I hit until these women ran across the road from their car and screamed at me, 'You killed Charlie'. They got in their car and left. You are the first car to come along."

I grabbed my flashlight and went down in the ditch. Charlie was lying there awfully still. His face was an ashen gray. His right leg of his bib overalls was torn and bloody. There was about a four-inch piece of leg bone severed from his leg and his foot. His foot was twisted backwards from his body. I heard a car come from the north and stop. A man came down by me. I turned and saw who the person was. It was Adolph Petrowski. I shined the light on Charlie, and Adolph recognized him right away. Then I noticed something puffing up Charlie's overalls on his right leg above the knee. I made the remark, "He is still alive. That must be a severed artery."

Adolph said, "How can we stop the bleeding?" I climbed up the ditch, to my car, to get my first aid kit. I had a tourniquet in there that might slow the bleeding down. I came back with the tourniquet, got it around his leg, and really pulled it up hard until the puffing stopped under his overalls. I went back to the car and grabbed my raincoat, opened it up alongside Charlie, and between Adolph and I, we got him onto the coat.

I told Adolph, "Let's get him in the car and head for Baudette." With Adolph on one side and me on the other side we wrestled him up to and across the back seat of the patrol car. I asked Adolph, "Can you crawl in on the floor and hold Charlie so he doesn't roll onto the floor?" Adolph held Charlie up and he didn't roll.

I told the fellow that hit Charlie I had his license number and that he should stay right there. There was a patrolman on his way from Bemidji, sixty-five miles south of there. The patrolman would be there within the hour to take his statement. He assured me he had no intention of moving.

We took off for Baudette as fast as the old state car would go (ninety-three miles an hour). I called Thief River Falls and told them, "I have the man, who was hit in the accident, in the back seat. I am headed north on Highway 72. Please send the ambulance south to meet us." I let him know how critical the situation was and requested he alert the hospital because time was of the essence.

Then I got to thinking, I had no business hauling Charlie. If he was dead when we got to Baudette, the Hermans would sue me and the state, and my supervisor would probably fire me. All

I could think of was, I was in a hell of a mess. If he lived, some of the old wardens would be down on me. They would have thought that this was the chance to get rid of an old problem. I've always said I was a worrier. I asked Adolph how Charlie was doing and his response was, "I don't know if he is alive or dead." We had gone about twenty-five miles when I saw flashing lights coming toward us. I was so thankful, thinking we would transfer Charlie to the ambulance. It turned out to be the highway patrolman from Baudette, Dennis Mattfeld, but right behind him was the ambulance.

We all met and came to a stop. I wanted to transfer Charlie. The two men from the ambulance took one look in the back seat and they said, "No, just keep going."

Denny swung around with the patrol car and took off with the lights flashing and I came as fast as my old car would go. Then Denny came over the radio and screamed at me, "Come on. Let's go."

I was at ninety plus and I called Denny and said, "She won't go any faster."

Eventually, we pulled up at the front door of the hospital. They were waiting for us. They had a table on wheels and we all turned to and lifted him out of the patrol car onto the table. While we were doing this, Charlie spoke up and begged us, "Hit me in the head." He was alive! I was so thankful for that.

We wheeled him into emergency and I looked around. Then, I just screamed, "Where's the doctor?"

A man in a nice business suit spoke up and said, "I'm the doctor."

In the emergency room, we slid him onto a larger table and I was able to retrieve my raincoat. When I saw what a mess Charlie was, I almost passed out. The doctor said, "I'll get your tourniquet."

I said, "Forget it. I'll draw a new one." Then I bolted out the door and sat down on a bench in the hall. I was sick to my stomach.

I really felt sorry for that doctor and those nurses. I heard they contacted the air base and got some soldiers to come over and donate some whole blood that night. They had quite a time keeping Charlie alive that night.

The highway patrolman from Bemidji contacted the driver of the vehicle and made out all the papers. Denny Mattfeld made out the reports on Charlie. The doctor wrote in his summation that if I hadn't put on that tourniquet, Charlie never would have made it.

The next day Charlie's grandson who had just come home on leave from the Navy came to my house. He wanted to know what I did with Charlie's wallet. I told him I never saw a wallet anywhere, anytime. He then accused me of taking Charlie's wallet and told me that Charlie had $200.00 in it. I was really indignant about that and I let the young fellow know it.

Charlie was gone for almost eighteen months. Half the bones in his body had been broken. They were able to save his knee but he had to have prosthesis from there on down.

Then one day, an attorney in Bemidji wrote me that he would like to have me come down and make a statement regarding Charlie's accident. This attorney was a man named Herb and he was born and raised near Saum. He was ambitious, studied hard, and became a lawyer. When I first came to Waskish he was the county attorney for Beltrami, and he was a good prosecuting attorney.

He asked me a series of questions and he had a court reporter taking a record. Then he asked, "Just how drunk was the man the night he hit Charlie?"

I told him, "He wasn't drunk, and he hadn't even been drinking." I was really upset. He wanted me to say the driver who hit Charlie was drunk at the scene of the accident. I told him if he had me on the stand and asked me that question I would flat out deny it and I would tell the court he tried on an earlier occasion to make that statement. I told him, "The man that hit Charlie was not at fault. It was a rainy, misty, overcast

night and Charlie had on dark blue bib overalls. He ran in front
of the car going to Cole's mailbox. The guy never saw him."

Waskish Man Is Seriously Hurt In Auto Accident

An elderly Waskish resident was seriously injured Sunday night when he was struck by a car as he crossed Highway 72 near his home.

Charles Herman, 61, was taken to Baudette Hospital by a game warden for treatment of a serious leg injury and other hurts. Highway patrolmen said Herman was struck by a car driven by Robert C. Powell, Cushing, as he crossed the highway to his mailbox about three miles north of Waskish. Herman was listed in serious condition Monday by hospital authorities.

The accident occurred at 8:45 p.m. Damage to the Powell car was estimated at $35.

Newspaper article about the accident

Chapter 45/ THE INTERNATIONAL CARRY ALLS

One afternoon in the summer of 1970, I got a telephone call at my station in Waskish from my neighboring warden at Baudette, Harland Pickett. He said there are four men in a tan-over-green International Carry All that left Baudette a short time earlier, and they had too many walleyed pike in their possession.

As Waskish is forty miles south of Baudette on Highway 72 and there is no place to turn off, he assumed I might be able to intercept them. However, he did say they might go east on Highway 11 so he would call Marv Smith at International Falls to watch for them if they took that route.

I immediately got into my patrol car and started north on 72. About seven miles north of Waskish, I met a tan-over-green International Carry All with four men in it. I made a "u" turn and caught up with this vehicle, pulled alongside, gave them the red light and motioned for them to pull over. They complied and after both vehicles were stopped on the shoulder of the road, I walked up to the Carry All, identified myself and ordered the men to get out of the vehicle and stand in front of it. I then came on kind of strong and told them that I had information to the effect that they had over their possession limit of walleyed pike and I would give them just thirty seconds to hand them over to me or I was going to pile all of their gear right out along side of the highway until I had the fish. Within ten seconds, I had both arms full of fish. Then I got a long story about taking home several extra limits to some of their co-workers who were going to come with them, but for various reasons couldn't or didn't come.

So I gave the vehicle a visual once over, and satisfied I had all the fish, I started the tedious procedure of counting fish, making out summons (seizure receipts), and explaining their rights to them. I was almost done with the paperwork, when I heard a vehicle coming towards us from the north. To my surprise, it was another tan-over-green International Carry All with four men on board. I flagged the vehicle down and pulled them over. I identified myself and checked their fishing licenses. Like the first vehicle, each fisherman had a Minnesota angling license and an Ontario angling license, so they could legally possess forty-eight walleyes, which was what they had.

However, with my first vehicle still waiting for me to complete the paperwork with them, and when I was half-way through checking the contents of the second vehicle, a third tan-over-green International Carry All came along. To make a long story short, eventually I had six tan-over-green International Carry Alls, each with four men and lots of gear, lined up along the shoulder of Highway 72. Some of the men became a bit impatient with me, but eventually I checked all the other vehicles and only the first one I had intercepted had too many fish.

So I sent them all on their way except the one with too many fish. This vehicle I accompanied to Kelliher and located the justice of the peace, Clara Quale. She heard the complaint, to which they plead guilty. She assessed a fine or the alternative jail sentence. They paid their fine and continued on their way minus all of the fish and with lighter pocket books.

That evening I called Harland Pickett and told him the mess he had gotten me into. At that time, he told me he had just found out that the International company had just completed a three-day sales persons' meeting at the Sportsman's Lodge on the Rainy River and there were over four hundred salespeople with over one hundred identical tan-over-green International Carry Alls for transportation.

There may have been other vehicles going east or west on Highway 11 that may have had too many fish but how lucky I was to have the first vehicle I stopped have too many fish.

Chapter 46/ DAVID MOHSTAD—BATTLE TOWNSHIP

I was staked out north of Saum in the latter part of October 1970. It was a sharp, clear night and I was sitting on the hood of the car. I hadn't seen a car all night nor had I heard anyone on the radio. I could hear flocks of whistlers and golden-eye ducks overhead on their migration flight south. Then, way off to the north, I thought I heard a shot just about in the direction of Hank Wistrom's farm. Hank lived next to the Red Lake Indian Reservation so it could be an Indian off the reservation, which could be illegal, or they could be on the reservation over which I had no jurisdiction, or it could be old Hank Wistrom himself. He was known to knock off a deer occasionally.

So I headed up that way. The sky was clear and I could see the road well even without lights. I did not see any vehicles or any lights. I passed a farm that had just acquired a new tenant, but there was no light on or anything to arouse my suspicions so I continued on west to Hank's farm. When I drove into the farmyard, the dogs started barking, then a light came on and eventually Hank came out of the house. I asked him about the shot and with the aid of my flashlight checked his fingernails and could see no blood or tallow under his nails. Then Hank said the shot came from the new neighbor east of him. He said this fellow moved up from South St. Paul with his family. Hank said he used to work in the slaughterhouse at the packing plant in South St. Paul.

I drove back east past this new resident in my area. Again I looked the building site over with my binoculars and could see no activity so I went home and got about three hours sleep. I got up about 7 a.m. and called Leo Manthei, my neighboring warden, and told him I wanted to make a search and wanted him to accompany me. Our supervisor always wanted at least two men to carry out a search warrant and he preferred three men. I told Leo to meet me in Kelliher at 8 a.m. at Clara Quale's house. She was the justice of the peace in the northern part of Beltrami County.

Leo and I met at the justice's house and I told her what I had heard and that Hank Wistrom, who was closer, confirmed it. The only thing we were concerned about was if Hank didn't like someone and he had a chance to sick the dogs on him, he would do it.

I assured the justice that Leo and I would go into the farmyard and talk to the new tenants and just generally look around and if we did not see anything suspicious, we would not use the warrant.

When we pulled into the yard, a small rugged man came out of the house dressed in blue bib overalls. We introduced everyone all around. The man did not seem nervous. When we asked if he had heard a shot about 3 a.m., he said he didn't. I then told Leo to take a hike out onto the field south and west of the buildings and see if he could see a fresh drag mark or anything else.

After Leo left, I pointed out to this man two blood spots on his overalls each about the size of a dime. His excuse for that was he had a part-time job butchering animals for a small slaughter house two miles north of Blackduck, and that he had been called in the day before to kill, dress-out, and half two beef. I got on the radio in my patrol car and called the dispatcher at Thief River Falls. I instructed him to make a telephone call to the Blackduck locker plant and slaughterhouse to see if, in fact, this man had been employed the previous day to slaughter two beef cattle. In about ten minutes, the dispatcher called back and said this man had worked at the slaughterhouse.

Eventually Leo came back into the yard and said he could find nothing suspicious. Then Leo and I got off to ourselves, and we had a private little conference. I wanted to use the warrant and search the buildings, but Leo warned against it and reminded me of my promise to Justice Quale. So the two of us went over and thanked the new farm resident for his cooperation and wished him well in his new home.

Leo got in behind the wheel of my patrol car, and I crawled into the passenger seat, and we started back to Kelliher to return the warrant and report to Justice Quale. I'll admit I was disgruntled because I felt sure someone had killed a deer on me and gotten away with it.

As we proceeded down this gravel road, I thought I saw a large spot of blood on the road. I told Leo to stop and back up so I could check it out better. He insisted it was my imagination. I finally had to get real insistent, and he did stop and back up. I got out of the car and checked. It was blood and there were deer tracks in the gravel. Then I could see down in the ditch that the weeds were matted down as though something had lain there.

Then looking into the brush, I could see where something had gone and there were patches of blood on the ground. I followed this for about a hundred yards and I came across a gut pile from a deer and on top of the pile were the testicles of the deer. This is some outlaws' way of showing disdain for the DNR.

I noticed the deer then had been dragged south about one hundred feet to an old abandoned gravel pit. At this point, I met Leo. He had found where the violator had driven his vehicle off the country road back into this pit site where he apparently dressed out the deer. Leo also called my attention to the strange vehicle tracks. In fact, he said they look like turkey tracks.

These tracks came out to the county road and proceeded south to a crossroad. I got out of the car and walked to the intersection and noted the tracks turned west. This is a dead end road and about a half a dozen people live down this road. Half of these people think it is their God given right to shoot a deer any time they want fresh meat. So as we came to each farm, I checked at each driveway, but the car continued down the road. Eventually we came to the last farm and there the tracks turned in. I walked following the tracks right up to what looked like a brand new car. It had tires that created this strange track. These were the first steel belted tires we had ever seen. The car was a sedan backed up to a closed garage door. Leo and I looked the back end of the car over and found one small blood spot on the bumper and several small blood spots in the leaves on the ground behind the car. A Mr. Mohstad owned this farm. I had picked his son up a year before for possession of venison in closed season. His son, David Mohstad, had lived in a farm across the road and at that time had just completed twenty years in the U.S. Navy.

So, I left Leo to stay by the car, and I went over to the house and rapped on the back door. Eventually, Mr. Mohstad came to the door and I told him who I was even though I'm sure he knew who I was and why I was there. I asked Mr. Mohstad who the car belonged to. He said it was his son David's car. So I told him to send him out. The father then advised me he was shaving, but that he would be out as soon as he finished.

In about ten minutes, David came out and obviously he had cut himself in a least a dozen places. He had little pieces of toilet paper stuck all over his face and you could see a red blood spot in the middle of each piece. The whole situation was starting to become funny.

However, when I told David to open the trunk of the car and the garage door he became real belligerent and asked if I had a search warrant and if not to get the hell off his dad's property. I then asked David, "Do you really want a search warrant?"

And he said, "Yes."

So I turned to Leo and told him to go into Kelliher, find Justice Quale, and get a search warrant for all the buildings and grounds of the Mohstad farm. At that point, David ordered me off the property. Then I let him know I was in what the law calls hot pursuit and no way would I leave this car or garage unguarded until Leo got back with the warrant.

At that point, David gave up, unlocked the trunk of the car and opened the garage. The deer was in the trunk skinned out and quartered, and wrapped in a clean sheet. I then advised David I could seize the car and eventually it would be confiscated, and he rather sheepishly said, "I figured I would lose the car when you guys turned in the driveway." So I told him if he would give me the gun he shot the deer with I would not seize the car, and also I advised him I could charge him with a gross misdemeanor. However, if he would promise to stop this taking deer illegally, I would just charge him with taking a deer in closed season which is a misdemeanor and he would probably pay a fine of 300 dollars and his rifle, a Ruger 44 caliber with a scope, would be confiscated. He promised me he would mend his ways and the above was the penalty. I also told him if I ever caught him again I would write the maximum charge and seize everything involved. To my knowledge, he kept his promise to me while I was stationed at Waskish. I have reason to believe he shot a big buck in closed season during the tour of duty of the third warden at the Waskish station after I left.

And, oh yes, about four days later while on patrol in an area about a half mile north of the new farmer tenant I heard crows and ravens hollering back in the woods so I investigated and found the remains of chunks of deer meat all cut up. Some of the meat had been packaged but the paper had been torn open and the meat pretty well eaten and starting to smell and covered with raven droppings. I should have used the search warrant on the new tenant.

Chapter 47/ EMMET AND LLOYD CARRIGAN

It was around noon on an early September day in 1972. I was at my residence in the state house at Waskish, Minnesota when I received a telephone call from Leo Manthei, my neighbor warden at Blackduck. He asked me to meet him at his residence as soon as possible. He suggested I bring my sleeping bag and anything else I might need for a possible long stake out.

I threw some things together and took off for Blackduck within a half an hour. When I got to Leo's house, I asked him what he had. He said some farmer living in Hornet Township came in with the back leg of a deer that his dog had just brought home. He showed me the leg and it was obvious it was off a fresh kill. Anytime something like this shows up in Hornet Township, our suspicions are aroused that it could be one of the Carrigans. The Carrigan old folks have a farm there and they have some young men that have a history of killing anything that can be sold. Leo was still busy gathering up some grub.

Then Leo dug out a Beltrami County map and showed me where the old Carrigans lived, and also the location of the farm of the farmer who brought in the deer leg. It was Leo's idea to hide our car about a mile west of the Carrigan's then come through to the back side of Carrigan's farm and see if we could find any other deer parts.

We drove out to this area where we ditched the car. We left most of our supplies in the car. We only took with us, in a small packsack, what we thought we might need. We finally got in an area where we could just barely see the old Carrigan's house. We started hunting around. There was evidence of a car being driven back on the pasture. Within a half an hour, we found, in a small stand of white spruce, some tubs and boxes full of quartered-out deer carcasses. We were able to determine that there were three deer for sure.

We could just barely make out the farmhouse through the brush and trees. We were elated to find something so quick. Also, we were pretty sure that within a short time someone would come to pick it up. We were pretty sure that the boys had a buyer some place and they would be anxious to get their money. We discussed what kind of charge to put against the perpetrators when and if we caught them. Leo said we would wait until the people came and started to pick up the meat. Then we would come out of hiding and make our arrest. I told Leo that would be a misdemeanor charge and the maximum fine could only be $300.00 and/or ninety days in jail. I suggested to Leo, "If this is the Carrigans, why don't we take them on a gross misdemeanor?"

Leo then asked, "How can we do that?"

I told Leo we will stay hidden until they get all the meat loaded. Then when they get in the vehicle, we will rush them, one of us on either side. Then we can charge them with transporting a big game animal in a motor vehicle in closed season and we will have the authority to seize the vehicle. That will really cut into their profits.

Leo was a bit apprehensive and made the statement, "What if they get in their vehicle, get it started, and get away from us? Our car is almost a mile away and we would end up with nothing."

I told Leo that's not going to happen. So we located a good place to hide. We would be separated by about forty feet. I told Leo when I said "Now" go for his side of the vehicle and I would go for the other side. We would be about fifty feet from the meat.

Along around five-thirty, a car came into the backside of the Carrigan house. Leo took up our binoculars and he announced it's Emmet and his brother, Lloyd, who works for the mill in International Falls. The two men went into the house.

Then Leo spoke up and said that pretty well confirms the rumor that Lloyd contacts the buyers from his fellow employees at the mill and then Emmet and he go out and fill the orders. The rumor at the time was that a deer dressed out brought twenty-five dollars delivered.

Game violators sentenced

Emmett Carrigan, Blackduck, and Lloyd Carrigan, International Falls were sentenced $600 fines each and up to one year in jail in district court Tuesday on charges of transporting a big game animal taken in violation of the law.

In Emmett's case, 9 months of the sentence was stayed and he was ordered to spend 90 days in the Beltrami County Jail under the Huber Law, which means he will be released to go to his job and

must serve his sentence on weekends.

Lloyd's jail sentence was stayed for one year and he was placed on probation for that period of time.

Both brothers will not be allowed to hunt, fish, or trap during their year - long probations.

Newspaper article

On another incident when Emmet was caught, I casually asked him how many deer he had killed that year. He said he thought it was around two hundred and twenty. That constitutes a pretty fair operation.

After about an hour and a half, the two men came out of the house, got in the car, and turned on the headlights as it was starting to be a bit dusky. They drove right back to us and backed the car right to the meat. They both got out and loaded all the meat into the trunk of the car. Then the men got into the car. Emmet was the driver and on my side. Lloyd was on the passenger side. Just as the doors slammed, I hollered, "Now!" We fairly shot across that space. I jerked Emmet's door open, just as he was trying to start the motor. I grabbed his arm and ordered him out of the car. Emmet turned sideways with both feet on the ground. He lowered his head and said, "You got us good this time." That was a typical response from Emmet. He would usually try to make the decision right at the first contact. However, he usually said, "You ain't got us good this time."

So we made out the summons, seizure receipts and we all piled into the car. I believe Leo drove. We took them down to Bemidji to lock them up. We went back and got Leo's patrol car and came back to Leo's house. Leo then started to growl, "What am I going to do with their car? I'm responsible for that car until after the trial and that probably won't come 'til next year."

I told Leo, "Quit your bitching. You got them and you got them good!"

Chapter 48/ WHEN GOOD FRIENDS PART COMPANY: ADNEY LAKE

One day in late summer of 1976, I was on patrol in Crow Wing County. I came down to Adney Lake and I noticed several boats fishing in the northwest part of the lake. I maneuvered my car as close as possible to these boats without being noticed, shut off the motor, and hooked up my spotting scope on the window mount and settled down for a bit of surveillance. One of the boats had three black men and they seemed to be far more successful at catching fish than the fishermen in the other boats. In fact, there hardly seemed to be a moment that at least one of the men wasn't pulling in a fish. They were catching crappies and they appeared to be about three to the pound. Also I noticed that they put their catch into one of two wire mesh fish bags hanging on either side of the boat. They were in a 16-foot aluminum Lund boat with about a ten-horse power motor on the back and they were anchored. They were about 100 yards from shore. I could make out the boat license numbers, so I called them into the dispatcher at Brainerd to find out who the boat owner was.

Before the dispatcher got back to me, the man up in the bow of the boat started pulling in the anchor. The other two men lifted in the fish sacks and I could see both bags were stuffed full. Now the limit on crappies is fifteen fish and there was no doubt in my mind they had way over their limit. The man in the back started up the motor and headed the boat in a southeasterly direction across the lake. There are a number of summer cabins plus Smith's Resort on the lake, and as I would have to drive on the road around the lake and at no time would I be able to see the lake or where the boat would pull in, I decided to sit tight until I knew where the boat was going to land. When the boat was still moving, however, it was close to the southeast shore. I got a call from the dispatcher that the boat belonged to Smith's Resort. I took off immediately and it took me about fifteen minutes to drive to Smith's Resort. On the way, I heard Art Gensmer check in on the radio. He is the conservation officer from Pine River. He advised me that he was only about fifteen miles away so I asked him to join me, as I believed we would find other boats with too many fish.

When I arrived at the entrance to the Smith Resort, I positioned my car at the entrance so no cars could get out. Then, I went in on foot. I checked two or three cabins and they were vacant. Then I heard an outboard motor start up. I hurried down to the lakeshore past the resort lodge and I could see what looked like the boat with the three men that I wanted to question heading back to the crappie bed in the northwest end of the lake. I checked the lodge and a couple of other buildings. As near as I could make out, there was no one in camp. Also, there were no boats tied up to the dock. Eventually, I came to the fish-cleaning shack located east of the lodge and at the lakeshore. Inside was a counter the full length of one wall with a double-bin kitchen sink in the middle. In these double sink bins were crappies— lots of crappies! Using a tub that was in there to count the fish into, I counted 110 crappies and one small northern. About two-thirds of these fish seemed to be alive.

I went out to my patrol car as I had decided to move it to a neighboring cabin, just east of the Smith resort, where I could watch out on the lake for the return of my fishermen. Also, I checked to see where Art Gensmer was. He was still coming but was not familiar with my area so he had to check his maps. I told him the status up to that point and where he would find me.

When I found a good place to park my patrol car so that I could observe without being too obvious, I stepped out of my car and walked slowly over toward the lodge. I heard an outboard motor start up over east of me. It seemed to be coming towards me, so I hunkered down. Two men in a red Lund boat came into sight, pulled up to the dock, tied up their boat, and came walking toward me carrying fishing poles, tackle boxes, and all the other good things fishermen have to have. As I had an old jacket on over my warden shirt, they thought I was another fisherman. I asked them what kind of luck they had and they told me they caught a nice mess of crappies, however they did not fill up. They had twenty-eight big black crappies averaging about three-fourths of a pound each—nice fish. So I opened up my jacket, identified myself, and told them I wanted to see their licenses. One man had a resident Minnesota angling license (he was about thirty years old and he lived in Minneapolis). The other man handed me a sportsman's license from the State of Arizona. I told him that license was no good in Minnesota. He told me that license was good anywhere in the United States. He was a young man about twenty-three years old. He said he was studying for the ministry at some college in Wisconsin. He had come over to Minnesota to visit his friend and they had decided to spend the weekend fishing.

I took the fish and their gear and walked them over to my patrol car. At this point, I had not told them my intentions. Also, now I could hear an outboard motor coming across the lake and I told these two men that that boat coming was the prime reason for my being there. I told them to sit down on a bench until I checked these other people out. Also, I advised them another warden was due any minute so don't get any goofy ideas of taking a powder.

Shortly, this other boat pulled in and tied up to the dock. These were the same three black men I had seen earlier. I asked to see their licenses and they all handed them to me. I examined the licenses and then shoved them in my shirt pocket. I looked in their boat for fish and the bottom of their boat was literally covered with fish. They must have bit so fast they couldn't put them in the fish bags. However, there was a gunnysack there, so I started counting and stuffing them in the sack. There were forty-two crappies in the boat. I looked up and noticed one of the men was missing. I ran with the sack of fish to the fish-cleaning shack and found the one man throwing handfuls of the crappies back in the lake. I ordered him to stop and told him I had already counted the fish. The crappies were dead and floating on top so I managed to salvage most of them. I acquired another gunnysack to put the crappies from the cleaning shack in, and also the ones I picked up along the shore and in the water where this man had thrown them.

I carried the two sacks of crappies to my car and put them in the trunk. At this time, Art Gensmer arrived and I started to fill him in when I heard a lot of shouting down at the dock. I ran over there and I could see the three men waving at three women in another boat about 200 feet out in the lake from the docks. These three women were throwing fish out of their boat back into the lake. Eventually, the boat with the three women came into the dock. They didn't have a fish in the boat. These women were black people also and I assume probably the wives or girl friends of the three men whose licenses I had in my pocket.

Now these two men that I had encountered earlier started to get a little hostile and wanted their fish and wanted to be on their way. These two men by the way are white people, not that it makes any difference. I gave the three licenses of the black men to Art Gensmer and told him to either make out a summons for each of them for over the limit, or if he didn't want to, he could tell them I would take care of them as soon as I could get the other two men taken care of.

I then turned to the two white men who were by my patrol car. I told the younger man with the Arizona license that I was going to write a summons on him and the charge would be "angling for fish in public waters without first procuring an angling license." He asked what that would cost him. I showed him the bail schedule and he would have to post $50.00 cash with me or the clerk of court before I would release him. At this time, I got to thinking I hadn't actually seen him fishing and I told him so. At that, he let me know in no uncertain terms that he was not fishing.

I turned to his partner from Minneapolis, who had a valid fishing license, and told him I would have to write the summons against him for having thirteen crappies over his legal possession limit. He got a shocked look on his face then he said, as he pointed to his partner, "Let me tell you, officer. That son-of-a-bitch was fishing." I charged the man from Arizona, collected $50.00 cash from him, gave him a receipt, and sent the two men on their way with fifteen crappies.

Now I turned my attention to the three black men with Art Gensmer. Only now, instead of three black men, there are about fifteen black people. They all claimed they put those crappies in the fish-cleaning shack. I knew better, so I told Art to give me their fishing licenses and I would write them up. Then Art said he had returned the licenses to them. At least I had their fish and I told them no way were they going to get them back. I also told them if I saw them fishing any more that day on the lake and taking crappies, (as I, for sure, had these three with 42 crappies) and if they took more than three crappies, I would write them up.

At that, I left and so did Art Gensmer. I thought I had better call my supervisor because I was sure there would be some fall out from the N.A.A.C.P. The chief warden told me that I best go back and return the fish. I did so but it was a bitter pill to swallow.

Chapter 49/ THE NEW SCHOOL SUPERINTENDENT

I was on my way home to Waskish. I had been in Municipal Court in Bemidji to testify on a Division of Waters charge.

Leo was out in North Dakota goose hunting for four days. He had asked me if I got down near Blackduck Lake or Chinaman Lake to check around especially at Tennis Shoe Pass. He asked me to do this just to show there was some law enforcement around.

I stopped off at Tennis Shoe Pass and checked a dozen or so hunters. It was around 3:30 p.m. There were several high school lads down at the pass and they were well schooled in migratory waterfowl hunting laws.

About that same time, a duck boat with two men in it came out from a small clump of bull rushes and maneuvered around a bunch of decoys. They picked up a couple of dead ducks.

They had an outboard motor on the transom and a five or six horsepower engine. They were using that for propulsion. They moved out into open water. Then the man up in the bow came up with a double-barreled shotgun and they started chasing cripples and shooting at them.

About then, I was wishing Manthei was home to take care of his own problems. Several of the hunters asked me, "Are you a witness to that?"

I told them, "Yes, but I don't have a boat."

One of the lads said, "I think someone will loan you a boat and motor."

I started walking to the west. Two of the lakeshore residents were reluctant to let me take their equipment. At the third place I checked, there was a woman. There was a small boat and motor tied up to their dock. Her husband was at work and she was reluctant to let me take their boat. She saw I was in a game warden uniform. She asked, "Where's Leo?"

I told her, "He's out in North Dakota goose hunting."

She mumbled something like; "He's always out there." Then she got my name and said, "Go ahead and use the boat."

I started up the engine, untied the boat and took out after the two men. When I caught up to them and we all shut off our motors we could hear the hunters at the pass holler. "Yeah!"

The man in the front with the shotgun was from Iowa. He had all the correct licenses and stamps. So I wrote him up for shooting from a motor propelled vehicle at migratory waterfowl. I seized his gun and gave him a receipt for it.

Then I turned to the man operating the motor. He offered up his resident small game license with all the proper stamps. On checking his license he claimed Kelliher, Minnesota as his residence. I told him, "I know everyone in Kelliher and you're not one of them." Then a thought hit me and I asked, "Are you the new school superintendent?"

He acknowledged, "Yes I am and I'm in the process of moving my family into our new home."

All I could say was, "I hate to meet you this way, but I'm Bill Callies the game warden out of Waskish. Kelliher is in my district and every spring the former school superintendent allowed me to teach firearm safety for one hour every day in the school during school hours. I always taught all the sixth graders. I hope this thing I have to do won't change that."

He said, "It won't."

I wrote him up for the same charges as his partner. I had to run them to the local Justice of the Peace. Leo got two pinches and I got two assists.

The school superintendent kept his word.

Chapter 50/ *QUESTIONABLE ATTORNEY'S DECISION*

This incident occurred during the firearm deer season of 1973. It was in the middle of the week. I had made a decision to go to bed early with the intent of getting out checking hunters the following day. I rolled out of bed at 5:00 a.m. Legal shooting time started that day at 6:55 a.m.

I was out and rolling south of Waskish on Highway 72. I checked a couple of deer camps down near the old C.C. Camp. The hunters were just getting out of their sleeping bags. The day promised to be bright and clear. There were three or four inches of snow on the ground. It was getting a little light when I turned west on County Road 23. At the same time, I turned my lights out. County Road 23 goes straight west for a short distance then it swings south and then back west for a long straight stretch of six or so miles.

At this point, I could see two red taillights on the right hand side of the road about a half-mile past old Highway 72. I passed Renemo's home and farm buildings and then I could see several men out on the field behind Renemo's buildings. I stopped behind their car and picked up my state binoculars. I could see this group was standing around a small deer lying in the snow. I checked my pocket watch—it showed 6:10 a.m. I immediately called the dispatcher out of Thief River Falls for time confirmation. He said it was 6:12 a.m. I gave him my location and told him that I was going out on the field and to see what was going on. I noticed their car had their headlights on and the motor running.

I walked out on the field about a hundred yards to where the men were standing. Seems to me there were four men. I asked to see their deer licenses. Upon receipt of them, I stuck them in my pocket. Then I looked at the deer. It was warm and flexible and the entrails were not removed. There was blood coming out of the bullet hole and the mouth. I told these men, "Legal shooting time is 6:55 a.m. and it is now only 6:20 a.m. Do you have permission to shoot on Renemo's private property?" I also asked them, "Was the deer shot from the car?"

They said, "We don't know who owns the property and the shooter got out of the car before he shot."

I told them, "I could charge all of you with taking and possessing one deer in closed hours. However, if the shooter will come forward I will only charge him. I am going to seize the deer."

One of the hunters stepped forward and admitted to being the shooter. So I booked him into Justice of the Peace Court in Kelliher. I showed him the bail schedule and told him the Justice of the Peace Clara Quale would probably fine him $100.00 and $5.00 court costs. So I made out the arrest summons and the seizure receipt and he signed it. Then I dragged the deer to my car.

Later on I was informed that he had hired an attorney, a change of venue had been arranged and the whole thing had been dismissed and according to a letter from the county attorney it was all done in the interest of justice. It is my opinion that one attorney was taking care of another attorney and I would bet that hunter paid a lot more than the fine would have been. However, no record of this would be on file and he would not be denied the purchase of a deer license the following year. ·

In a way, I did get my licks in. I approached Esther Renemo and told her of the shooting on their back forty. I wasn't sure about her reaction because basically she and Ingvar had a strong dislike for game wardens. I was surprised when she approved of my actions but when I told her what the courts had done — one of the Renemo's attorneys had been involved. Their legal work was quite substantial. She told me that was the last nickel he would ever see of their money.

Chapter 51/ TULLIBEES IN MILLE LAC LAKE

When I moved to the Crosby-Ironton station, I became aware that the younger men knew little or nothing about gill netting for white fish and tullibees. The season was coming up in the early part of October. Back in the sixties and seventies, each fisherman could use two one hundred foot by three-foot gill nets. The cost at that time was one dollar for the license for each one hundred foot net. Also, you had to have an angling license and this type of fishing was restricted to resident anglers only. Gill nets could not be set in water more than six feet deep. Also, the licensee could clerk only his own net. All nets had to have the owner's name and address on one of the locator floats.

Brad Burgraff, my neighbor at Garrison, had as part of his district the northwest part of Mille Lacs Lake. He requested my assistance to check netters on Mille Lac. I don't believe there are any white fish in the lake but there are tons of tullibees.

I went down to Garrison Sunday morning around sunrise and picked up Brad. We started up Highway 169 to an area where we could see a big area of the lake. I hooked up my spotting scope and started looking for the flags of the gill net markers. I spotted quite a number about three quarters of a mile from shore. I asked Brad if he had any idea how deep the water was out there. He told me he had no idea. I rather assumed the nets had to be set in over six feet of water. So we sat and waited hoping for the owners of the nets would show up and clerk the nets.

Along around ten o'clock, a pretty nice boat with two men pulled into the area where the net markers were. I could see with the aid of the telescope one of the men grabbed one of the flag markers and started pulling the net in over the side gunnel of the boat. I could see that there were lots of fish hanging in the net. On completion of that net, they moved over and pulled in a second net, then a third net, and then a fourth net. That's the most two men could legally have. However, they pulled in a fifth net then on up to a total of nine nets. They had picked up five nets more than they could legally have. That, in itself, is five violations so we have to watch where this boat goes, intercept it, and check out the fishermen. It was a fair size boat with an I.O. motor. It seemed to be heading into a marina northeast of us, so we hurried to get ahead of them. We pulled into the marina and stayed out of sight. The boat pulled into one of the slots and the two men started unloading square type washtubs. Each tub contained a net and lots of fish.

We approached the men and told them who we were and that we wanted to check their angling licenses and netting licenses. The one man had neither angling nor netting license. The other man had an angling license and two netting licenses. He also had four netting licenses that belonged to other people. He was a hog and wrong too many ways. So, we started in writing summons and seizure slips. Then this boat owner started to get ugly and using abusive language.

I told him, "That's enough. You open your mouth one more time and I will seize your boat." That shut him up.

We loaded all of the tubs of nets and fish and headed for the justice of the peace, Bill Dewitt, on Borden Lake near Garrison. We dumped all the fish in a stock tank and counted them. There were over fourteen hundred tullibees.

I can't remember what the justice of the peace penalized these men, but I'm sure they knew they had been in court.

Brad and I went back to the marina and talked to the manager. He was pleased that we had caught them. He also told us these two had taken that many tullibees the day before. Later on that day, we went out to check the water depth about where they were netting. It was a reef with an average depth of five and a half feet.

Chapter 52/ END UP WITH A DUCK KILLER-1976

It all started one day in the fall of 1976. I had become acquainted with a property owner on Lower Mission Lake that offered to donate a piece of property to the State of Minnesota providing the DNR would develop a good public access for watercraft. This property is located on the northwest end of Lower Mission Lake in Crow Wing County. As I remember, this property was about one hundred feet wide and a quarter of a mile long. This would require building a road a quarter of a mile long for which, at the time, the department would be hard pressed to come up with the money. I located the property survey stakes. However, the state sent in one of their survey crews and confirmed the existing property stakes.

On this day, I spent some time cruising the property to try to locate the best place to run a road through from the county road to the lake for a minimum of cost. I came across a small area where there was evidence of fresh digging. There were eight or nine spots about two feet in diameter. One of the spots looked real fresh and the sandy loam soil was loose, so I started digging with my hands. I moved about a foot of earth in this hole when I came across about a half a dozen of nice sized sunfish. I went back to the patrol car and got my shovel, came back to the site, and at each hole I found buried fish in the round. I found a lot of nice size sunfish, some crappies, and a couple of black bass. This was wanton waste and there was no excuse for anyone taking these fish and not making use of them. If they didn't want them after having the fun of catching them, release them back into the water. The fish were not salvageable so I covered them and tried to make the area look the way I found it.

It was late in the afternoon and I knew I should go home because my wife said she would have supper ready around 6 p.m. Also I knew the individual that buried those fish might be coming out to catch some more sunnies or crappies. I thought of calling the dispatcher at Brainerd on my radio and have him call my wife that I might be late getting home. However, I cancelled that thought because there were so many monitors in the area and I might inadvertently alert the party I would be watching for.

I drove the patrol car north around Upper Mission Lake and then down a small road on the east side of Upper Mission and finally to a small opening on the northeast portion of Lower Mission Lake. It was located almost directly across from the location of the proposed access site. I would have a clear view with the aid of my binoculars from this location.

I brought the patrol car to a stop and just stepped out of the vehicle when I saw four teal fly past coming from the south flying in a northerly direction. They were about 30 feet from shore and about ten feet in the air. One bird seemed to have a hard time flying to try to keep up with the other three. They all seemed hell bent on getting out of there. I had not heard any shooting so I assumed something had disturbed them. I froze on the spot, hanging onto the car door so as not to make any noise. There was a heavy growth of brush to the south of me and it extended from the lakeshore to about fifty feet back from the shore.

Within seconds, a man burst out into the water. He had on

work clothes and rubber boots and he was obviously in a hurry. Then I saw him pick up a duck in the weedy water, then a second duck, and a third duck. I started running south on the small open ridge and I could see through the brush that this individual turned and headed back for shore. He came into the brush, picked up his shotgun, and with his gun in one hand and three ducks held by the neck in his other hand, he came right toward me. He didn't seem to see me until we were about ten feet apart. I stepped forward and said, "Game Warden, I'll take that gun and those ducks." He almost seemed in a state of shock. His only problem was the duck-hunting season wouldn't be open for a couple of weeks.

I instructed him to come over to the patrol car where I made out a summons to appear before Judge Longfellow that coming Friday. I also made out seizure slips for the three ducks and his shotgun, which as I remember was a rather expensive, gas operated, semi-automatic 12 gauge in like-new condition. I then released him on his own recognizance as he was a Minnesota resident and had signed the summons that he would appear in court at the time set on the summons.

The following Friday, I went to the courthouse in Crosby, Minnesota. I checked in with one of the clerks of court. I submitted the court's copies of the summons I had issued so she could put them on that day's calendar. The Honorable Henry W. Longfellow was one of the county judges and he was usually the judge from Brainerd, the county seat that heard the complaints from that part of the county on Friday. Judge Longfellow was an intelligent man, however, he seemed to know little or nothing about game and fish violations and often I had to show him the specific law in the book that the alleged violator was in violation of. Also, because he did not consider violations of the game and fish laws too important, he was inclined to reduce the fines as recommended by the State of Minnesota and other judges. This was a very popular situation enjoyed by any violator that was found guilty.

The Department of the Interior controls ducks, being a migratory bird, and it was usually the policy of the federal government at that time to recommend a fine of $100.00 per bird. Finally it was the time for my illegal duck hunter to appear before Judge Longfellow. The complaint was read to him —"did take, possess three green wing teal ducks in closed season." The man entered a plea of guilty. The judge did not ask me for any of the circumstances he just said, "I accept your plea of guilty, the fine is twenty five dollars, and pay the clerk of court." He got his billfold out, paid the clerk of court and he received a receipt. He then sat down in the back of the courtroom.

After court was over, I walked to the back of the courtroom where a rather ugly duck hunter confronted me. He asked me if I was satisfied with what I had done to him. Then he said, "I want my gun back now." I told him he came out of that courtroom smelling like a rose.

Then I told him you aren't getting that gun back and I showed him in the law book where if someone takes or attempts to take wild animals, the instrument that was used to take can be confiscated by the State of Minnesota. At this point, he became quite belligerent so I let him know that the gun would appear at the annual gun auction in St. Paul the following spring and he could attend the auction and if he bid high enough he could get his gun back.

This did not seem to appease this man one bit so I told him I would give him one other option. "What's that?" he said.

I told him, "You bring one of those three ducks back to life and I will give you your gun back." He yelled something unfriendly and off he went and that's the last I ever saw of him.

Later that fall, during the deer season, I was checking deer hunters in an area south of Lower Mission Lake. One deer hunter that checked out okay made the statement I'll bet you're that old white haired fart that pinched my partner. Not knowing who he was talking about, I inquired who that might be. He mentioned his name, which meant nothing to me, and then he went on to say I got him with three ducks before season and wouldn't give his gun back.

Not knowing this man's feeling on the subject I was really pleased when he stuck his hand out and said I want to shake your hand. He said they worked for Potlatch at Brainerd and he said this partner of his bragged about living off the fat of the land. He told me that the day before I caught him he had killed four ducks out in front of his house. He went on to say he moved up there from northeast Minneapolis, bought some property on Lower Mission Lake, built a house, got a job with Potlatch, created a big garden in his yard, and lived off of deer, partridge, squirrels, rabbits, and fish the year round.

The guy then said, "I'm glad you got him. He was long overdue."

Chapter 53/ RACCOON

It was in the fall of 1976. I was stationed at the Crosby, Ironton station in Crow Wing County. It was about a week before the mink and muskrat trapping season was to open. I was patrolling my area south of Crosby near Clearwater Lake. There were the remnants of a huge blow down of trees caused by a tornado that had gone through this area a couple of years before. I could see off to the west what looked like a small stream. Curiosity got the best of me. It looked like an area an early trapper might try to pick off some early mink.

Due to the tangle of trees, it took a little time to get to this small stream. I followed this stream looking for places I would make a mink set if I were trapping. Sure enough I found one trap, then another. Eventually I located a half a dozen sets of #1½ traps. Also, I came across a snare made out of #14 wire. It was a crude set but it could take a small deer.

Realizing these traps were probably set by some local person and he might come along and see my patrol car, I thought it best to get back to the patrol car and get out of there. I did snap one of the traps. Occasionally, a trap that is set real lean will snap without anything touching it. Hopefully, the trapper doesn't become suspicious so he will reset the trap. That way, I could assume he hadn't seen me, or the patrol car, or that I had just missed him.

The next morning I was up early and out in the vicinity of the trap line. I parked my car in an out of the way place and walked into the creek where the traps were. I set up in a place where I could see if the trapper came to clerk his traps without him seeing me. I lay there from sunrise until noon and no trapper showed up. So I checked the trap that I had snapped off and it was still snapped.

Raccoon in trap before Bill released him

So, now I'm reasonably sure the trapper is wise to me and never will show up. All he will be out are his traps. So I started to pick up his traps. I noticed, also, he did not have his name or address on any of the traps. That is a requirement in the State of Minnesota.

Down near the far end of the trap line, I found a big old male raccoon caught by one of his front feet in the trap. The season for trapping raccoon was open, however, you aren't allowed to set a trap within fifty-feet of any waterway for raccoon.

This old raccoon has got a problem and now I've got one. Raccoon have got a mouth full of sharp teeth and they are fighters. I didn't want to kill the raccoon and I had nothing with me to hold him back if I tried to release him. So, I sat down on an old log within ten-feet of him and started talking to him. He would chatter back. It was a Mexican stand off for almost a half hour. Me telling him in a soft voice, "If you won't bite me, I'll turn you loose." I had my camera along so I took his picture. Then real slowly he backed under the roots of an old tree as far as the chain on the trap would allow him. His foot with the trap on it was extended out.

I approached real slow talking to him all the way. I extended my right hand out real slow, took hold of the spring on the trap, squeezed it, and shook the trap jaws. That old raccoon pulled out his foot and started down stream. He went about twenty-feet, turned and looked at me, and then disappeared into the brush.

Chapter 54/ DONALD LARSON: STAR ROUTE DEERWOOD

On February 1, 1976 about 3 p.m., I was in my patrol car and accompanied by conservation officer, Duane Lohtka, driving east on County Road 12 (Deerwood short cut) when the aircraft observer advised us by radio that there were four snowmobiles approaching County Road 12 from the north. The aircraft observer put us in a position to intercept the machines to make a routine check of their licenses. When the machines appeared, I got out of the patrol car and went across the road to check the licenses. The first sled was owned and operated by Danno Mahoney. The machine was properly licensed. A Mrs. Larson operated the second machine. It was a new Scorpion with an expired license application receipt (a summons was written earlier in the day on this machine by Brad Burgraff). The next two machines stopped about 100 feet back. I proceeded to them. The third machine, owned by Danno Mahoney, was properly licensed and operated by a woman. I then proceeded to the fourth machine. This machine, a Scorpion Stinger, had a set of numbers on one side, E4473. There were no Minnesota decals on either side. When I asked the operator if he had an ownership card, he told me, "Get out of my way and you are not giving me any ticket."

When I told him the machine was not licensed, he told me that was none of my business. I asked the man to turn off his machine. He pushed at me with his hands and told me there was something wrong with his clutch. He also said that he could not hold the machine and that he might run me down. I stepped off the sled trail to the right of the machine, noticed a crutch on the machine foot rail and that he had an unusual boot on one foot. When I asked again that he turn off the machine, he took the key and turned off the machine. Before the motor stopped spinning, he turned the key back on. The motor backfired once and then continued to operate properly. Then the man dropped onto the machine with one knee, took hold of the throttle, and started to leave.

I ordered him to stop and I grabbed the lift bar on the back of the machine. I called to him to "Hold it" but he ignored my commands. He jerked me to the ground and proceeded toward the other machines. As he went past my partner, Duane Lohtka, Duane took him off the machine. As soon as his hand came off the throttle, the machine came to a halt. I got to my feet and turned the key off on the machine and stopped the motor. Officer Lohtka was holding the man around the chest from the backside. Officer Lohtka said he thought the man should be put in jail, however, the man with him asked me not to do this and that he would be responsible for him. I got a summons book from Lohtka and wrote the man, Donald Larson, up for operating an unlicensed snowmobile.

During the process of writing the summons, Larson made the statement, "For your own good you had better not ever be brought into the emergency ward at the hospital when I am on duty." At this time, he told me he was a doctor.

I questioned that he could be a doctor the way he was acting. However, later that evening, I checked with the Crosby police and they confirmed his position.

The man and woman (Mahoney's) that were with the Larsons seemed ashamed of his conduct and assured me they would be responsible for him and get him home if I would overlook his actions and not put him in jail. So I told them to see to it that he took the machine straight home and that he was not to operate it until it was licensed. All the while, I was talking to Mr. Mahoney; the doctor was standing on one foot and violently kicking the snow with his other foot. All this time the crutch remained on the machine. Officer Lohtka told me he thought I should charge him for failure to stop under M.S. 84:873.

That evening, Dr. Larson called me to tell me he was going to sue me. On February 2, at 11:15, Dr. Larson called and left a message to return his call. I returned his call at 4 p.m. and he advised me he would be in court with his attorney. He said he lost a days work because of the way we handled him. He talked some more of suing. I just told him to appear in court and answer to the complaints.

"P.S. For your information, Brad Burgraff was the conservation officer from Garrison. This Donald Larson dragged me the 100 feet from where he stopped to the roadway with his snowmobile."

The above statement that I wrote up was for the county attorney because the man said he was pleading not guilty and intended to contest me in court. Copies of my statements were given to the defense attorney.

When I testified, the defense attorney really tried everything, short of shooting me, to keep me from stating the threat Doctor Larson made to me.

Also later, I found out Doctor Larson had a broken leg and foot that occurred about two months earlier when he kicked his lawn mower. I am reasonably sure when he was kicking the snow, while I was making out the summons, that he was attempting to re-break his leg.

I met more nuts around Crosby. Anyway, Judge Longfellow found him guilty, but I can't remember the penalty.

The attorney that attempted to defend Larson got the word out that he would take any case for people I arrested for whatever the bail schedule was set up for that particular offense. The attorney said if he lost, he would not collect a fee.

That fall, this attorney invited me to his house and apologized for taking this position. He lost every case. He even told me I was doing a good job. He said the people around Crosby, Deerwood, and Emily just weren't used to having to obey game and fish laws.

Chapter 55/ DEAN LAKE - INDIANS - POLITICS 1976

It was the middle of August and the wild rice was getting ripe. I had at least a dozen areas in my district that had some outstanding wild rice patches. The rice buyers would be paying from a dollar and a quarter to two dollars a pound for good long-grain, ripe rice.

I had some characters in my district that would be harvesting rice before the state opened the season if they felt they could do it without getting caught. I heard rumors of two young men the year before that had harvested five thousand pounds in about two weeks. I had caught these two men shooting too many ducks the fall before, shortly after I had transferred to the Crosby station.

The various rice fields are monitored as to the ripeness of the rice. When the state authorities get notice from the various wild rice commissions that the rice is ripe, a notice goes out via newspapers, radio, telephone, and word of mouth.

The season usually opens for two hours (ten to twelve a.m.) on the first day, closes on the second day, and opens again on the third day for two hours. It usually continues like this for the first week. However, it always closes on Sunday. Usually on the second week, the state allows four hours every day starting at nine a.m.

As a rule, these wild rice thieves work at night. During the day, the conservation department aircraft can easily spot the thieves.

I had one lake in my district that had a super crop of wild rice. It was Dean Lake in the northeast part of Crow Wing County. There were three trails at that time to get into the lake. One road led into a farm on the southeast corner of the lake. The farmer used to keep a locked gate into his place so he could charge ricers for the privilege of going across his property with access to Dean Lake.

Bill checking the rice

A second trail ended up on a government lot on the southwest corner of Dean Lake. The Indian band from Mille Lacs Lake claimed this property was part of their reservation. Then there was an old logging trail located in the northwest part of the lake that usually was not navigable most of the time. I thought this might be the route some early rice thieves might try.

Night after night, I sneaked in there hoping to catch an early ricer. On a quiet night, you could hear the ricer's flails swishing the rice kernels into the canoe or boat. If you had a clear night you could see out onto the lake with binoculars. I put in a week of nights on Dean Lake waiting for an illegal ricer and none ever showed.

Tuesday night at midnight was the end of our workweek. So the first thing Wednesday morning I would complete my weekly reports and get them in the mail.

That Tuesday, the state announced the ricing season would open at ten a.m. on Wednesday. After I had made out my reports and put them in the mail, I went back to Dean Lake to see to it that the ricers waited until ten a.m. There were no early harvesters.

There is a clause in the law that says if there is a rice area in your district where the rice is not ripe, the local warden has the authority to post the lake for "No harvesting" until he knows the rice is ripe.

I did receive a letter from my regional supervisor suggesting two Indians thought the rice was too green in Dean Lake to harvest. The rice was ripe so I ignored the letter. I heard later these two men were flown over Dean Lake in a state plane and they made this observation from the air going about a hundred miles an hour.

I checked with several rice buyers that bought rice from the ricers just as the harvesters came off the lake. They were very pleased with the quality and the ripeness of the rice on the first day.

Seventeen Mile Lake was in my neighbor's district. He is Warden Duane Lohtka of the Aitken district. He apparently thought these two Indians knew more than he did so he posted Seventeen Mile Lake to pacify the Indians and the politicians.

Checking the rice

The following Friday was the day the county court judge came over to Crosby to hear the cases accumulated for the week by the game and fish, the highway patrol, and the Crosby city police. The judge usually started court at nine o'clock a.m. I would make it a point to get to the courthouse about eight fifteen to turn in my arrest charges to the clerk of court so she could get them on the docket for that day. I had one case where Duane Lohtka assisted me on an arrest. I had requested that he be present that day in the event the judge wanted to hear both of our testimonies.

About twenty minutes to nine, Fred Hammer, my area supervisor, came into the clerk's office and wanted to speak to me in private. Fred, Duane, and I went into a closed office. It was then and there that I was told to go out to Dean Lake and post it for "No rice harvest". I told Fred the rice was ripe and I would not close the lake to rice harvest. Fred then told me I was subject to a thirty-day lay-off for failing to obey a direct order. I told Fred to go ahead and give me thirty days off but that lake is staying open. He then said if I didn't go post the lake, he would have to go post the lake and stop the rice harvest.

I told Fred if you post that lake I will go up and take the signs down. Then I went on and told him that rice was ripe four days before the season opened and he could check my reports for confirmation. Then too, how could he tell the people that had harvested rice last Wednesday or the rice buyers that bought the rice that the rice from Dean Lake was green?

Fred backed off a bit and told me to call Joe Jovonovich, our regional supervisor. I told him I would right after court because the judge had arrived and had gone up to the courtroom with the clerk of court.

After court was over, Supervisor Hammer, Duane Lohtka, and I went to my home. I called Joe Jovonovich, the regional supervisor. He gave me the same instructions and threats that Fred Hammer had given me. He did say he hoped I would cooperate because he didn't want to suspend me for thirty days. He also advised me that this was a direct order from the commissioner's office in St. Paul. I told Jovonovich I was getting tired of cow towing to the Indian politicians. The Mille Lac Band had a fantastic stand of rice on their reservation that they would harvest on the opening day and then they would go to Dean Lake at a later date that would be controlled. At least that was what they were trying to do.

At this point, Supervisor Jovonovich said those were his instructions from the commissioner's office. So I told Joe if you want me to call the commissioner, I would be glad to and explain the facts of wild rice harvest. He gave me their number. I ended up with the assistant commissioner, Clarence Buckman. I told him who I was and that I had been verbally told by my immediate supervisor to close Dean Lake for the harvesting of wild rice. However, it was my knowledge that the rice on Dean Lake was ripe and had been ripe over a week and I had no intention of posting the lake for no harvest.

He still insisted I post the lake and failure to do so, at his command, would cause me to be suspended for thirty days.

I told him the ricers and buyers harvested and purchased wild rice the day before yesterday and were at that moment harvesting rice. Those people know more about the wild rice in Dean Lake than the whole conservation department. The rice was and is ripe and no way was I going to knuckle under to a couple of Indian politicians.

Buckman told me I hadn't heard the end of this problem and he slammed down the telephone. I never was suspended and eventually my regional supervisor wrote me and congratulated me.

Footnote: About a year later, Regional Supervisor Don Fultz denied me the transfer to the Orr station. He used my "aggressive attitude to authority" as the reason. It took me almost eight months to gain my right to the Orr station.

The Representative Doug Johnson and Senator Bob Lessard championed Don Fultz. Don Fultz was eventually fired for stealing money and possession of illegal firearms.

Bill poling during ricing to check ricers

STATE OF MINNESOTA

DEPARTMENT OF NATURAL RESOURCES-ENFORCEMENT

Office Memorandum

TO   : William Callies

DATE: 8/17/76

FROM   : Joe Jovonovich

SUBJECT: Wild Rice

Roger Head and Art Garbo were wondering about closing up Dean Lake and 17-Mile Lake for approximately a week because the rice is green.

I made no commitments stating that I would check into it and that it would be up to the local warden and his decision.

JJ/cb

STATE OF MINNESOTA

DEPARTMENT OF NATURAL RESOURCES-ENFORCEMENT

Office Memorandum

TO   : Bill Callies

DATE: 8/23/76

FROM   : Joe Jovonovich

SUBJECT: Congratulations

Congratulations on your being a good officer and taking pride in your judgement, knowledge, and expertise in the field, whereby your personal pride and high principles dictated to you that you were right in not closing Dean Lake for ricing.

Keep up the good work.

JJ/cb

Notes from supervisors about controversy

Chapter 56/ THE STATE LOSES

One day in August of 1976, I was cruising my district with the state's fourteen-foot Alumacraft boat and a twenty-five horsepower motor on a trailer behind the patrol car. My usual approach to a lake was to maneuver my patrol car to a place where I could have a good view of the lake. I would park, hook up my spotting scope on the window mount, and look for an infraction of the law. The usual infractions were an unlicensed watercraft or a fisherman with too many lines.

This particular day I had come to an opening on the north end of O'Brien Lake. There were a half a dozen boats out on the lake with the occupants fishing.

One boat had two men in it fishing. The boat did not have a current sticker, so that was sufficient reason to unload the boat and go check those people out.

There is no access on this lake but there is a creek on the north end of O'Brien where I could unload the boat. I then pulled up to the boat with the two fishermen. Both men were fishing with spinning outfits and using minnows for bait. I told the men who I was and that I wanted to see their angling licenses. I also wanted to know who owned the boat and why there was no current sticker. The man in the back by the motor said it was his boat and he was sure he had renewed his boat license but apparently forgot to attach the current sticker. He got his billfold out and he sat there for fifteen minutes going through the papers in the billfold. He found his angling license but could not find his boat ownership card for that year.

He finally admitted he must have failed to renew his watercraft license. So I wrote a summons for operating an unlicensed watercraft.

Then I turned to the older gentleman and asked for his

angling license. He took out his billfold and searched and searched but could not find his angling license. He finally told me it must be up in the cabin that belonged to his son-in-law. I noticed when he was shuffling the papers in his billfold that he had an Iowa driver's license.

I told the two men we would go up to the cabin because I had to see his angling license. We maneuvered the two boats over to their dock and tied them up. Then the three of us climbed the steps to the cabin. The two men went inside and they offered to let me in. I told them I would wait outside for the older man from Iowa to produce his license.

About twenty minutes went by and no one came out. It got real quiet inside the building so I pounded on the door and hollered for the older man to come out. There was dead silence from within the building. So then I really went to work pounding on the door and I hollered if the man didn't come out, I would break the door down and I would sign a complaint against everyone in the house.

A woman's voice then responded with, "Just please go away and leave us alone." I then told them they had thirty seconds to come out or I would break the door down. That was too much for the old fellow and he came out.

I told him if he had failed to buy a non-resident license to be a man about it and take his licks. He told me he was a minister from some church down in Sioux City, Iowa and they had come up to their son-in-law's and daughter's home to stay with them for about ten days. He said he usually only goes out fishing about a half a dozen times while he was there. He went on to say that he was reluctant to buy a license for a whole year because he was only up for about ten days. I told him you could have acquired a short-term license for three days. He came back with I would have to buy three of four short-term licenses and that would cost him more than a year license. I asked him how many years he had been coming up to O'Brien Lake. He said he thought it was about fifteen or sixteen years. So I let him know he beat the State of Minnesota out of a lot of money.

I then told him I was placing him under arrest and taking him to the justice of the peace. I also informed him that the normal fine was fifty dollars so he best have at least that much money on him or more. He squealed about that so I told him his other option would probably be ten days in jail.

I took him in my boat to my patrol car, loaded the boat on the trailer, and we went to Emily to look up the justice of the peace. The gentleman plead guilty and paid his fine. Then the judge started to figure how much the man saved by not buying a non-resident fishing licenses over the years. The judge then announced you are still ahead of the state by three hundred and eighty-five dollars.

That didn't make the preacher feel any better.

Chapter 57/ ME AND MY BIG MOUTH

Every year in the State of Minnesota there is a requirement of all law enforcement personnel that they qualify in the use of a handgun.

I was stationed at Orr, Minnesota when I received a letter to the effect I would have to go to Grand Rapids at some later date to try to qualify. Grand Rapids is one hundred miles from Orr and I would be spending a whole day or longer driving to and from the Rapids plus the shooting time.

I met one of the Indians from the Nett Lake Reservation and he told me he too was notified to be qualified for using a handgun. However, all the Indian wardens and Indian police in the state were to go to Nett Lake to do their qualifying shoot. I asked him if I could shoot with their group and he said he was sure it would be okay if it met with approval of my regional supervisor, Don Fultz. Nett Lake is only about ten miles from Orr.

I sent a letter to Fultz requesting shooting at Nett Lake and that the shooting would be supervised by Doug Parisian of the Bureau of Indian Affairs. Fultz approved and sent word back via the state radio. I am sure Fultz was pleased that I wouldn't appear at his Grand Rapids shoot as he hated my guts.

Minnesota State House in Orr for wardens

So on the morning of September 8, 1978, I met with a whole bunch of Indian officers at their handgun range located on the Nett Lake Indian Reservation. The Nett Lake range is small in that only three men can shoot at a time. However, the course, distance, and all other requirements are set up by the F.B.I. so that all enforcement nationwide meet the same standards. You must shoot a score of at least seventy out of a possible one hundred.

I was the only white officer so I was kind of conspicuous. Doug Parisian asked for the first three volunteers and no one moved. Doug spoke to me and said I should shoot with the first group. Then he pointed to two of the Indian wardens to complete the trio.

The three of us completed the course then Doug went down to the targets and totaled up our scores. While Doug was down by the targets one of the officers approached me with a big red coffee can. There was quite a lot of money in the can. This officer told me if I wanted to, I could put a dollar in the can. All the money would go to the officer that shot the highest score. When Doug gave the scores I was high with 93.2 out of one hundred.

One group after another shot the course. Around noon, some of the women from the reservation came to the range with a big tub full of ice cubes to which they added a couple of cases of pop. They also had several cartons full of sandwiches each individually wrapped in wax paper. The people invited me to join them for lunch. I really enjoyed that, as I was getting hungry. Although I had shot, Doug wouldn't authorize me to leave. He did tell me I still had the high score and I should stick around until the shooting was over to collect the money. A lot of the men failed to qualify so he was having them shoot over. It seemed the more they shot the worse their scores were.

It was getting near four p.m. and Doug was getting impatient. He made the remark to all of us, "No one is going home until you all qualify. If you don't settle down and start shooting some better scores, we are all going to be shooting out here under the lights."

Now I had spent fifteen years at Waskish and the Red Lake Indian Reservation was on the west side of my district. I had caught many Indians shooting deer at night with spotlights off the reservation. At one time, I witnessed an Indian with a single shot 22-rifle plop a bullet right into the eye of a deer under a spotlight at three times the distance these men were shooting.

I don't know whatever came over me. I just blurted out, "If you end up shooting under the lights, you won't have any trouble hitting the target."

There was dead silence. I knew I was in the wrong place to

make a statement like that. All of a sudden that money in the coffee can had no appeal for me. I walked over to my patrol car and got out of there.

Obviously, there was no way I was going to get that coffee can of money.

Chapter 58/ LAWYERS

On this day of June 2, 1979, I was stationed in Baudette, Minnesota. There were several rivers in my patrol district to patrol but only one lake. To be more precise, I was assigned only the southeast portion of this lake. Al Markovich, the warden at Warroad, had the southwestern part of this lake. The Canadian wardens from Manitoba and Ontario had twice the area on this lake to patrol as we two Minnesota wardens had. This lake, of course, is Lake of the Woods.

This is a very popular lake for taking walleyes and saugers. The Minnesota limit on Lake of the Woods is six walleyes and eight saugers. The Minnesota limit on Lake of the Woods was more generous than any of our inland waters or neighboring states or provinces. And at one time, our commissioner increased the possession limit to ten walleyes and/or twenty saugers. This was an added incentive to those fishermen who wanted to take home lots of fish.

Consequently, I end up with lots and lots of fishermen on a huge body of water fishing day and night the year around. I used to feel about as effective as a fart in a windstorm. On this particular day, I was using the state's 16 foot, model K Alumacraft, with a twenty-five horse Johnson motor, operated by a tiller bar. I had a light tan jacket over my warden shirt so as to be as inconspicuous as possible. I used to bring my fishing gear along and would troll slowly among the fishermen watching for people angling with too many lines, unlicensed boats, people throwing trash and cans into the lake. Occasionally, I would pull along side and check for angler's licenses, life preservers and quantities of fish.

I was cruising on the lakeside of Pine Island from Morris Gap to the lighthouse gap a distance of roughly five miles. It was a typical nice day. The waters were almost calm. I could see about a hundred watercraft, most of them were sixteen-foot open boats with two to five fishermen. There were some cabin cruisers and a few resort launches. Fishing seemed to be slow so over limits were not too much concern.

About midway down Pine Island, I noted a 16-foot open boat with four persons aboard. What really caught my eye was a young bearded man standing on the back seat of the boat urinating over the transom and motor of their boat. I don't know if he was showing off or trying to raise the lake level. To me it was a disgusting act, especially in light of the fact there were women and children in nearby boats. I was about two hundred yards away. I reeled up my trolling line and proceeded over to this boat. I met their boat on the starboard side of my boat against the starboard side of their boat.

There was a young man in his early twenties in the front seat with a fishing pole in his hand. I opened my blouse and told him I was a Minnesota game warden and I would like to check his license. He produced a non-resident three-day license. I noted his name, that he was fishing on one of the three days granted by the license, and that he was a resident of Council Bluffs, Iowa. The young man in the next seat also was angling, so I requested to see his license.

He produced a Minnesota resident full year angling license. His last name was the same as the young man in the front seat, however, his address was St. Louis Park, Minnesota. I was a bit suspicious so I asked for his driver's license, at which time, he let me know he wasn't driving. I told him I just wanted it for confirmation of his residency. He then said he had left it at home because another member of the group furnished the car and did the driving.

So as I was still holding the license he had submitted to me, I asked him what his birth date was. He seemed confused and finally blurted a month, day, and year, which didn't agree with what was written on the license. I then asked him what his home address was. The only thing that he said that agreed with the license was St. Louis Park, Minnesota. He then suggested the person that made out the license apparently misunderstood him. So I told this young man I felt this was a license he had borrowed from a third brother who did, in fact, live in St. Louis Park. I stuck that license in my pocket and told this young man we would check into this later.

The next man in the next seat was quite a bit older. He said his license was back at their cabin at the resort where they were staying. I asked him what his name was and his last name was the same as the two men's license that I checked. I asked him if he was the father of the two men. He let me know that was not a pertinent question for me to ask. I did suggest there seemed to be a similarity in their appearances.

I then came to the young man who had urinated into the lake. I told him I witnessed this act even though he denied it. He, too, was fishing so I asked to see his license. He presented me with a resident Minnesota angling license. I asked him his name and he gave me the same name as on his license. However, when it came to the birth date and the house address, he showed signs of confusion. He showed a rather aggressive attitude, so, I stuck his license into my pocket and told him I would make further checks on this license.

In my mind, I felt sure I had a father with no license and two sons that had borrowed resident licenses from two other brothers who lived in the metropolitan area. To top it off, I had the feeling they were all attorneys. At this point, the only person in this group that was legal was the youngest man I had checked first.

I then instructed the older man to get in the boat with me. I told the other men to pull up their anchor and follow me back to their cabin. Also, I took possession of the three fishing rods that were used by the three men with questionable licenses.

Left to Right: Bill Callies, Ces Richards (retired),
Al Markovich

We tied up the two boats at the resort dock and started walking towards their cabin. The older man stopped about half way and turned to me and said, "I guess you know I don't have a license."

I told him, "I thought that out on the lake." Also I told him it was my opinion that the two lads with the resident licenses had somebody else's license. I informed him that I was going to make a call to the dispatcher at Thief River Falls and have him call the St. Louis Park police and the sheriff in Council Bluffs, Iowa to confirm or deny my suspicions. Also if my suspicions were right, I would charge the two people with loaning their resident angling licenses to other people. I then blurted out, "This is a real serious situation, and this is a felony."

To which the older man said, "Oh no, this is not a felony. A misdemeanor or maybe a gross misdemeanor in Minnesota, but not a felony." I knew this was a misdemeanor, but it also made me more certain I was doing business with attorneys and that I should be careful to conduct myself so they could have no complaints.

At this point, the older man decided to make a clean breast of the situation. He admitted to not procuring a license and also to the two sons from Council Bluffs borrowing their brothers' resident angling licenses. I may not have gotten to the very bottom of this sordid mess, but I decided to back off a bit and just charge the three men with angling for fish without first procuring a license.

We all went into the cabin. I sat down at the kitchen table and made out the summons, which each man signed and I gave each man their copy. Due to the fact that Judge Hemstad only comes to Baudette to hear cases one day a week, I had to set the hearing date for June 7th, which would be five days hence. I then told the men I would have to put them in jail until the trial date because they were non-residents and could take a powder, or they could post bail and I would release them. I showed the men the county court bail schedule. The bail for non-residents angling without a license is forty dollars cash. They still had the opportunity to appear in county court on June 7 to enter a plea of guilty or not guilty, in which case I would submit my evidence to the court.

The elderly man at this point pulled out a large roll of money. He took three fifty-dollar bills out of the roll and threw them on the table. I told the man I did not have change, so he sent one of his sons over to the resort office to break one of the fifty-dollar bills and gave me one hundred twenty dollars for which I gave him a receipt.

I then made out a seizure receipt for the three fishing rods and reels to seize them for the state. I knew I should sign complaints against the two brothers that loaned the licenses and get them into court also, but I had so many other activities going on that I should look into. I decided on not getting involved in a bunch of paper work so I just wrote void on the licenses, the date and my initials. I hope these people got the message.

About a week later, I was at the Baudette bridge customs' office checking fishermen coming in from Ontario. I met a nice group of men in a motor home. Their Ontario angling license indicated they were residents of Council Bluffs, Iowa. I then asked them if they knew anyone by the name of the men I had picked up. They all knew them. I then asked what the elder person's occupation was and the one gentleman said he thought the whole family were lawyers...I thought so.

Chapter 59/ BORDER VIOLATIONS

Quite frequently when I wanted to work the Rainy River, which is the dividing line between the State of Minnesota and the province of Ontario, I would contact my counterpart from Ontario, Ted Biggs. If he were free, we would travel together in either a boat or a snowmobile to check fishermen, hunters, trappers, etc. Our respective laws are quite similar so regardless of which side of the line we were on we knew what to look for in the way of violations. The dividing line for all practical purposes is the center of the river. However, when you get out into the Lake of the Woods you had to be more careful. I will give you a working example.

Ted and I were in the Minnesota State boat, a sixteen-foot Alumacraft, with a twenty-five horse motor. There was a boat in the center of the lighthouse gap. There were two men anchored there and they were each angling with two or more lines. I told Ted I believe they are in Ontario. It is against the law in both Ontario and Minnesota to fish in open water with more than one line.

We pulled along side and held onto their boat and told the men they were in violation of the law. They had too many lines out. Ted asked to see their Ontario licenses and they only had Minnesota licenses. Then we told them they were actually in Canadian waters and Ted told them he should charge them for angling in Canadian waters and angling with more than one line. However, they were only about fifteen-feet in, so, he would turn them over to his counterpart—me. I wrote them up for angling with more than one line. Ted told them to either get a Canadian license or get over on the Minnesota side.

There were border buoys and I'm sure these men knew where they were but neither Ted nor I ever cut it that fine.

On another occasion we were using the Ontario boat and we were working the border up behind Sable Island to Burton Island and Ted made a pinch for someone from the states fishing in Ontario waters without an Ontario license. In those days, when we caught someone in violation of the game and fish laws that was from another state or province, we were authorized to take bail for which we had a schedule. If they didn't have enough money for bail, we had the option of seizing a lot of their gear or take them to the closest jail and lock them up until the court date for a hearing. Or, they also had the option of posting bail and picking up their gear that had been seized.

We continued on up into Canadian waters where we came upon a man and a woman with two young children. They had a real fancy, expensive boat, loaded with all kinds of gadgets.

The man and woman were fishing. When we came along side them, Ted asked to see their angling license. The man got out his billfold and pulled out a Minnesota resident combination license. Ted advised him that they were over three miles into Ontario and they must have an Ontario angling license to fish these waters. This man said he thought he could fish anywhere on Lake of the Woods with a Minnesota angling license. I corrected him on that subject and I am reasonably sure he knew he was in Canada and hoped he wouldn't be checked.

So Ted made out the summons for the man and the woman. I used to feel sorry for any Canadian warden that had to make out a summons. Some super dumb higher echelon person must have designed their summons book. The book looked like one of those full-size school tablets. I believe there were five copies so there were four full-size sheets of carbon paper to insert each time you made out a new summons.

Our summons book had four copies with built in carbon paper.

Ted had to have a brief case to carry all of the papers along to make out an Ontario summons. Just imagine what a mess that is out in a boat or snowmobile on a windy or rainy day.

When Ted got done filling in all the blank places, he submitted the summons for the violator's signature. Then he would explain the violator's options.

When Ted told the violators how much bail they would have to post, the man and woman said they didn't have any money—just credit cards. So Ted started to select some items in the boat that would exceed the amount of the bail so that it would behoove the individuals to come up with cash money at a later time to regain his seized items. Everything Ted tried to seize was securely bolted down and connected to the electrical system. If Ted could not seize items, we would have to transport them clear to Fort Francis to incarcerate them and have the children turned over to Social Services. Our day would be really screwed up.

Then the fellow said if he could get back to his resort he could draw enough cash from the resort operator to post bail. So we started back a total of about twenty-five miles. Ted instructed this party to follow right behind us, in that way they were in Canadian waters. I advised this man to follow Ted's instructions because if he broke and crossed into Minnesota water I would have jurisdiction over him and I would put the man in jail until the County Judge came to Baudette from International Falls for his one day a week appearance to hear complaints.

There is a law that says any illegal activity that occurs in another state or province will be dealt with in the Minnesota courts so just to get across the line will not absolve him of his or her wrong doing.

So this party complied with Ted's instructions. Both boats stopped on the Canadian side of the river directly across from the resort. At this point, Ted told the man to get in our boat while his wife took their boat and went over to their resort to get bail money. The lady told us she didn't know how to drive the boat. So the man asked, "How would it be if my wife stayed with you while I go get the bail money?"

Ted was kind of surprised. We both had the feeling that if they crossed the border that would be the end of the Ontario charges and I would have to take over. I was not too keen on having to carry out my part of the problem. The local sheriff would really growl about the cost of holding this man.

Ted finally said O.K. so we held the boat tightly together and the lady climbed into the Canadian boat. The man with the two children went across the river to the resort. The man tied their boat up at the dock and went up into the lodge.

We waited and waited for at least twenty minutes, and then the man came out the front of the lodge and stood looking out over the river. Finally, he came down to his boat, came across the river, and submitted the bail money to Ted. Ted made out a receipt and then we very carefully held the two boats while the lady transferred to their boat and returned to the Minnesota resort.

After that was over, I said to Ted, "That man may have had some thoughts of not redeeming his wife." We both agreed there has to be a better way. Today there is but I won't take time to explain it.

On another occasion in the spring of the year when the walleye pike season opens we had a real problem. I believe it was the year 1979. The Minnesota pike season opened on a Saturday, one week before the Ontario season opened.

I called Ted to set up a time and place where we would meet on the Rainy River Saturday morning. It was then that he told me the Ontario season wouldn't be open for a week and he hadn't planned on working. I told Ted that for sure he should come along and work because he was sure to have people fishing on his side of the line. He finally agreed that he would be available.

I could be wrong but I have reason to believe that was the day Ted wrote the most summons in his career. At first as we checked fishermen and we would find Minnesota fishermen on the Ontario side, Ted would politely tell the people to get on their side of the line.

It was days like this that made me ashamed of being a Yankee. They would tell us that the law was they could fish bank to bank on a Minnesota license. That is a true situation between states in the United States but now we were dealing with another country. In Canada joining provinces or states don't enjoy that privilege.

Eventually, we came to a river in Ontario across from the Rainy River Marina. This river has a huge bay, just at its mouth where it enters the Rainy River. I ran our boat in there and we found a huge inboard, outboard boat with two men in it, both of them fishing. The boat had two motors built into it.

When we came along side and stood up in our boat, our chins were on the gunnel of their boat. Ted told these two men they were in Ontario and the pike season was not open and if it were they would have to have an Ontario angling license. Also, the live minnows they had for bait were supposed to be purchased from an Ontario minnow dealer who would have given them a receipt.

The fellow in the back submitted his Minnesota angling license to Ted and then made the mistake of telling Ted that he could fish in the Rainy River bank to bank and also he could fish in any river that flowed into the Rainy River.

Ted finally had it up to his armpits with all this arrogance. He reached for his brief case, took out his summons book, wrote this man up and collected the bail and turned to the operator of the boat for his license. This man said he just worked for the big man in the back and he had been told by him to run the boat into the mouth of this river. Ted made out the summons anyway and told the operator, "Maybe you can get your boss to post the bail or we will take you with us and put you in jail." The big man paid his bail also.

They started up the motors and the big fellow said he would contact his legislators about this problem.

While Ted and I were involved with these two people, an open boat with two more fishermen had come into the bay and were trolling for fish. We approached them and came along side them. This time Ted didn't hesitate at all, he just took their Minnesota angling license and started writing them up. Before we finished writing them up another boat with three fishermen came trolling into the bay. I tried to motion to them to go back and I think one man gave me the finger.

So when Ted got done with the two men, we just went over and pulled the three men over. Ted collected their Minnesota angling licenses. Then, because the wind was coming up, the boats were bouncing. I suggested to Ted we pull into the access site. There were several large tree logs cut into stumps just about the right size to sit on. It would be easier for Ted to make out the summons sitting on a stump.

When the first man found out what the bail was going to be, the three men realized they weren't going to have enough money to bail all of them out. So Ted told the first man that he would release him to go back to their resort to get some more money. Ted asked me to follow him in my boat to see which resort these men came from.

So, I followed him back to the Minnesota resort. The fellow either made out a check or submitted a credit card. Anyway he got the money. He also told the resorter what was happening. The resorter implied it was kind of a chicken shit thing for his guests. I advised him to warn his guests. Ted tried to be nice at first but he finally got his belly full of the arrogance shown by so many of the fishermen.

We came back to where Ted was waiting and I found another boat with some people fishing in the bay. I pulled along side the boat and told the fishermen who I was. I pointed out Ted sitting on one of the stumps at the access and told them to go over there and see Ted—he would take care of them.

I sat out there in the bay, if a boat came in and the occupants were fishing, I directed them over to Ted. If they didn't have lines out I told them where they were and suggested they get back where they belonged. And, so the day went. Sometimes there were two or three boats pulled up on the access waiting their turn with Ted.

This went on for over two hours, without a break. Then, I happened to look into where Ted was. He was on his feet waving both arms. It seems to me he was running out of summons. I don't know how much money Ted had to account for but he sure had a pile of it in his briefcase and it would take him several days in his office to make preparations with the court in Fort Francis for anyone who chose to make an appearance to enter a plea of guilty or not guilty.

The Baudette newspaper made a big blurb about this incident and of course the game wardens were at fault. We just did what we were hired to do.

Chapter 60/ RAINY RIVER GILL NET

Late one day in May of 1979, a young man came to my house in Baudette. He said he lived with his folks on the shore of the Rainy River, about seven miles northwest of Baudette. He had gone out for a little motor boat ride after school and came across a place he thought a net was set. He knew that was an illegal act so he thought he should alert me.

I asked him if he would show me this location. We went to his house got in his boat and proceeded down stream alongside some bulrushes. As we passed over this area I could see two of the floats about a foot below the surface on the water. I told him, "Let's get out of this area quickly in the event the owner of the net is watching."

We returned to his house. I told this young man and his father, "I will go back through the woods and sit on this."

The father offered me a warm coat to wear with the suggestion, "It might get cool through the night."

I walked back through the woods until I was about in line with where the net was located. I found a big tree to lean on while sitting on the ground. The mosquitoes had good eating up until about 10 p.m. when they quit. It did get quite cool and I was thankful for the coat the man loaned me.

I did doze off a couple of times but the cold woke me up with my shivering.

Then I started to imagine the guys that set the net while I was dozing off came in a canoe or rowboat and lifted the net.

Finally, around 4:30 a.m. it started to get light and the gulls were flying up and down the river looking for some dead or crippled fish to feed on.

Then to answer my question, if the net was still out there, two herring gulls could evidently see some fish caught in the net. They lit on the water and made several attempts to reach the fish in the net. So the net was still there and there were fish in it.

Shortly the sun was coming up and my body just soaked the warmth of the sun's rays. I got so warm and cozy I had a super hard time staying awake sitting there leaning on the big basswood tree. I did catch myself several times dozing off and then apparently I lost all control because I woke up by the squeaking of oars in the oar locks.

I opened my eyes to see two older men in a sixteen-foot Lund rowing toward the area of the net. I was sitting right out in the open about seventy feet from this boat. Apparently they hadn't seen me so I very slowly slid down until I was flat on the ground.

The squeak of the oars didn't change their rhythm so apparently these two men didn't see me.

I was elated lying there. My dad had taught me to crawl up on ducks when I was a kid. I used everything he taught me to slowly, very carefully, slither back in to dense cover.

From there I was able to observe these two men lift the gill net. I could hear the excited voices as they came upon each fish. They left the fish stuck in the gill net and just piled the whole net on the floor in the boat.

I looked at my watch; it was around 7:00 a.m. I must have slept for over an hour. My wife accused me of snoring but obviously I didn't snore this morning.

The two men were quite elated rowing their boat down stream, while I paced them from tree to tree. Eventually they pulled into a dock near where the Winter Road River comes into the Rainy River. I watched them tie their boat at the bow and stern to the dock and then I broke cover and ran about two hundred yards. About the time I hit the dock one man saw me and the expression on his face went from jubilant to pure misery. He knew they were had.

Actually what I had was a couple of old men that had a little devilment left over from when they were kids. However, they both had plenty of money. When I wrote them up for 'taking fish with the aid of a gill net in public waters', which is a violation of 97C.325 Section 3.

I showed the men the bail schedule in Lake of the Woods County. It called for $200 bail from each man plus I seized the net and the fish.

One man said he came across the net in his tool shed and coerced his neighbor to go along with him in this act so consequently he would pay both of their fines. He gave me a check made out to the Clerk of Lake of the Woods County for $400 with the statement. "It was fun while it lasted."

DNR patches

APPENDIX

GAME WARDEN?

Game Warden? I couldn't believe it, not Jerry Liemandt, my brother-in-law! He had a good job as a tool-and-die maker. He had just acquired a new home in Robbinsdale. This happened around 1948. Our family went out to visit him the weekend before he was to leave on some kind of training program to become a Game Warden for the State of Minnesota.

I had been brought up to avoid Game Wardens like a plague. They were enemies of the people according to my father. I had never met or known a real Game Warden before in my life. My father had always admonished me that while hunting, fishing, or trapping, to avoid any human being regardless of whom they were.

That following fall, Jerry had acquired permanent status and had been assigned to his station at Thief River Falls. Our family went up to visit Jerry, Monica, and their children, more out of curiosity than anything else.

Jerry took me out with him on his patrols a couple of times. At that time, they were living in a big old rental house near the Red River. Also, Jerry took me to see a lot he had acquired where he was in the process of building a house by himself. My trade at the time was installing floor covering. It seemed to me, I went back up there on a weekend to assist him on that part of his construction.

At about this time, Nate Pliam, my employer, had put me in charge of the installers for installing floor covering in all of his stores. This was a job that put a lot of stress on my whole family and me. There also was a lot of prestige and more money.

On a visit to Liemandts, I was quite envious of the freedom this Game Warden position allowed, so I asked Jerry, "How did you acquire this kind of employment?"

He told me that I would have to take and pass a civil service test. If I managed that, I would subsequently have to take an oral test. If I passed that, I would be put on the list for the job. I then asked Jerry, "Where do I accomplish all this?"

Then he let me know that the pay was considerably less than what I was earning. I countered with, "The freedom is worth it."

He said, "If you're really serious, go over to the capitol in St. Paul. Go to Civil Service and they will give you a sheet with all the Civil Service Jobs available. You mark which jobs you would be interested in taking." He went on to say, "I would recommend Game Warden, Highway Patrol, and Refuge Patrolman." He told me some men have gotten on these other units and then made a lateral transfer to Game Warden.

So I went over to the capitol and checked off those three categories. In the spring of 1950, I took the test for a Refuge Patrolman; and within a month, I was advised I had passed it and I was on the list.

Early that summer, two men that were factory representatives of Sloane Blabon and Matico approached me about going into business for myself. They would come in with me as silent partners. We would each put up $5,000. It would be a corporation. I would be the President and Treasurer and to all outward appearances, I would be the sole owner. I would make all the decisions. We located a building under construction in St. Louis Park at 5810 Excelsior Boulevard. I couldn't see how I could lose. They had me on an ego trip. I had to sell our home in order to come up with my share and we moved into a rental on Nicollet Avenue. I really took on an obligation. I was amazed that my wife and children went along with me.

I went into Nate Pliam and told him I was going into business on my own. I told him I would stay with him for two weeks until he broke in a new man, or I would leave right then, whatever he wanted.

He told me I could never make it on my own. He said I would go belly up within six months. Then he said, "You go ahead and have your fling. When you're broke, you come on back. I'll always have a job for you." I thanked him and we parted on real good terms.

I took leave of Pliam Linoleum and took the job of buying, selling, estimating, hiring installers and the thousand and one things you can be faced with in starting up a new business with a minimum of financing—no help from Uncle Sugar. In fact, he was my worst enemy.

Two months after I opened this new business, Modern Floors, I received a letter from the State of Minnesota that there was an opening for me at the Thief Lake Wild Life Management Area, which was located about forty miles Northeast of Thief River Falls where my brother-in-law was the Game Warden.

Jerry and I had married sisters at a double wedding. Apparently, Jerry and Monica heard about the State offering me this job at Thief Lake about the same time I received notice of the job. At any rate, Monica who is not one to assert herself too much, got on the phone and called my wife, Patricia, who is her sister, and said, "If Bill takes that job, leave him." She was dead serious.

I had other problems. All of our money was stuck in the business. I had about eight or ten employees. I had several thousand dollars of installations sold and scheduled. I had a wife and two children I was responsible for. This free and easy job had its merits and appeal but it would have to wait.

I took a few minutes the next day while out estimating, to run over to the capitol to see if they could give it to the next person on the list and keep my name on the available list.

The person I saw said, "No way, you have ten days to get up to Thief Lake or submit a letter to us that you are turning down the assignment. That's final!"

It was obvious to me of the two options I had; I would remain in the floor covering business. Four years later, I got fed up with my two silent partners. Every time a major change in the operation would come up, it was put to a vote. They had always consolidated their opinion before any meeting and I was always faced with a losing vote. It was always two to one.

Frank, who had been a representative for Sloane Blabon, was pensioned off and he wanted to work at Modern Floors as a salesperson with the same salary I drew. Again the vote was two to one, now it became confirmed to me that Frank, who used to be a social drinker became a full-blown alcoholic. He was so unsure of himself that he started drinking early in the morning and by noon he was plowed.

The three of us in the partnership had a real go around one Saturday morning, and I ended up buying both of them out.

We ended up with a real mom and pop operation. We had about fifteen employees. I put in an average of fifteen hours a day, every day, except on Sunday. The whole family would turn to, on Saturday and Sunday, cleaning up the store and warehouse. I had a fabulous wife and she took any chore I hung on her with a vengeance. I could see the kids got bored real quick and it was not fair or interesting to them.

An old buddy, a floor installer friend of mine, was always calling me to move out to Montana. He had a job for me as an installer working for Western Floors in Great Falls. He talked about the hunting and it was too much for me. I put the store up for sale and one of my employees bought it.

A year later, (I'll not bother you with the details) I came back to Minneapolis hired out to St. Paul Linoleum and Carpet as an installer. A year-and-a-half later, they put me in charge of the installation department.

On February 8, 1958, I took the test for Game Warden. I passed the written test and the oral test with a final of 86.50. I was 23rd on the list. There were eleven hundred people that took the test.

On the first day of July 1960, I received a letter to the effect that the department was filling some vacancies around the State. Was I still interested?

You bet I was! My income would be reduced to about one-third of what St. Paul Linoleum paid; however, we had enough set aside to get both of our children through college.

I notified my employers, Bill Groth and Howard Commers, owners of St. Paul Linoleum and Carpet, that I was going to try to get this job as a Minnesota State Game Warden. I even suggested to them the name of another person that could easily replace me.

I went to the Chief Warden's Office. F. W. Johnson was the chief and I let him know I absolutely wanted the job.

He told me I would have to go through one more interrogation to be conducted by Gordon Wallen, Richard Tarte, and F. W. Johnson. If the majority approved, I would have to take and pass a rigid physical before they would hire me.

Dick Tarte, the Area Supervisor from the Northern part of the State, objected to me being hired. The department had set an age of thirty-five years as the maximum age of anyone they would hire. I was forty-three years old at the time and my hair was snow white. At the same time, John Kennedy was also forty-three and he was trying to become President of the United States. I commented that we were both the same age and he was being touted as too young to be the President of the United States and yet they were saying I was too old to be a Game Warden. Also, the Legislature had approved a law that any service man that was honorably discharged from the Armed Services would have the age requirement waived if he was trying to get a civil service job. Gordon Wollen backed me up on that statement then he added, "But you still have to pass the physical." I didn't worry too much about the physical in those days. I was in pretty good shape and used to hard work.

I did pass the physical and I was hired. I was given a law book, a set of commissioner's orders, and told to read and study them.

I was actually hired on July 24, 1960. I was advised that I would be involved in a training program for the next six months. I would spend two-week increments with various Game Wardens who would impart their knowledge to me.

Thus began my twenty years as a Game Warden for the State of Minnesota.

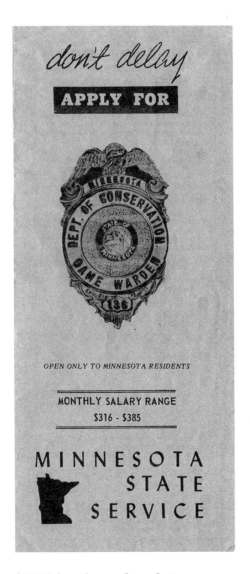

Cover of 1960 brochure about being a game warden

FIRST TRAINER, AL HOGER

My first assignment was to start on July 26, 1960. I was to go to Walker and work with Al Hoger for ten days. Then I would have four days off to go home before my next assignment.

My brother-in-law, Jerry, heard I was being sent up to Al Hoger and he called me and said Al Hoger is recognized as the 'ax man' for trainees. I told Jerry if he can find anything wrong with me and he is a fair person then I have no business taking this job.

I got up about 3:00 a.m. on July 26, had breakfast, took leave of my wife and children in our home in Minneapolis, and struck out with good wishes from my wife for Walker, Minnesota. I arrived in town about 7:45 a.m. and made inquiries where I would find Al Hoger. Someone directed me to his home.

I drove into his driveway, went to the front door and knocked. Mrs. Hoger answered and told me Al was not expecting any trainees. In fact, he had taken four days off to celebrate some kind of a Muskie Fishing Celebration. However, she said, "He has gone downtown to pick up the mail and he always spends fifteen minutes on a certain corner to answer any questions. He would be smoking a cigar. Maybe you can catch him there."

I immediately took off for the downtown area about a mile north. I found a man near the post office standing on the corner smoking a recently lit cigar. I parked my car and approached this man. Just the way the man stood on the corner I got the feeling that this man was an outstanding individual. I offered my hand in a handshake and announced my name. There was absolutely no sign of recognition. Then I said, "I am the trainee assigned to you for the next two weeks."

His response was "Oh no you're not! I'm on four days off." I thought, what a way to start. Then Al backed off a bit and said "That damn office, I told them two months ago I wanted these fours days off for the Annual Muskie Derby Celebration. I sent in my leave slips and alerted the dispatcher. I'm not working, and I don't know what you are going to do."

Then Hoger started to cool down some and made some unintelligible remark about the office. Al said, "You come along with me for now and I'll try to figure something out." He directed me to the hotel to get a room and then told me to meet him at his house.

I did this. Al introduced me to his wife. She was ironing warden shirts. There were at least a dozen freshly ironed shirts hanging on clothes hangers in a closet off the front room. I always enjoyed the smell of clean, freshly ironed clothing.

Al was letting off some steam about a lot of different personnel in the various offices. I almost started to think I should go back to Minneapolis and start over.

Then Al said, "Well, it's not your fault but damned if I'm going to change my plans." With that he said, "Come on." We went down to a marina where he had a small boat tied up with a ten-horse motor on the back. We went out on to the lake and pulled up to a large pontoon boat with an enclosed building on it.

When we got inside, there was a big welcoming group sitting around a big round card table. Everyone had a glass of starting fluid or a bottle of beer in front of him. The cigar and cigarette smoke was so thick you could almost cut it. Hoger introduced me to some of the people. It was obvious I was like a thorn in his side, although it was not my fault.

Al kept looking at his watch. Finally, he told his cronies, "I've got to meet someone in town but I'll be back shortly."

We got back in the boat and came back to the marina where we met Dick Heinlen, the warden at Longville. There was a conversation between Heinlen and Hoger. Then the two men came to me. Hoger said, "I'm sending you with Heinlen until Sunday morning. However, you continue to stay here at the hotel and you drive back and forth every day. You are to work with Heinlen through Saturday."

Heinlen and I did spend some time checking fishermen on small lakes but most of the time he showed off a project he had going. He was building cabins on lots on one piece of property on a real nice, small lake. Heinlen told me that he had a partner who was the manager of the State Capitol Credit Union. Money was not a problem. He had several cabins in various states of construction. I got along good with Heinlen. In fact, I was thankful to him that he took responsibility for my predicament.

When Al got back off his leave, we really went to work. He was an excellent teacher and he knew his job. We made several arrests every day and he would have the violator appear at eight or nine p.m. before a judge in the city courthouse at Walker. There are many small lakes in Hoger's district. We worked some of them until dark. We spent some time servicing his equipment.

One evening, we worked Leech Lake and it was on this evening I really made points with Hoger. He was using an open aluminum boat with a steering wheel up front and a thirty horse Johnson to move us along. It was a bare bones boat—no fancy seats, no windshield or top, but he did have a pair of oars if we broke down.

There were several groups of boats and as we would pull up to a group, Al would select his first boat to check. When he pulled along side the first boat, I'm sure the other fisherman knew who we were because you could see some of the people looking through their billfolds for their licenses.

It was on the third or fourth group that we pulled up to that Hoger started to pull up to one boat then he made a fast turn to another boat. A man was standing up with a fly rod in his hand winding the small rod as fast as he could when suddenly a fish grabbed his hook. The pole almost bent double. As we pulled along side, I saw a casting rod lying in the boat with the tip just up on the gunnel and a line down in the water. I heard Hoger say his name then something about I gotcha this time. The fisherman conceded that. While Hoger was writing him up for angling for fish with more than one line, I was holding the two boats together and saw the rod tip was near me. I used my free hand to work the line up to see what he was using for bait. He had on a clamp type sinker and a single hook with a small shiner minnow on it. I dropped the whole mess back down in the lake. Hoger had this man booked into court along with three or four others the following night.

The next day, we checked two or three small lakes then we quit in order to attend court. This one man that Hoger caught on Leech Lake the night before plead not guilty. Al then told the judge he was fishing with one casting rod and one fly rod. When he tried to get the fly rod out of the water a small northern grabbed his hook and we had him. The fellow then told the judge that the casting rod had line on it hanging in the water but there was no hook on it. Hoger's jaw just dropped when the judge asked, "Is that right, Al?" The fisherman was all smiles because he knew Al didn't check the casting rod line.

Then I spoke up and told the judge when I was holding the two boats together I lifted the line and saw there was a sinker and a hook with a minnow on it. That saved the day for Al.

I ended up with six checks of standard and two checks of outstanding on my report card for this first training session. Al Hoger, in spite of our bad start, was one of the best instructors I had and he exemplified what I thought a Game Warden should be.

SECOND TRAINER, LLOYD HOFFMAN

My next assignment of August 10 through August 23, 1960, was with the Area Supervisor, Lloyd Hoffman, at Sauk Centre. Lloyd gave me two books to read and implied he would question me on the contents at a later date. He gave me a brief run down on an Area Supervisor's duties. Lloyd obviously had a lot of duties to perform as an Area Supervisor because he would drop me off at my motel with instructions to read and study the law book and the Commissioner's Orders.

On one occasion, he picked me up, took me to his house for coffee and some bakery goodies. He questioned me on the books I was reading to see if I understood the contents. After an hour or so, he asked if I played cribbage. I spent three years in the Navy and that was a Navy man's pastime, so, of course, I played cribbage.

Some time into our second or third game, we had a visitor, Elmer Lenzen, one of Lloyd Hoffman's men. Elmer sat down and we started playing three-handed cribbage. While playing, Elmer started to complain about his job. Everything was wrong. He couldn't understand why I quit my job at St. Paul Linoleum to become a Game Warden. He went on and on for fifteen or twenty minutes. I spoke up and told him "If the job is so bad why don't you quit. There are eleven hundred other men that would be glad to take your place." Elmer jumped up, threw his cards, said something about a smart-ass and left.

Don't get me wrong on Elmer Lenzen. I was to find out he was and is one of the most dedicated Game Wardens in the State of Minnesota.

There was one night we worked that I never understood. It seems there was a rumor of some butcher shop over near Camp Ripley that was making sausage using venison for the meat.

This shop was paying hunters to kill and deliver the deer to some unknown location. It was further believed that the hunters worked at night. Lloyd Hoffman spent some time showing me a portable radio telephone and how it worked. He made some remarks about the poor quality of this portable. One could not be sure if it was transmitting or receiving properly.

Lloyd advised me to take the rest of the day off to pick up whatever I needed for a midnight lunch and that I should go back to the motel and take a nap. He would pick me up at about 7:00 p.m. and explain my duties after that.

I was too excited over what might happen that night to lie down and sleep. I had my lunch packed and I was hot to go. Around 7:00 p.m., Lloyd picked me up. There were four men in the car. Kermitt Peterson, Lloyd Hoffman, another man whose name I can't remember, and Art Tonder. I remember Tonder because he had a baseball uniform on.

We rode out to some place and there I got instructions to get out of the car, take my lunch, the portable radio, and Lloyd gave me a heavy coat in case it got cold later on. He pointed to a field that had some high ground about two hundred yards from the road. I was to go to this area where I would have good vision all around. If a car showed up, I was to call them on the portable radio and give them an account of what was transpiring. I was also told there was another warden car in the vicinity with four men in it. With that, they left.

I got myself and gear up to where I was to go. I had good unobstructed vision all around. Also, I was sure if someone shined a light up to where I was, I could lie down in the weeds and wouldn't be seen. I was told to turn on the radio every half-hour and let them know if I was O.K.

Around 10:30 p.m., a car came down the road and stopped about where I was dropped off. Two men got out of the vehicle. Then the car left and the men went into an area across the road from where I was. They turned on a pretty strong light and I could see they were walking through an area with some big conifer trees and several old buildings. They went past this area, then, I could see they made a big sweep of their light, a very slow and meticulous sweep. I was so excited I could hardly find the switch to turn the radio on. Then the light went out. I had given a running account as things happened. No one answered the radio. I called several times before someone answered. They said they thought they heard all my transmission. I told them again two men were across the road in back of some buildings shining a light but the light was not on now.

About fifteen minutes later, I saw a light come on at a location further away and to my left. I reported this but got no confirmation. The light went out. Some time later, I saw a light about a half-a-mile away and to my right. I reported this with no confirmation. A short time later, I saw a light that looked like it was shining in the same area that I first saw the light only a bit to my right. I reported this with no confirmation. A short while later, I saw the light come on in the building area. Then I saw a match light. I thought I saw the glow of a cigarette or a cigar. I called on the radio and told them, "I think I can sneak up and catch these people." I was told to stay put.

About twenty minutes later, a car came down the road and stopped. A few minutes later two people came out of this dark area and got in the vehicle and drove off. I reported this.

Then I heard someone say on the portable, "Are you going to stop that car?"

Another voice said, "You're closer than we are."

Then someone said, "Do I have to do everything."

I think things were getting a bit testy. Some time later, Hoffman's car stopped down below. The horn beeped and I went down and got in the car. Things were pretty quiet all the way back to Sauk Centre where I was dropped off at the motel. Someone thanked me, and to this day I don't know the whole story.

I got a good report from Supervisor Hoffman. He gave me four outstanding and four standard checks.

I went home for my four days off. I reported to my brother-in-law that I thought I was doing pretty well so far. I told him my next stop was International Falls with Marv Smith. He let me know Marv was a real top notch Warden. He went on to say Marv had been a Refuge Patrolman then he took a lateral transfer to Game Warden. He also advised me when I got notice back in 1950 that I was to go to Thief Lake as a Refuge Patrolman and turned it down, Marv was the next man in line and he took the station.

THIRD TRAINER, MARV SMITH

I was to put in ten days with Marv Smith between August 24 and September 6 at International Falls. Marv had made arrangements for me to stay with a super couple in their home—Mr. and Mrs. Otto Kuehne. Otto was and is one of the finest dedicated citizens to his fellow man that I have ever known.

I had the feeling Marv had something else upper most on his agenda and that I had made an untimely move to his station. He was not like Al Hoger but acted like he would do his best to put up with me. Also, I had the feeling he was also employed by the M. and O., a paper manufacturing company. The first day, we spent removing beaver dams at the request or complaint of the paper mill. The second day, we went out in the woods and cut down two large birch trees. Both of the logs had straight areas and a bent area. We cut the logs so the bent area was the same distance from the cut ends so that both sections were almost identical. We ended up constructing what resembled a stone boat that some Iowa farmers towed behind a team to remove rocks and stones in some fields. I guessed it was to be used as a pulp hauler out to a landing area.

Marv turned me over to Ray Thorpe at Kabetogoma. About all we did was fish and visit at various resorts. I was with him four or five days. The warden at Little Fork had just transferred to Tower. His name was Jim Charles. A local representative complained that Little Fork could not be left without a game warden during the fall. Jim Nickish, who had been a refuge patrolman and had made a lateral transfer to the warden service, was sent to Little Fork for the fall. Jim asked for assistance from Marv Smith so Marv wished me off on to Nickish. I don't think that was what Nickish had in mind. He wanted Marv to come to Little Fork to show him where to look for trouble. I spent one night patrolling the area around Little Fork with Jim Nickish. I, for one, didn't really know what we were doing. We did happen to come on to a yearling doe that had been hit by a car. Jim gave me a knife to dress the deer out. I turned the carcass over to drain out the excess blood. Then Jim asked me to give him a hand to throw the deer up on top of his car. When we did that, there was some blood in the body cavity and Jim got a big smear of it on his refuge patrolman uniform.

Then one night, Marv said there was going to be a small work party. I was to ride with Marv. I had gotten to know his call number on the radio. We were on a small trail somewhere out of Ray. Marv backed his car down an old logging trail about a hundred feet from this small trail we had been on. We broke some brush and piled it on Marv's car so it wouldn't show up too much. Then he told me to go to the small trail. If I saw or heard a car coming, I should come back and alert him. After about two hours of this, I heard someone calling Marv's call number on the radio. He kept repeating it and he seemed quite excited. Finally, I got up and walked back to the car. I thought Marv might have seen something and took off through the woods. Instead, I found him sound asleep. I woke him up to tell him someone was calling him. He took the mike in his hands and made some odd sounds. I realized he wasn't fully awake, so I shook him and repeated that someone was calling him on the radio. I do remember the dispatcher at Virginia had an all points escape out on a man from a mental institution that had threatened someone with a butcher knife.

I did get to attend a jury trial that involved Ray Thorpe and Ray Appleby finding evidence of Frank House trapping beaver before the season. Marv Smith was in on the search of Frank House's home. Minnesota won the case and House got a fine of $100.00 or ninety days. He took the ninety days in jail. I remember Mrs. House crying and Ray Thorpe trying to console her.

Marv did give me a good report—six outstanding and four standard checks.

I went back to Minneapolis for my four days off.

FOURTH TRAINER, MATT BLAESER

My next learning station was Virginia with Matt Blaeser from September 7th through September 20th. This instructor was a lot like Al Hoger. He obviously knew his job and patiently imparted his knowledge to me. On the third or fourth day, Matt's neighboring Warden from Hibbing, Louie Pelican, came over to Virginia to see Matt about something or other. Matt introduced me to him and we shook hands. Louie started to complain that the office never sent any trainees to him. Matt then said, "Would you like to take Bill for a few days?" Louie Pelican seemed real pleased. I could appreciate these training officers being tied down to these trainees. When I was a floor covering installer, I used to have to put up with apprentices. Occasionally, you would get one you could tolerate.

Matt told me to report to Pelican the following morning at 8:00 a.m. I was to maintain my motel room in Virginia. So I would be driving back and forth every day until I was told to stop.

The following morning I reported to Louie Pelican at his home. He made the statement, "I understand you know something about cement finishing." I allowed that was a part of my former trade. However, I did not really consider myself a top-notch finisher. All this time, I was remembering my brother-in-law telling me the Wardens sometimes got together to build a boathouse or do some repair work in a State building.

I did go on to say, "I don't have any of my tools with me."

Louie came back with, "I've taken care of that." He took me to an establishment that rented tools.

I countered with I should know what this job was and where it was; in fact, I wanted to see the place this work was to be done. He took me to a house with a double garage and a dirt driveway.

Louie said we are to put in a concrete driveway for the double garage. He had made arrangements for the first load of ready mix to be delivered by noon.

I really began to think the man didn't have all his marbles. However, I was on probation. It was not for me to neither wonder why nor even ask questions. I did start in to tell him we should have a better base and there were no framework, grids, or wire mesh. I told Louie he better hold up the ready mix for a couple of days while we got the forms in, got the two-by-fours for the forms, shot some levels, and I had selected some of the tools I would need. I couldn't believe what a mess I was in.

All I can say is, it was sheer panic and at the very best it would be a smickety-smack installation. To this day, I don't know how we did it but I got the forms in and the mesh down just as that first ready mix truck came down the road. You can believe me or not but I worked. Louie helped me spread the cement. I had over two-thirds of the driveway in-floated, darbied, troweled, and brushed. I was on the final third which was the second load of ready mix. I was in the process of finishing troweling around 5:00 p.m. when some young man came on the scene and started to complain that the part I had finished was brushed and pretty well set up. He wanted it all smooth troweled. I told him I never saw a driveway left smooth troweled. They get too slippery when wet.

Then I asked who the hell he was. Louie spoke up and said he was his son and he was the Manual Arts Teacher at some school. I couldn't believe I was conned into this mess on a private home.

I threw the trowel at him and said, "Finish the damn job yourself." I got in my car and returned to Virginia. When I got back to my motel I didn't know whether I should say something to Matt Blaeser or not. I might even get kicked out of the program so by the following morning I swallowed the previous days experience.

I went to Louie's house and neither one of us even hinted about the concrete driveway. We went down in Louie's basement where he had an office. He talked some on how to make out daily reports, arrest reports, etc. He brought out some cleaned and ironed warden shirts and tried to sell them to me for a $1.50. I didn't buy any, so then, he came up with two new shirts. He wanted $2.00 for them. I didn't buy any. Then he tried to sell me some finished wild rice for two dollars a pound. I didn't buy any.

About 11:30 a.m., Louie said we would take a run out into a wooded area and check around. First he went out into this garden and pulled out an onion. He put the onion and a one-gallon jug of water in the trunk of his car and also a plastic bag that looked like it had bread inside into a box in his trunk.

We drove to an area at the end of a trail that had a small trampled area about 30' X 30'. Louie parked the car and told me to make a note in my notebook that we were in section so and so, range so and so, and township so and so. He told me to enter that in my daily report as to where we had lunch. Then he told me to give him the dollar and twenty-five cents we were allotted for lunch. I gave him the dollar and a quarter. Then he opened the trunk and took out this wooden box he had put the bread into. He opened the box and there were some tin plates, tin cups, knives, forks, and a single gas burner. He set this all up. There was also a can of soup that was marked ten cents.

Eventually, he concocted two bowls of soup, two onion sandwiches, and two cups of tea. We ate this little snack, cleaned everything up, put the box back in the trunk, got in his car, and returned to his home in Hibbing. Again, he was submitting things for me to buy. At 5:00 p.m., I returned to Virginia. I tried to locate Matt Blaeser but both he and his wife must have gone away.

The third day was a duplicate of day number two, except we had lunch at a different location. That evening I got a hold of Matt Blaeser and requested not to have to go back to Hibbing. I did not tell him what happened nor did I complain.

I spent the balance of my time with Matt Blaeser and he eventually graded me out with three outstanding and five standard checks.

Matt Blaeser was an excellent instructor and a very patient man.

FIFTH TRAINER, HARLAND PICKETT

My next stint was with Harland Pickett, a feisty character. He raised labrador dogs as a hobby and he was an enthusiastic hunter. He was also into hockey in a big way. He was instrumental in getting the community to build a hockey dome. He didn't just talk about hockey, he was physically involved. I was to be at Baudette from September 21 through October 4. The ruffed grouse and sharp tail season was open so we spent a lot of time checking bird hunters for small game licenses and the number of birds in possession.

We spent one whole day down in the forest area stopping cars and checking for loaded or uncased firearms. Harland had a real aggressive and firm attitude at this particular phase of the training. It was his opinion that this was an important part of our job. We should be firm, in control, but fair and impartial when checking these sportsmen out.

We spent two days out on Lake of the Woods and Rainy River checking fishermen. When he worked he was extremely meticulous. In a lot of ways, he was a lot like Al Hoger.

One day, we went down to Waskish on the shore of Upper Red Lake. He told me this used to be a Refuge Patrolman Station. When Al Markovich moved out two years before and took the Game Warden Station at Warroad, the Waskish Station was transferred to the Enforcement Division of the Conservation Department.

The north one-third of the Waskish Station was added to Pickett's duties. The southwest portion was added to Leo Manthei's area out of Blackduck, and the southeast portion of this station was added to Don Claude's district out of Northome. All three of these men had plenty of work in their original area without adding these additional parts of the Red Lake District on to them.

Harland told me the Waskish Station had been open for two years and no one would bid on it. This station had a State house, a big old log building, a double garage, a boathouse, a workshop, and two bunk houses.

The house had been cannibalized. The section of game had removed the furnace, the waterheater, and the sump pump. These items were obvious, but they probably removed other things too. The house and grounds were in a sad state of repair. The Tamarac River was in the backyard. The dock too needed replacing. The whole set up had an appeal to someone like me who likes to fix things up. The rent was also very nominal.

I would have to get my wife up to look at this place. I was aware I had a selling job on my hands.

Then, too, I had another problem. Dick Tarte was the Supervisor of this area and he probably would rather put up with things the way they were rather than put up with an old forty-three-year-old green horn.

Harland gave me five outstanding and two standard performance ratings.

I suggested I was somewhat interested in the Waskish Station. I asked him if I were to get it, how would he feel about having me as a neighbor. His response was he would do business with the devil if he could be relieved of his responsibility to the Waskish Station.

At the end of my ten day work period, I went to Minneapolis, picked up my wife and took her up to see Waskish.

Fortunately, it was a nice, warm, sun-shiny day when she took her first look at Waskish, the log house, and the out building. Her first comment was "Are you out of your mind? This is no place for us at our age."

Our daughter was just in her first quarter at the University of Minnesota. Our son would be starting his first year in high school which would be in Kelliher, fifteen miles south of Waskish. I told Patricia, "Don't worry. I don't think they want anyone to take this station. After all, there were only about twenty-five people living in Waskish." I also told her, "I don't believe Dick Tarte, the Supervisor, would want me in his district." Then there was the possibility that someone with some seniority would bid on the station. Time would tell.

I took Patricia back to Minneapolis where we did a rush job to clean up my clothes to get ready to go to the next training session.

SIXTH TRAINER, BURT ELLIG

My next tour would be with Burt Ellig of Pine City. I believe he had been a Refuge Patrolman up around Ely. I had the feeling he was a college graduate with a degree in Game Management. Burt was like a good schoolteacher. He had unlimited patience. I was to be with him from October 5 through October 18.

The duck season opened that first Saturday. We spent a long day checking duck hunters for the proper guns, license, and federal duck stamp.

He spent a lot of time with me regarding Public Relations and Work Planning. I had been a dispatcher planning the work for up to forty men every day, plus, I had lots of experience collecting money and taking care of complaints. So this part of my training was old hat, and it showed up when he graded me. In every one of the performance ratings, Burt gave me a grade of outstanding.

A week into my training period, I was told to go to Orr, contact Ray Appleby and accompany him to the State cabin on Namakan Lake to install the sheet rock and pine paneling. When I met Ray, he told me to give him the money I had allotted and would spend for meals for the next four or five days. He said he would need it for supplies. When he came back to his house, his packsack clinked—Christian Brothers.

We lived off walleyes he found at night in Canadian gill nets. On the second day, Ray said he was going elk hunting out in Colorado and Merle Bystrom from Cook would come up to help move the gas refrigerator from the house boat to the new cabin. Merle was really P.O.d about this task.

It took me about five days to finish this job and I returned to Pine City. Burt graded me and I returned home to clean and rest up.

SEVENTH TRAINER, MIKE CASEY

I was scheduled to go to Carlos Avery Game Farm just out of St. Paul from October 19 through November 1.

At this station I met a lot of Biologists and Game Managers. They each had their own expertise, from cottontail rabbits up through moose. I was given a lot of reading material and was allowed to move about the compound and observe all the birds and animals. Also, I checked some duck hunters under the guidance of Walt Rohl. Midway through this period, I was sent to St. Peter to assist in a game check—predominantly pheasants. That was a learning experience. Some hunters had chickens, Peking ducks, and small pigs along with a lot of hen pheasants that you really had to dig for.

Mike Casey gave me three outstanding and five meets standard grades on my report.

EIGHTH TRAINER, VERNON GUNVALSON

My next training period was at the Section of Game at Bemidji from November 2 through November 10. Gunvalson turned me over to a Roger Lehman who constantly epitomized Gunvalson as the "Leading Authority on the white tail deer in the North American Continent." I think that is how he kept his job.

One day I accompanied Lehman to an area Northwest of Bemidji. Some farmer wanted to purchase a forty-acre piece of land that adjoined his farm. These forty acres belonged to the State of Minnesota. We located the piece of property, walked around it a bit and appraised the timber on it. He made out some papers that approved the sale of this forty for $400.00. Roger was quite upset that day because we would not be able to get back to Bemidji by noon to pick up his wife to take her home for lunch. I don't know where she worked, but that noon arrangement was high on his daily list of duties.

I spent most of my time washing the windows at the Game Office Building, changing the screens to storm windows, sweeping, and mopping the office floors. Roger kept me occupied.

Bemidji was where Supervisor Tarte lived and had his office in his basement. I spent my evenings cruising around with McPhall, the local warden.

On the last day, Gunvalson elected to spend some time with me. Roger Lehman drove the vehicle, I was in the middle and Gunvalson was on my right. We went out on some back roads in the Chippewa Forest where Roger Lehman said he monitored ruffed grouse drumming.

When we came back to the office, Gunvalson took me into his office and asked me a bunch of questions. At one stage in the interrogation, he made the statement. "I'm sure by this time you are aware there is friction between the Warden Service and the Biologist Game Managers." I told Vernon Gunvalson that is the first time I had heard of that.

He graded me out. I got one outstanding grade, six meets standard grades and one improvement needed on my knowledge of methods, tools, materials, equipment, etc. grade. The only tools they gave me were a mop, broom, dustpan, stepladder, pail, and rags to wash windows.

SPECIAL ASSIGNMENT, CAMP RIPLEY

On November 11th, I was sent to Camp Ripley for a special rifle deer season to work with Lloyd Hoffman. The state had installed a radio in my car. I made lots of pinches. I was told to call on the radio every time I found a violation and someone would come from the office to take the violator off my hands. Every time I called, Bill Henry, from Little Falls, would come tearing down to meet me. The best pinch I made was a hunter who had sneaked into the camp and shot a deer with a twenty-two high power—two illegal acts. Old Bill Henry was eager to take that fellow off my hands.

SPECIAL ASSIGNMENT, ST CROIX PARK

The second weekend of the deer fire arms season, I was sent to St. Croix Park. It was a special season in the park to a limited number of deer hunters and I was to report to Burt Ellig on November 16th.

One hour before the season was to open, one shot was fired. It turned out that one deer hunter killed another deer hunter.

I made lots of pinches here and was allowed to make out each summons. Everyone was to be scheduled into J. P. Court at 9:00 p.m.

That evening, Bernard Mantheis collected my tickets and ran the violators through court.

NINTH TRAINER, CON OHMAN

My next training site was at Waterville, Minnesota, with Con Ohman of the Minnesota Fisheries. I was to be here from November 21 through November 29.

Waterville was where my father was born and started his career with the Minneapolis and St. Louis Railroad. A lot of my dad's relation live out in the rural area around Waterville, Elysian, and Le Center.

I spent some time visiting with some of them in the evenings. They were shocked that I would take up this new vocation.

Con Ohman showed and explained their operation and its benefits to the State of Minnesota. The plant is located on the south side of Lake Tetonka.

Back in the early forties, three game wardens were shot and killed by a local illegal fish buyer who later committed suicide in the town of Waterville.

My dad and uncle used to sell fish to this man when they were young teenagers. Dad told me they used to sell and ship a barrel of fish every other day. The fish (crappies, sun fish, northern, walleyes, and bullheads) were shipped to Minneapolis and St. Paul to be sold in butcher shops.

Con gave me eight meets standards grades.

TENTH TRAINER, BILL JOY

My next training period was with Bill Joy, the Manager of the Minnesota Fisheries at Detroit Lakes, from November 30 through December 13, 1960.

At this station, I accompanied various personnel to various shallow lakes that were frozen over. They would dig a hole in the ice and drop a device to determine the oxygen content of the water.

Fisheries had various methods of taking care of their lakes if the oxygen content dropped below certain standards. This was a constant on-going monitoring program.

Bill Joy graded me out with eight meets standards grades.

ELEVENTH TRAINER, DALE PETERSON

My next and last training station was with Area Supervisor, Dale Peterson of Owatonna.

We spent a lot of time together doing all sorts of tasks and meeting sportsmen and other game wardens under his jurisdiction.

It was an easy, relaxing station to be at.

Dale gave me good grading and sent me on my way.

WASKISH APPOINTMENT

I was able to be home for Christmas with my family in Minneapolis.

I had sent in a letter requesting Waskish as my first choice for a station. For some reason, I was concerned that they were going to assign me to Little Fork. I found out that Gil Keeler took the Little Fork Station.

I stopped at the St. Paul Office and talked to the Chief, Fran Johnson. He told me that I was the only one that put in for the Waskish Station, and if I still wanted to go there, the station was all mine.

He went on to say the state house and grounds would require a lot of work and material. I told him I was aware of that. He said he would have to find some extra funds to replace the equipment the section of game spirited out of the building. I told him I would like to leave my family in Minneapolis until school was out in June. Hopefully, by that time, I would have the old log house made livable. Chief Johnson thought that might be a wise arrangement.

Then, I asked the Chief if I could work with someone near the cities for the next two weeks so I could be with my family through the holidays.

He said he would assign me to Owen Josephson at Minnetonka through the 15th of January 1961.

He told me to plan on being in Bemidji on the 16th of January to meet with Dick Tarte who would be my Supervisor. I told the Chief I would be there but I was a little apprehensive about how Tarte would accept me.

He told me Tarte would treat me the same as all his other men. He would set me up in the station and would let me know what was required of me.